The Sexual Politics of
Jean-Jacques Rousseau

Joel Schwartz

The Sexual Politics of Jean-Jacques Rousseau

The University of Chicago Press
Chicago and London

The University of Chicago Press, Chicago 60637
The University of Chicago Press, Ltd., London
© 1984 by The University of Chicago
All rights reserved. Published 1984
Paperback edition 1985
Printed in the United States of America
94 93 92 91 90 89 88 87 86 85 6 5 4 3 2

Library of Congress Cataloging in Publication Data

Schwartz, Joel, 1950–
  The sexual politics of Jean-Jacques Rousseau.

  Bibliography: p.
  Includes index.
  1. Sex. 2. Dependency (Psychology) 3. Autonomy
(Psychology) 4. Rousseau, Jean Jacques, 1712–1778.
I. Title.
HQ23.S35 1984   306.7   83-18141
ISBN 0-226-74223-7 (cloth)   ISBN 0-226-74224-5 (paper)

To My Parents

Contents

Preface

This book grew out of work which I did as a graduate student, when it was my good fortune to study first with Allan Bloom and then with Judith Shklar; it was easy to become devoted to the study of Rousseau when introduced to it by such teachers, and it is with gratitude that I acknowledge my intellectual debt to them. Among my other teachers, I must particularly thank Harvey C. Mansfield, Jr. I am also grateful to Harvard University for providing me with the fellowship support which enabled me to begin the study of this topic in Paris; to Christopher Kelly, Arlene Saxonhouse, and particularly Arthur Melzer for their thoughtful criticisms of earlier versions of the manuscript; to Patrick Anderson, both for his word-processing and his miscellaneous advice and encouragement; and to Lynn Sanders, for preparing the index.

Whenever possible, I have cited English translations of works which originally appeared in other languages; I have occasionally altered the translations, but have always indicated when I have done so. All translations of passages from works cited in French are my own.

Abbreviations

References to works of Rousseau appear in the text in parentheses immediately after the citations. The references employ the following abbreviations.

Botanique   *Fragmens Pour un Dictionnaire des Termes d'Usage en Botanique.* In *Oeuvres Complètes*, vol. 4. Paris: Gallimard, Bibliothèque de la Pléiade, 1969.

Confessions   *The Confessions of Jean Jacques Rousseau.* New York: The Modern Library, n.d. References provide book number as well as page number in the Modern Library translation.

Correspondance   *Correspondance Complète de Jean Jacques Rousseau,* vols. 5 and 9. Ed. R. A. Leigh. Geneva: Institut et Musée Voltaire, 1967, 1969.

Corsica   *Constitutional Project for Corsica.* In *Rousseau's Political Writings.* Trans. and ed. Frederick Watkins. New York: Thomas Nelson and Sons, 1953.

Dernière   *Dernière Réponse de J.-J. Rousseau [a Bordes].* In *Oeuvres Complètes*, vol. 3. Paris: Gallimard, Bibliothèque de la Pléiade, 1964.

Dialogues   *Rousseau Juge de Jean Jaques. Dialogues.* In *Oeuvres Complètes*, vol. 1. Paris: Gallimard, Bibliothèque de la Pléiade, 1959. References give dialogue number as well as page number in the Pléiade edition.

Emile   *Emile, or on Education.* Trans. Allan Bloom. New York: Basic Books, 1979. References give book number as well as page number in the Bloom translation.

Émile et Sophie   *Émile et Sophie, ou les Solitaires.* In *Oeuvres Complètes*, vol. 4.

Essay   *Essay on the Origin of Languages.* Trans. John H. Moran. In *On the Origin of Language.* New York: F. Ungar, 1967.

Événements   *Essai Sur Les Événements Importants Dont Les Femmes Ont Été La Cause Secrète.* In *Oeuvres Complètes*, vol. 2. Paris: Gallimard, Bibliothèque de la Pléiade, 1964.

Femmes   *Sur Les Femmes.* In *Oeuvres Complètes*, vol. 2.

First   *First Discourse.* In *The First and Second Discourses.* Trans. Roger D. and Judith R. Masters. New York: St. Martin's Press, 1964.

Fragments   *Fragments Politiques.* In *Oeuvres Complètes*, vol. 3.

Geneva	*Geneva Manuscript*. In *On the Social Contract with Geneva Manuscript and Political Economy*. Trans. Judith R. Masters. Ed. Roger D. Masters. New York: St. Martin's Press, 1978. References give book and chapter number as well as page number in the Masters translation.
Heros	*Discours Sur Cette Question: Quelle Est La Vertu La Plus Nécessaire au Héros*. In *Oeuvres Complètes*, vol. 2.
Julie	*Julie, Ou La Nouvelle Héloïse*. In *Oeuvres Complètes* vol. 2. References give part and letter number as well as page number in the Pléiade edition.
Letter	*Letter to D'Alembert*. Trans. Allan Bloom. In *Politics and the Arts*. Ithaca, N.Y.: Cornell University Press, Agora Editions, 1960.
Lucrèce	*La Mort de Lucrèce*. In *Oeuvres Complètes*, vol. 2.
Malesherbes	*Quatre Lettres à M. Le President De Malesherbes*. In *Oeuvres Complètes*, vol. 1. References give letter number as well as page number in the Pléiade edition.
Montagne	*Lettres Écrites de la Montagne*. In *Oeuvres Complètes*, vol. 3. References give letter number as well as page number in the Pléiade edition.
Narcisse	*Narcisse, Ou L'Amant de Lui-Même*. In *Oeuvres Complètes*, vol. 2.
Poland	*The Government of Poland*. Trans. Wilmoore Kendall. Indianapolis: Bobbs-Merrill Library of Liberal Arts, 1972. References give chapter number as well as page number in the Kendall translation.
Political	*Political Economy*. In *On the Social Contract with Geneva Manuscript and Political Economy*.
Pygmalion	*Pygmalion*. In *Oeuvres Complètes*, vol. 2.
Reveries	*The Reveries of the Solitary Walker*. Trans. Charles E. Butterworth. New York: New York University Press, 1979. References give walk number as well as page number in the Butterworth translation.
Second	*Second Discourse*. In *The First and Second Discourses*.
Social	*On the Social Contract*. In *On the Social Contract with Geneva Manuscript and Political Economy*. References give book and chapter number as well as page number in the Masters translation.

References to all other works appear in the notes.

~ *1* ~

The Ambivalence of Politics and Sexuality

Of all the great philosophical writers about politics, Jean-Jacques Rousseau is the one who wrote most, and most profoundly, about the character of human sexual relations. That Rousseau wrote about both sex and politics should be apparent to anyone familiar with his writings. That there is a connection between his writings on sex and his writings on politics is less apparent, however: many of the writings most concerned with sexuality—his autobiographical *Confessions* and his romantic novel *Julie*—seem to be altogether apolitical, and his best-known political writing—*The Social Contract*—has next to nothing to say about human sexuality.

And yet there is a connection between Rousseau's political philosophy and his understanding of human sexuality. This connection is most apparent in Rousseau's educational treatise *Emile*, which culminates in the sexual education (interrupted by the political education) of its fictitious subject. Rousseau regarded *Emile* as "the best, as well as the most important, of [his] writings" (*Confessions*, XI, p. 594). I believe that his judgment on this point is correct; and the excellence and importance of *Emile* result in large part from Rousseau's success in that work at incorporating and combining the sexual and political themes which seem to divide so many of his other works. Upon reflection one can see that the relationship between politics and sexuality, explicitly attested to in *Emile*, provides a hitherto neglected key to the understanding of Rousseau's work generally. I have written this book to demonstrate this proposition, and to argue that no explication of Rousseau's politics which fails to take account of his understanding of sexuality can be a fully adequate one. Furthermore, not only can a thoughtful reading of Rousseau's writings on sexuality teach us more about Rousseau; I would make the further and more important claim that it also teaches us more about both politics and sexuality.

Rousseau is generally regarded as a paradoxical thinker, at times a contradictory one. This judgment is particularly applicable to his discussion of sexuality. Rousseau's work contains two different teachings about sexuality: one teaching celebrates sexuality, the other condemns it. Because of its apparently self-contradictory character, the Rousseauian presentation of sexuality is quite complex, but it is also remarkably comprehensive; one can learn from Rousseau the costs as well as the benefits of sexuality, for individuals and for societies.

The complexity of Rousseau's views is suggested by the contradictory character of the criticisms which they have recently elicited. Rousseau is seen as the archetypical male chauvinist who exaggerates sexual differences with the aim of subordinating women to men, as a proponent of the patriarchal family; but he is also seen as the intellectual progenitor of the most radical elements within the women's liberation movement, as the advocate of the abolition of the family. Susan Okin articulates the first criticism: "Rousseau argues all the most commonly held assertions that have, as part of our patriarchal culture, rationalized the separation and oppression of women throughout the history of the Western world."[1] She further faults Rousseau for "concluding that the patriarchal nuclear family is natural and inevitable."[2] By contrast, Brigitte Berger condemns the

> Rousseauian vision of human freedom which underlies all the demands of the current women's liberation movement. . . . Rousseau's famous dictum that "men are born free yet everywhere they are in chains" referred to all of traditional society as a prison, but above all, it referred to the family, which in Rousseau's view was the most powerful generator and reinforcer of wretched traditions, and must therefore be destroyed. It is this view of the family as the major obstacle to a better social order—a view of long standing, for which Rousseau provided particularly persuasive arguments—which has come to occupy the forefront of current women's liberation theory.[3]

Although these two very different criticisms of Rousseau indicate that his views are controversial, they do not show why his views need to be taken seriously. But Rousseau should be taken seriously, because he has more to teach us about human sexuality than either of these critics suggests. Both critiques are too narrow; neither one is able to account for the existence of the other, in part because neither adequately presents Rousseau's concern with sexuality in its larger social and political context. This is not to suggest that Rousseau's position is wholly correct; it is to suggest that his position is complex, and that the criticism of a complex position must be preceded by the position's comprehension. My task throughout this work will be to make his position comprehensible by explaining the two teachings about sexuality, which I shall now proceed to sketch.

The two teachings are very different. They have one important element in common, however; both begin by noting the bodily differences between men and women, and both contend that the differences are extremely important. Sexuality is crucial to Rousseau's understanding of humanity because Rousseau is a materialist;[4] human beings can be understood, he would say, only on the basis of human bodies, some of which differ from others because some are male, others female.

Rousseau does not believe that the differences between men and women are only bodily; he does believe, however, that all the other differences between them find their root in what is bodily. Because of their bodily differences, men are more likely to acquire some virtues, women others. Rousseau realizes (as we all must) that all bodies are not identical, and he also believes that the nature of our bodies decisively influences our experiences in the world and our reactions to the world. Not only do the bodily differences between males and females lead them to differ from one another in certain moral and emotional respects; similarly, old people are likely to differ from young people, and healthy people from invalids. In general, people who have greater reason to fear physical attacks will behave differently than will others. Materialism is generally thought to be an egalitarian doctrine, but in fact it is not wholly egalitarian; if we are all alike in having bodies, we may also all be differentiated by virtue of having different sorts of bodies.[5]

Rousseau is in many respects an egalitarian thinker; but if his egalitarianism in part depends upon his materialism, in part it is also tempered by it. His egalitarianism consists largely in arguing that under some circumstances (in the primeval state of nature, and to a considerable extent in the political arrangements of the very small number of legitimate civil societies) physical inequalities are irrelevant—he does not believe that physical inequalities are nonexistent.[6] Where physical inequalities do exist—as they do, he would say, between men and women—relevant and important moral consequences may follow therefrom.[7]

Men and women differ from one another in many ways, all of which result from bodily differences. What follows from these differences? Rousseau answers this question very differently in his two teachings regarding sexuality.

The first teaching is criticized by Okin; as she notes, Rousseau there emphasizes the dependence of women upon men. But it is important to realize that he also emphasizes the dependence of men upon women. Rousseau stresses the lack of self-sufficiency of men as men and women as women; his purpose in doing so is to make men and women understand themselves as social beings who are necessarily dependent on others, so as to lead them to act less selfishly as members of society.

In his first teaching, Rousseau suggests that the political betterment of mankind is in large part to be accomplished by heightening the differentiation between the sexes, with the goal of heightening their mutual dependence as well. Although he denies that human beings are naturally political, he nevertheless argues that humans in many respects benefit from the mutual dependence characteristic of members of communities. Human beings may by nature be fundamentally independent of others; but if they are to be social beings, that very independence must be broken down, and people must learn to become mutually dependent, or to be parts of a larger social whole. Sexuality is important for Rousseau because it is the most natural indicator (he would say the only possible natural indicator) that we are meant to depend on one another, and not merely on ourselves alone. This first sexual teaching of Rousseau suggests that we can achieve freedom through sexuality, or that sexual energy, directing us toward one another physically, can be manipulated so as to enable us to depend upon one another politically as well; from sexuality we can learn to cooperate with one another without exploiting one another.

Sexual differentiation gives men power over women, but it also gives women power over men. Rousseau believes that this power has historically been exercised by women both for better and for worse, and that it could be so exercised again. He is in short quite ambivalent about the power of women over men. His ambivalence is evident in a brief discussion in the *First Discourse*.

There Rousseau discusses the unfortunate aesthetic consequences that follow, he thinks, from the dependence of male artistic creators upon the likes and dislikes of their female critics: "Men have sacrificed their taste to the tyrants of their liberty" (*First*, p. 52).[8]

Women tyrannize men and cost them their liberty. That is to say, men once had liberty (or else women could not have deprived them of it), but no longer do so. As soon as Rousseau makes this argument, however, he proceeds to reverse himself and to argue for the conceivably beneficial effects of this loss of male liberty. Men now depend upon women, but Rousseau wishes to argue that this dependence can be legitimated or justified. The note in which he makes this contention is worth quoting in its entirety.

> I am very far from thinking that this ascendancy of women is in itself an evil. It is a gift given them by nature for the happiness of the human race. Better directed, it could produce as much good as today it does harm. We do not adequately suspect the advantages that would result for society if a better education were given to that half of the human race which governs the other. Men will always be what is pleasing to women; therefore if you want them to become great and virtuous, teach women what greatness of soul and virtue are. The reflections occasioned by this subject and made long ago by Plato greatly deserve to be better developed by a writer worthy of following such a master and defending such a noble cause (*First*, pp. 52–53).[9]

Not only can men's sexual dependence upon women be legitimated, but such a legitimation would have favorable political consequences.

"Society" can be improved, men can be made "great and virtuous," as a result of the fact that women "govern" men.

Rousseau repeats and amplifies this argument in his *Dernière Réponse*, a defense of the *First Discourse* occasioned by the publication in 1751 of Charles Bordes's *Discours Sur Les Avantages Des Sciences et Des Arts*. Once again he addresses the question of the morality of sexual relations in a footnote to the body of the text.

> Men and women are made to love one another and to unite together; but outside of their legitimate union, any relation of love between them is a frightening source of disorders in society and in morals. It is certain that women alone could lead honor and probity back among us; but they disdain from the hands of virtue an empire which they want to owe only to their charms; thus they do nothing but harm, and often receive themselves the punishment for this preference (*Dernière*, p. 75).

Again we see the same historical ambiguity that was evident in the note to the *First Discourse*. Women *could* in the future lead to that "purification of morals" so manifestly not accomplished by "the restoration of the arts and sciences." But women *do* in the present simply further the moral corruption or degradation so characteristic of the times. The key to the transition from present corruption to future redemption, we are told, is the improved education of women. Women make of men what they wish; they are in other words the educators of men. Since this is so, men can be redeemed if (perhaps only if) women are reeducated. Rousseau's task, as he conceives it, is therefore to educate the female educators.[10] In the last sentence of the note to the *First Discourse* he sees himself as the one who is to improve upon Plato in this regard: because women educate men, Rousseau attempts (through the depiction of his fictional heroines Sophie and Julie) to reeducate women.

Because contemporary women abuse their influence, modern societies are corrupt; were women to exert their influence beneficially, modern societies could be reformed. The influence of women is always politically decisive, but they can exert it both for better and for worse. Rousseau believes that historically they have exerted it both for better and for worse; different political regimes have depended on different arrangements of the relations between the sexes. In other words, the manner in which sexual relationships are conducted is relative to (and relevant for the understanding of the preservation, transformation, and destruction of) the political regimes in which they occur.

In his first teaching, Rousseau praises sexuality (and the power over men which sexuality gives to women), because sexuality can help to promote human interdependence. In the context of this teaching, Rousseau undeniably expresses doubts about the beneficence of the power exercised by women over men: but if he is uncertain whether women lead men for better or for worse, at any rate he is certain that women *can* lead men for better and not for worse.

Rousseau's second teaching is very different. The second teaching condemns sexuality (and the power over men which sexuality gives to women). As we have seen, sexuality socializes us or makes us mutually dependent; but since Rousseau is uncertain as to whether human beings are better off mutually dependent than they would be were they all totally isolated and independent, he is uncertain as to whether sexuality benefits or harms us. In other words, Rousseau praises sexual differentiation because it can make a nonexploitative society possible, but he also blames it because it makes society (regardless of a society's character) unavoidable.

Both teachings agree that women are more social than are men, and that women are the agents of men's socialization. They disagree as to whether men are inevitably harmed by the socialization to which women lead them. The second teaching is based upon a vision of a radically individualist autonomy and independence of others, to which Rousseau believes (a few) men but no women could reasonably aspire. The second teaching is thus a critique of society and a critique of sexuality, both of which lead Rousseau to a critique of femininity.

Like the first teaching, the second begins with a materialist analysis of the differences between the male and female bodies. The first teaching holds that the differences make possible a praiseworthy mutual interdependence between male and female. The second teaching, by contrast, denies the mutuality of male and female. Rousseau argues instead that men are naturally better situated than are women to attempt altogether to avoid dependence upon others, in particular to attempt altogether to achieve independence of the other sex. He argues that women, being physically weaker, are naturally and necessarily social; they inescapably depend upon men, so they must also induce men to depend upon them. Men, being physically stronger, could conceivably be altogether independent and asocial (though this is admittedly quite unlikely); instead, he contends, the less natural and necessary sociability of men follows largely from feminine artifices and constraints upon men. In practice men and women depend on one another; in theory women must depend upon men, whereas men could conceivably avoid depending on women. It is in this sense that Rousseau can most fairly be charged with sexism, with a belief in the superiority of men to women. He does not believe that men can, should, or do unilaterally dominate women; for if men dominate women, it is also the case that women justifiably dominate men. Men are instead superior in that men and not women can more easily be imagined altogether escaping from what Rousseau at times describes as the vicious circle of mutual domination.

Thus Rousseau is ambivalent about sexuality not only because it can result in both good and bad politics; he is also ambivalent because it can result (for males) in any politics as opposed to no politics. Politics involves our attempt to dominate one another. Since sexuality provides a natural basis for this interaction and mutual domination, if males would be better off without politics, they would also be better off without sexuality. In Rousseau's view nature essentially condemns women to be sexual and political, whereas nature treats men less imperiously, and might perhaps allow at least a few men to transcend the domination characteristic of politics and sexuality.

The identification of politics with domination, culminating in the distrust of politics, lies at the heart of Rousseau's second teaching about sexuality. In the first teaching, sexuality is praised because it makes us individual parts of a larger sociosexual whole; but if humans cannot be happy as parts of a larger whole, they cannot be happy as sexual beings. Instead they could be happy only as wholly autonomous and independent selves, transcending sexuality and its attendant dependence.

Rousseau's second teaching is criticized by Berger. As she observes, Rousseau often writes in opposition to the family. His reason for doing so, however, is not always (as she suggests) that the family makes a sound political order impossible; more interestingly, it is often because the family (and the sexual differentiation upon which it is based) make social interaction of any sort inevitable. Nevertheless, Berger perceptively sees Rousseau as the originator of the cult of "personhood" as opposed to masculinity or femininity.[11] The "person" is someone who is essentially neither male nor female, who therefore stands in need of neither a complementary female (for his maleness) nor a complementary male (for her femaleness). The "person" then is someone who transcends sexuality; someone who is not essentially dependent upon others (either in the family or in society), but who is instead radically independent of all others, fundamentally self-sufficient. We shall see that the ideal of personhood was in many respects exemplified by Rousseau himself, who appears to us on occasion in his autobiographical writings as the prototype of the individual who achieves radical independence by means of transsexuality or bisexuality.

Thus one of Rousseau's teachings aims to convince us that we can live happily only if we live morally in social relations of mutual dependence whose natural basis is to be found in the difference between the sexes. The other teaching, however, aims to convince us that we could live happily only if we lived amorally in an asocial individualistic condition of radically independent self-sufficiency, which condition could be achieved only through a transcendence of the natural difference between the sexes, or through an incorporation in some way of the principles of both sexes within one person. Happiness is seen here not as the lot of the domesticated dependent member of a family, but as the lot of the radically autonomous and self-sufficient individual. Asexual anarchy would be the best condition for those few who might be capable of attaining it. Freedom could not be achieved through sexuality (as in the earlier teaching), because freedom and dependence are by definition incompatible; freedom could therefore be achieved only by those males who were able to achieve freedom from sexuality.

As I already indicated, any serious attempt to assess the validity of Rousseau's two teachings would have to follow upon a more detailed explication of them than is possible in an introductory chapter; such an attempt is therefore reserved for this work's conclusion. Nevertheless, it is now possible to provide some preliminary indications as to the importance of the study of the Rousseauian teachings on sexuality.

Both teachings emphasize the differences between men and women; because they associate sexuality with domination, both teachings emphasize the political character of sexuality. The first teaching legitimates its political character; it argues that, because of their differences, male and female dominate and are dominated by one another. The first teaching therefore implies that the differences between men and women need not mean the superiority of men to women; that the differences between men and women can point not to the impotence of women but to women's power and to women's justifiable attempts to exercise their power; that equality between men and women can be based on the differences between men and women, or that (contrary to what is often believed today) equality need not be based on the nonexistence or irrelevance of those differences.

The second teaching is far more disturbing than the first, not only (though to be sure largely) because of its misogynistic character. Nevertheless, the second teaching deserves study for two reasons. To begin with, since the pleasures and benefits of sexuality are so obvious to us, any exposition of the costs and pains which sexuality entails—any assertion that the costs and pains are inseparable from the pleasures and benefits— is necessarily of interest, if only to serve as a partial corrective to our habitual presuppositions. In addition, Rousseau's second teaching, after undergoing transformations, has in our time come to be surprisingly influential. Rousseau thought that the goal of radical self-sufficiency could be achieved by only a few exceptional men; most men would continue to depend upon women (and all women would continue to depend upon men). Rousseau's goal has today been democratized; many now believe it to be easily attainable by all. The goal of fundamental independence of all others, of the rejection of commitment to all others, explains much that was characteristic of the America of the "me decade" (and much that is still characteristic of America today). In particular, the connection made by Berger between some elements within the women's liberation movement and the Rousseauian ideal of personhood is, I believe, correct. This is to say that the most radical wing within the women's liberation movement inverts and universalizes the Rousseauian teaching; it contends that the goal of radical self-sufficiency should be sought after not by a few men, but potentially by all women.

It would be absurd to assert that all feminists want to have nothing to do with men; but it would be false to assert that no feminists want to have nothing to do with men. The radical feminist claim that women would be better off were they to be fundamentally independent of men can, I suggest, be understood in the context of the earlier Rousseauian contention that at least a few men would be better off were they to be fundamentally independent of women. Both moderate and radical feminists have cause (often, I would say, good cause) to find some of Rousseau's arguments offensive. But insofar as Rousseau celebrates the power of women (in the first teaching) and points to the desirability of the avoidance of contact between the sexes (in the second), feminists, paradoxically, also have cause to recognize in him a sort of ancestor.

Rousseau's understanding of sexuality is all-encompassing; if, as I suggest, there are feminist elements within his thought, Okin is also correct to point to patriarchal elements within it. One gives an indication of Rousseau's influence (though hardly an indication of his profundity) by saying that he is the unrecognized intellectual source of both Phyllis Schlafly and Kate Millett. The important thing, however, is not to label his thought or to trace its impact, but to comprehend it. In order to begin to do so, we must now consider in some detail his discussion of sexuality as it exists by nature.

∽ 2 ∾

The Natural History
of Sexuality

Rousseau believes that by nature human beings are independent of one another. He also believes that they can benefit from mutual interdependence (though unfortunately they can also be harmed if their dependence is not truly mutual but exploitative). These beliefs explain Rousseau's ambivalence about politics. Politics for him is clearly unnatural; it is unclear, however, whether the political departure from nature represents an improvement upon it or a disfigurement of it. He expresses this ambivalence in a very important statement in the *Social Contract*:

> The passage from the state of nature to the civil state produces a remarkable change in man, by substituting justice for instinct in his behavior and giving his actions the morality they previously lacked. ... If the abuses of [his] new condition did not often degrade him beneath the condition he left, he ought ceaselessly to bless the happy moment that tore him away from [the state of nature] forever, and that changed him from a stupid limited animal into an intelligent being and a man (*Social*, I, 8, pp. 55–56).

Sexuality is both important and an ambivalent phenomenon for Rousseau, because its understanding is central to his judgment of each of the human states discussed in the above quotation. He argues that in the state of nature the human being "considered only himself" (*Social*, I, 8, p. 56). For this statement to be plausible, Rousseau must have an explanation of the character of sexuality in the state of nature; for sexuality is the human characteristic which most clearly seems to suggest natural human sociability or gregariousness. (Speech, to be sure, testifies still more clearly to human sociability, but speech unlike sexuality is not obviously natural; one can imagine—Rousseau does imagine—human beings surviving without the power of speech; one cannot imagine them surviving without sexuality.) Because human beings are presumably "natural" sexual creatures (whatever else they may be in addition), one would immediately be tempted to assume that by nature each individual human being considers not simply himself or herself, but others in the species as well, or that by nature human beings are not radically independent of one another but necessarily interdependent.

Thus, insofar as Rousseau wishes to argue that humans are naturally independent of one another, sexuality is of great importance to him, since it appears as the most obvious, immediate, and natural threat to that independence. On the other hand, insofar as he wishes to argue that humans benefit from (unnatural) mutual interdependence, sexuality is again of great importance to him, since it appears as the most natural (he would say, the only natural) support of that mutual interdependence.

Both of Rousseau's teachings on sexuality are rendered more convincing insofar as they receive support from Rousseau's understanding of nature. If the two seemingly incompatible teachings are both according to nature, however, Rousseau must have not one but two understandings of nature. Natural independence must be possible in spite of sexuality; mutual interdependence can be confirmed as somewhat natural only as a result of the evidence provided by sexuality.

As he explains in *Emile*, Rousseau does have two different understandings of nature, one stricter than the other: "One must not confound what is natural in the savage state with what is natural in the civil state" (*Emile*, V, p. 406). That he can speak of "what is natural in the civil state" is revealing, since by the strict standard of the state of nature provided in the *Second Discourse*, civilized life is inherently unnatural. But in *Emile* Rousseau applies a different standard according to which it is possible (though assuredly difficult) to combine something approximating the freedom of natural man with the acquisitions described in the *Second Discourse*—the acquisitions that have civilized or humanized human beings, distinguishing them from all other animals. By this second standard, it is possible to speak of the natural sexuality of civilized human beings.

The sexuality of civilized human beings can be said to be natural, though it is different from the sexuality of human beings in the state of nature. It differs chiefly with respect to the question of independence or interdependence stressed above. The radical independence of all individuals from one another in the savage state of nature was possible in spite of natural sexuality; this belief in natural independence, we shall see in chapter 4, underlies Rousseau's second teaching on sexuality. The mutual interdependence of individuals in the civil state is in part generated by natural sexuality; this belief in natural interdependence, we shall see in chapters 3 and 4, underlies Rousseau's first teaching.

In Rousseau's account of sexuality in the state of nature (which is to be found in his *Second Discourse* and *Essay on the Origin of Languages*), he equates human nature with the physical equipment of human beings. He contends that sex there involved nothing but the very occasional employment of this equipment, and was altogether devoid of social or psychological implications. He attempts to explain how sexual relations can have been possible without creating social ties between men and women; how they can have been possible without creating mutual psychological dependence between sexual partners; how they can have been compatible with the total independence and self-sufficiency of the sexual partners.

In other words, in this account Rousseau attempts to explain how natural sexuality can have been altogether unlike the phenomenon of civilized sexuality as men and women experience it today. Because Rousseau's account depends on a discrepancy between what was once natural and what is now experienced, he must also attempt to explain the transition from natural sexuality to sexuality as it is experienced today.

Rousseau's account of natural sexuality in the civil state is to be found in his educational treatise *Emile* and in his *Letter to D'Alembert*. In these works he understands nature much more broadly, so as to encompass the intellectual and emotional development that the human species experienced after its primeval origins. Not surprisingly, natural sexuality in these accounts is completely unlike the natural sexuality described in the *Second Discourse*, and very much more like sexuality as experienced by socialized men and women. Sexuality is now presented as a phenomenon which is inherently psychological as well as biological. Rousseau contends that by nature sexual relations are inconceivable without the creation of social ties and psychological dependence between the partners; that by nature sexual relations necessarily imply that neither partner can be totally independent and self-sufficient.

If the two accounts differ in almost every respect, they are similar in one very important respect: both accounts emphasize the interrelationship between politics and sexuality. The *Second Discourse* account, as we have already noted, argues for the original compatibility of sexuality and individual self-sufficiency. As sexuality is transformed, this self-sufficiency is lost. But what is important for our purposes is that this transformation not only involves the origin of sexual dependence, but also leads to the emergence of social and political dependence. Sexuality is the bridge which links original human self-sufficiency with ultimate human political dependence. Sexual phenomena are of vital importance in Rousseau's genetic explanation of political society. Furthermore, sexual phenomena play a crucial role in bringing into being the psychology of political life—the desire to dominate others and to win public approval.

The *Emile* account, by contrast, presupposes the impossibility of individual self-sufficiency. Men and women, parts of a sexual whole, are necessarily dependent on one another. Here sexuality does not serve as a bridge to political society, because the existence of political society is assumed—no genetic account of it need be given. But one can say that the sexual relationship is itself a political relationship; for it is much more true of the Rousseauian than it is of the Aristotelian male-female relationship that "there is an interchange of ruling and being ruled."[1] In *Emile* sexuality is not simply a biological phenomenon; instead, sexual relations are inconceivable without the psychological desire to dominate. The desire to rule is not explained as an outgrowth of sexuality; rather sexuality itself is a specific manifestation of the desire to rule.

Sexuality: The Ambiguously Natural Need

As an introduction to Rousseau's two accounts of natural sexuality, it is helpful to examine three different statements of his concerning the status of sex as a need. This will enable us to situate sex in comparison to other needs, some of which are unambiguously natural, and others the clear result of unnatural human development.

In the *Second Discourse*, sex is presented as a natural need, no different from other natural needs. "Savage man['s] . . . desires do not exceed his physical needs, the only goods he knows in the universe are nourishment, a female, and repose" (*Second*, p. 116). It seems that his need for "a female" is no different in kind than his need for sleep or nourishment, notwithstanding the fact that only the first is a need for another human being. In denying that there is a qualitative distinction among these various needs, Rousseau implies that natural man does not depend psychologically on the woman with whom he sleeps, any more than he depends psychologically on the roots or berries he eats. His independence is possible, as we shall see, because natural man does not often want to make love; when he does, partners are readily available. He eats when he is hungry, sleeps when he is tired, and makes love when he must. But he would no more be choosy about whom he slept with than about what he slept on.

Nevertheless, Rousseau's very emphasis on the relative infrequency of sexual desire indicates that its status differs from the desire for nourishment and repose. He describes sex as "the appetite that invited [savage man] to perpetuate his species" (*Second*, p. 142). How then can it be wholly assimilated to desires necessary for the preservation of the individual? This obvious problem emerges in Rousseau's discussion of the natural evils that savage man confronts: "The only evils he fears are pain and hunger" (*Second*, p. 116). He responds to hunger by seeking nourishment, and (less directly) to pain by achieving repose. But neither pain nor hunger can be allayed with "a woman." One can starve to death or be worked to death; but can one die of celibacy? Thus even when sexuality is seen only as a biological function, it can still plausibly be differentiated in character from man's other biological functions.

Sex appears in the *Second Discourse* as a natural need, but not a particularly important one; although it seems to be a natural tie to other humans, it is in fact compatible with natural independence of other humans. In *Emile*, by contrast (where Rousseau argues that sex necessarily entails interdependence), he seems to deny *any* biological basis to human sexuality: sex is purely and simply the creation of human psychology.

> The senses are awakened by the imagination alone. Their need is not properly a physical need. It is not true that it is a true need. If no lewd object had ever struck our eyes, if no indecent idea had ever entered our minds, perhaps this alleged need would never have made itself felt to us, and we would have remained chaste without temptation, without effort, and without merit (*Emile*, IV, p. 333).[2]

To deny that sex is a need is to make an astonishing claim, and one that evidently contradicts the doctrine of the *Second Discourse*. Yet it is clear that Rousseau means for his claim to apply only to civilized human beings. (Recall that the subject of *Emile* is "the civil state," as opposed to the *Second Discourse*'s focus on "the savage state.") Rousseau does not deny that "the senses" of human beings in the state of nature are aroused without benefit of an imaginative impetus; in fact this is what he asserts: "Imagination, which causes so much havoc among us, does not speak to savage hearts. Everyone peaceably awaits for the impulsion of nature, yields to it without choice with more pleasure than frenzy; and the need satisfied, all desire is extinguished" (*Second*, p. 136).

But as we shall see, Rousseau contends that the sexuality of civilized men and women is inconceivable without the participation of the "imagination, which causes so much havoc among us." And if the imagination is said to be unnatural (the doctrine of the *Second Discourse*), then the sexual arousal which it produces can be said to be unnatural (hence strictly speaking not a need) as well.

Sexuality then both is and is not a true need. A third statement of Rousseau's is most useful in helping us to understand the in-between status of sexuality. This statement is found in a political fragment of Rousseau's, to which the title *L'Influence Des Climats Sur La Civilisation* has been assigned. "Man is not able to be self-sufficient; his needs, which are always reborn, force him to seek outside of himself for the means to satisfy them. He depends always on things and sometimes on his fellow men" (*Fragments*, p. 529). The distinction between dependence on things and dependence on men enables us to distinguish further between savage man's need for nourishment and repose (things) and his need for a female, the distinction not found in the *Second Discourse*. Things are more necessary than are fellow human beings. This gradation coincides with our observation that nourishment and repose are truly necessary for the individual's preservation, whereas a sexual partner is not. Furthermore, the preference for dependence on things as opposed to dependence on men is a very important tenet of Rousseau's thought. It is the guiding principle of the education of the young (i.e., prepubescent) Emile.

> There are two sorts of dependence: dependence on things, which is from nature; dependence on men, which is from society. Dependence on things, since it has no morality, is in no way detrimental to freedom and engenders no vices. Dependence on men, since it is without order, engenders all the vices, and by it, master and slave are mutually corrupted (*Emile*, II, p. 85).

The first order of needs discussed by Rousseau in the fragment consists of "nourishment" and "sleep" alone. These, as is already clear, are things "on which our preservation depends. They are such that each man would perish if he ceased to be able to satisfy them: these are called physical needs, because they are given to us by nature and because nothing can deliver us from them" (*Fragments*, p. 529).

In view of the presentation in the *Second Discourse*, we might now expect to see sexuality classified by itself as a second order of need, necessary not to the individual's but to the species' preservation. Yet this is not what Rousseau says. Instead of associating sexual desire with the preservation of the species, he connects it to the delectation of the individual. Because sex is not considered here as necessary for preservation, it is not seen as a natural need. In this view sex is less necessary; it is more a product of human choice, and not of natural inclination. Sex is humanized and moralized:

> Other needs tend less to our preservation than to our well-being, and are properly only appetites, but sometimes so violent, that they torment us more than do true needs; however, there is never an absolute necessity to satisfy them, and all know only too well that to live is not to live well.
>
> The needs of this second class have as their object the luxury of sensuality, of softness, the union of the sexes and everything that flatters our senses (*Fragments*, p. 530).

Rousseau then speaks of a third sort of need—stemming from human opinion, as opposed to preservation and pleasure. The examples he gives include "honors, reputation, rank, nobility" (*Fragments*, p. 530)—political goods we might say. The classification in the fragment therefore resembles but is not identical to the distinction between dependence on things and dependence on men expounded in *Emile*. First-order needs reflect our dependence on things: as in *Emile*, this dependence is truly natural, hence unavoidable and in no way to be resisted. Third-order needs, or "those which come from opinion," reflect our dependence on men. As we have seen, though, in *Emile* Rousseau condemns dependence upon men (though to be sure he qualifies and even retracts this condemnation at later stages of Emile's education). In the fragment, however, Rousseau's ambivalence about dependence on men is made evident immediately. On the one hand, such needs comprise "everything that has existence only in the esteem of men"; but on the other, concern for such esteem leads to "real goods which one would not obtain without it" (*Fragments*, p. 530). It is nevertheless the case that the first species of needs is wholly natural, reflecting our dependence on things and not on other humans, whereas the third kind is wholly conventional, reflecting our acquired dependence upon other humans and not upon things.

Needs of the second order, however, including sexuality, are particularly hard to classify according to the division between dependence on things and dependence on men. Like those of the first order, they are self-regarding and physical; they differ from first-order needs only insofar as they relate to our comfortable (as opposed to our bare) physical preservation. But like those of the third order, most obviously in the case of sexual union, the needs occasion reliance upon others. Thus the sexual need shares characteristics of both first- and third-order needs. Because it does so, it can serve as a bridge to third-order needs (in the *Second Discourse* account), and also be seen (in *Emile*) as itself a third-order need. Thus in each account sexuality is intimately related to the quest for "honors, reputation, rank, nobility," or to the political life and to its psychology. We shall see that Rousseau's ambivalence about sexuality is a special case of his general ambivalence about political life—the life whose worth "has existence only in the esteem of men," but which also leads to "real goods which one would not obtain without it."

Sexuality in the State of Nature

We now turn to Rousseau's discussion of sexuality in the state of nature. The sexual need, which we would expect to link human beings together, to socialize them, is so weak that it fails to accomplish this. It is therefore compatible with their retention of individual independence. Rousseau's demonstration of this proposition can best be understood if parts of his argument are compared to the views of three of his sources—the Roman poet Lucretius, the seventeenth-century natural law theorist Pufendorf, and the eighteenth-century natural scientist Buffon.

Rousseau contends that, in the beginning, human beings were promiscuous. "Males and females united fortuitously, depending on encounter, occasion and desire, without speech being a very necessary interpreter of the things they had to say to each other; they left each other with the same ease" (*Second*, pp. 120–21). But because of their promiscuity, sexual encounters play a remarkably unimportant role in the life of savage human beings. "Any woman is good" for natural man, because no woman is really important to him. "He heeds solely the temperament he received from nature, and not the taste he has not been able to acquire" (*Second*, p. 135). Sexual temperament is the generalized desire bestowed on the human species by nature. Sexual taste, by contrast, is the particularization of this desire that human beings acquire themselves. Rousseau contends that generalized desire is weak, that only its particularization strengthens it. All women are available to savage man as potential partners. In what is essentially an economic calculus, the consequence of this oversupply of potentially desired objects is the comparative weakness of the male demand for them. Only later, when humans are able to prefer some potential sexual partners to others, is the supply effectively reduced and the desire consequently augmented. For sexual preferences (the outcome of the development of sexual taste referred to above) "irritate the sentiment [of love] and augment its difficulties." Without such preferences, "men must feel the ardors of their temperament less frequently and less vividly. . . . Everyone peaceably waits for the impulsion of nature, yields to it without choice with more pleasure than frenzy: and the need satisfied, all desire is extinguished" (*Second*, p. 135).

The weakness of the primeval male's sexual desire enables him to maintain his individual independence. The weakness of desire is important to Rousseau in an additional respect: it allows him to deny or at any rate to minimize the extent to which sexual disputes would cause outbreaks of violence in the state of nature. If the state of nature is to be peaceful, the character of sexuality there must be such as not to occasion conflict. Weakness of male desire conduces to peace in two different respects: peace between men and women, and peace between men through the absence of disputes over women.

There is peace between men and women because their sexual unions result from mutual desires on the part of both men and women. Everyone (men and women) "peaceably" waits for the impulsion of nature. "Males and females united fortuitously, depending on encounter, occasion, and desire." Rousseau does not suggest here that there might be a significant difference between the sexes concerning those desires or their expressions, or even a relevant difference in physical strength between them.[3] In short, he does not suggest that there might be cases of rape in the state of nature, any more than there might be cases of robbery, or other oppressions. "What can be the chains of dependence among men who possess nothing?" (*Second*, p. 139).

> Since the bonds of servitude are formed only from the mutual dependence of men and the reciprocal needs that unite them, it is impossible to enslave a man without first putting him in the position of being unable to do without another; a situation which, as it did not exist in the state of nature, leaves each man there free of the yoke, and renders vain the law of the stronger (*Second*, p. 140).

While it is true that men and women are generally dependent on one another, no man is dependent on any specific woman. Let us suppose that one woman rebuffs a man's advances. Because Rousseau argues that human sexuality is naturally teleological, directed toward the end of reproduction, he hypothesizes that this might happen. "If in the state of nature the woman no longer feels the passion of love after the conception of the child . . . she no longer needs either the man who impregnated her or any other" (*Second*, p. 219). Should a man chance upon a woman not desiring to mate (because of her pregnancy or any other reason), one can suppose that rather than use his superior physical strength to compel her, he would simply search for another, more compliant partner. Because men desire relatively infrequently, such a partner ought to be easily available. The reluctant female therefore does the aroused male no harm. To summarize, peace characterizes the primeval relations between males and females because there is a disproportion between their physical strength and their sexual desire: the sexes are equal because each sex's superiority is compensated for by a corresponding inferiority. Men would have the strength to compel women but lack the desire to do so; women (whose natural sexual complaisance we have yet to discuss) might have the desire to compel men but lack the strength to do so.[4]

The two inequalities combine harmoniously to produce the natural mutuality of sexual relations. Rousseau, who in so many respects bases his account of the state of nature on Lucretius's poetic account of the origins of man, signally departs from his classical model here.[5] Lucretius mentions mutual desire as one cause of sexual union, but assigns two others as well, according to which the male takes the initiative: "And Venus would unite lovers in the woods; for each woman was wooed either by mutual passion, or by the man's fierce force and reckless lust, or by a price, acorns and arbute-berries or choice pears."[6] Rousseau's "encounter, occasion, and desire," none of which suggests male compulsion of the female, replace Lucretius's trinity of mutual desire, rape, and bribery—the last two of which clearly suggest the greater intensity of male desire.

Rousseau's lengthiest discussion of sexuality in the *Second Discourse* advances the second argument for the peaceful character of primeval sexuality: he contends that by nature there is no significant conflict among men occasioned by disputes over women. "The disputes [of natural man] would rarely have had bloody consequences had there been no more sensitive subject than food. But I see a more dangerous subject left for me to discuss" (*Second*, p. 134). This dangerous subject is sexual desire, described as an "ardent, impetuous, . . . terrible passion . . . which . . . seems fitted to destroy the human race it is destined to preserve." It is obvious that such a depiction is incompatible with the portrait of a basically peaceful state of nature. "What would become of men, tormented by this unrestrained and brutal rage, without chastity, without modesty, daily fighting over their loves at the price of their blood?"

Rousseau must oppose a contention of Pufendorf's in making his second argument in defense of a peaceful state of nature. Pufendorf asserts that human sexuality differs naturally from that of animals, and therefore "that it is not fitting that man [as opposed to the other animals] live without laws."

> The beasts sense only hunger, thirst, and the stings of love. Even these last movements press them only at certain times, and as much as is necessary for the multiplication of the species, and not simply to procure for them a vain pleasure. Have they arrived at their end? Then they are content, and their desires cease of themselves. In man, by contrast, the movements of love are not limited to certain seasons, and they are even excited much more frequently than seems necessary for the propagation of the species.[7]

Rousseau concedes that "the more violent the passions, the more necessary laws are to contain them" (*Second*, p. 136).[8] But he denies the validity of the premises which Pufendorf introduces in order to demonstrate that human sexuality is a naturally violent passion. For Pufendorf contrasts human and animal sexuality in two different ways. He argues first that animal sexuality is teleological, directed toward the goal of reproduction. Hence when the goal is satisfied, animal desires cease. Human sexual activity, by contrast, is undertaken partially in order to experience a "vain pleasure." Rousseau's response to this first contention is a simple one. What Pufendorf ascribes to animal behavior is ascribed by Rousseau to the behavior of savage (though not of civilized) human beings as well. "The need satisfied, all desire is extinguished."

Pufendorf's second argument is intended to substantiate the distinction that he draws between animal and human sexuality. That human desire is impossible to satisfy would seem to be indicated by the lack of periodicity of the human female's sexual receptivity. If human sexuality were intended only for procreative purposes, why should the sexual activity of the human female alone be unrestricted as to season? To which Rousseau responds with his own question: How could human sexual activity occasion conflict, since the sexual availability of the human female alone is unrestricted as to season? Rousseau does not deny that the female of the human species is unique among the animals in this respect. On the contrary, he insists on this distinction, because it alone guarantees the peaceful character of human sexual relations. For sexual combat among males does characterize other species, but cannot have characterized the human species as it was by nature. "Cockfights do not provide an inference for the human species" (*Second*, p. 136). Rousseau, who in the *Second Discourse* assimilates human behavior to that of the animals in so many other respects, explicitly rejects the analogy in this instance.[9] For the supply of potential female partners, the cause of peace between the sexes, is also the cause of peace within the male sex.

> These fights can have for causes only the scarcity of females with reference to the number of males, or the exclusive intervals during which the female constantly refuses to let the male approach her, which amounts to the first cause; for if each female tolerates the male during only two months of the year, in this respect it is the same as if the number of females were reduced by five sixths (*Second*, p. 136).

In the human species, by contrast, "the number of females generally surpasses the number of males," and females do not "have times of heat and exclusion." Male desire, then, is weak because females are so receptive to the males' advances. And as we saw earlier, men who desire weakly are men who desire peaceably. The absence of female modesty in the primeval state of nature explains the existence both of peace between the sexes and of peace within the male sex.

Generalized or physical love characterizes natural man. Rousseau contrasts this peaceful love with the particularized or moral love characteristic of civilized human beings. The basis for this distinction can be found in Lucretius, but Rousseau's more immediate source is his contemporary, the great French naturalist Buffon.[10] Rousseau and Buffon both agree that it is moral, not physical, love which causes human unhappiness. For Rousseau, as we have seen, natural man is "limited solely to that which is physical in love, and fortunate enough to be ignorant of those preferences that irritate its sentiment and augment its difficulties. . . . Imagination, which causes so much havoc among us, does not speak to savage hearts." A similar contrast is to be found in Buffon as well.

> Love! Why is yours the happy state of all other beings but the unhappiness of man?
> It is because only what is physical in this passion is good, it is because, in spite of what those who are smitten may say, its moral aspect is worth nothing.[11]

It is interesting to compare Rousseau and Buffon on the contrast between physical and moral love. One might think that Rousseau simply adopts Buffon's distinction. Their views differ, however, in one important respect: Buffon ascribes the happiness of physical love to the animal species (as opposed to human beings), whereas Rousseau ascribes it to natural (as opposed to civilized) human beings.[12] The sexuality of human beings in the primeval state of nature shares all of the positive attributes of animal sexuality, according to Rousseau; it differs only in that its expression is more peaceable than (hence preferable to) the expression of animal sexuality.

Nor is this the only respect in which Rousseau departs from Buffon's distinction between physical and moral love. Buffon is the harsher critic of moral love: for he reduces the moral aspect of love to "vanity," whereas Rousseau associates it with the acquisition of "ideas of merit and beauty which produce sentiments of preference" (*Second*, p. 148).[13] But in some respects Rousseau views civilized sexual morality less favorably than does Buffon. Rousseau says that moral love is "extolled . . . by women in order to establish their ascendancy and make dominant the sex that ought to obey" (*Second*, p. 135). Buffon celebrates the equality of conditions between the sexes that he thinks characteristic of civil society. Prior to the development of civilization, Buffon contends, women were subject to oppression because of their physical inferiority. "Women are not nearly as strong as men are, and the greatest use, or the greatest abuse, which man has made of his strength is to have enslaved and often treated in a tyrannical manner this half of the human race, which was made in order to share with him the pleasures and pains of life."[14] The savage state with which Buffon contrasts civil society thus differs markedly from Rousseau's natural state of liberty and equality between the sexes, which Buffon explicitly rejects.[15] The savage state, in which men enslaved women, existed from the beginning because women depended on men from the beginning to help them provide for their offspring: thus Buffon (unlike Rousseau) equates "man in pure nature" with "the savage in a family."[16]

In the savage state, then, according to Buffon, men "oblige their women to work continually, it is they who cultivate the earth, who do the painful work, whereas the husband remains lying nonchalantly in his hammock."[17] If at the origins men unjustly tyrannize their women, "It is only among the nations civilized to the point of politeness that women have obtained that equality of condition, which however is so natural and so necessary to the gentleness of society."[18] According to Buffon, women are the cause of civilizing society to the point of politeness, and are therefore the great benefactors of society. Women achieve "natural" equality (which was not granted them in the beginning) and benefit society by doing so. For Rousseau, women are naturally equal to men— they are equal in the primordial savage state, without having to alter that state to achieve equality. They are weaker than men but strong enough to be self-sufficient, because men lack the need and the desire to oppress them. For Rousseau, then, nature is the state of sexual equality, whereas the female sex achieves unnatural predominance in civilization. There is no predominance of either sex by nature because natural sexuality enables all members of both sexes to live independently or self-sufficiently. Despite the fact that sexual relations are natural, the independence of each human individual is equally natural; humanity itself, not nature, has made us dependent upon one another.

Pregnancy and Maternity in the State of Nature

Rousseau's argument for the natural equality and independence of women seems to be subject to the obvious objection raised by Buffon: How can women be truly independent of men, since pregnancy inconveniences them so much more than it does men? In order to support the case for natural equality between the sexes, Rousseau must discount the inconveniences of pregnancy for women (just as we have seen him discount the dangers of rape for women) in the state of nature.

Because pregnancy does not seriously inconvenience women, they do not require the assistance of men to care for their offspring. In other words, women are naturally independent of men, which is to say that the human family is not, strictly speaking, a natural institution. This is the teaching of the *Second Discourse*; yet in the *Social Contract* Rousseau affirms the naturalness of the family.[19] We shall therefore have to see how it is that Rousseau can both affirm and deny that the family exists by nature.

He says in the *Second Discourse* that "Males and females united fortuitously . . . ; they left each other with the same ease." The female is then left to nourish and protect her progeny by herself at the termination of her pregnancy. She does so because the maternal instinct is a natural one: "The mother nursed her children at first for her own need" (*Second*, p. 121). The question is why mothers were originally able to do so without the assistance of males, but not subsequently.

The human female can nurture her offspring independently because the human species is unlike all other species. Again we see that where humans differ from the other animals, the difference redounds to their (and in this case specifically the human female's) advantage. Humans are primordially the beasts without families not because they are like all other animals, but precisely insofar as they are unlike many of them. For only the human female is a biped.[20] Thus a mother can transport her child by carrying it, while simultaneously either seeking her food or fleeing her animal pursuers (*Second*, pp. 108, 112).

Rousseau states unequivocally that humans are bipeds (*Second*, pp. 183–86).[21] He is rather equivocal as to whether they are naturally omnivorous. In his text he suggests that they are: "Man . . . feeds himself equally well with most of the diverse foods which the other animals share, and consequently finds his subsistence more easily than any of them can" (*Second*, p. 106). Once again it seems that Rousseau distinguishes humans from other animals, and that the distinction favors humans. In a note commenting on this text, however, Rousseau hypothesizes that humans may in fact be naturally frugivorous, because they have "teeth and intestines like those of frugivorous animals." For it is apparent that there could be natural advantages to their being frugivores as well. "As prey is almost the unique subject of fighting among carnivorous animals, and as frugivorous ones live among themselves in continual peace, if the human race were of this latter genus it clearly would have had much greater ease subsisting in the state of nature, and much less need and occasion to leave it" (*Second*, p. 188).

In two other notes Rousseau indicates that the primordial eating habits of human beings are relevant to the determination of the status of the human family. Because carnivores are able to feed themselves more rapidly than are frugivores, they tend to bear more offspring (*Second*, pp. 191–92). But human females, Rousseau contends, cannot nurse (and hence cannot naturally have been intended to give birth to) a great many offspring, since they have only two breasts. He then claims that this anatomical consideration "furnishes a new reason to withdraw man from the class of carnivorous animals and to place him among the frugivorous species" (*Second*, p. 192).

In his final note relevant to this investigation, Rousseau takes issue with John Locke's contention that the human family must be natural because human beings are carnivores. "It seems on the contrary that if the help of the male were necessary to the female to preserve her young, it would be above all in the species that live only on grass" (*Second*, p. 216).[22] But this argument of Rousseau's suggests not that the human family is *not* natural, but that the frugivorous family *is* natural. To develop our earlier contention, if the human family is unnatural, it is not because humans resemble all other animals, but because they are unlike all other frugivorous animals.

As a frugivore, the human female experiences more difficulty in caring for her offspring than would a carnivorous female. This disadvantage is partially offset by the fact that she bears fewer offspring than a carnivorous female. She is additionally compensated for the disadvantage insofar as she is a biped, and hence can more easily nourish and protect them. Nevertheless, it is clear that this latter advantage as well is contingent upon the human female's producing few offspring and producing them seldom; a mother can carry one child while fleeing or foraging, but she can hardly carry four or five. In refuting Locke, Rousseau specifically observes that, in the pure state of nature, women conceive less often and children become self-sufficient more rapidly than is the case in civil society (*Second*, p. 217).[23] If the number of pregnancies were to increase, women could deal with the difficulty with which they would be presented in two different (but not mutually exclusive) ways: (1) females (and males) could become omnivorous, in order to facilitate the provision of food, and

(2) females could avail themselves of the assistance of males in order to guarantee the protection of their young.[24] Thus, although the family is unnatural in the pure state of nature, one could reasonably contend that the family "becomes" natural, so to speak, when women begin to bear more children. But why should they begin to do so?

The Causes and Consequences of the Invention of the Family

"The continual cohabitation of husband and wife provides such an immediate opportunity to be exposed to a new pregnancy that it is very hard to believe that chance encounter or the impulsion of temperament alone produced such frequent effects in the pure state of nature as in the state of conjugal society" (*Second*, p. 217). Rousseau suggests here that the invention of conjugal society is the cause and not the effect of women's more frequent pregnancies. Men do not become husbands because mothers require their assistance as fathers; such a transition would depend on men's recognition of a moral obligation, and as Rousseau observes, "moral proofs do not have great force in matters of physics" (*Second*, p. 215). Instead, mothers require men's assistance as fathers because men become husbands. The earlier fortuitous unions of males and females resulted from human beings' "having neither houses, nor huts." Thus "everyone took up his lodging by chance and often for only one night" (*Second*, p. 120). This situation is altered by a technological innovation, described by Rousseau as the "first revolution, which produced the establishment and differentiation of families."[25] The cohabitation characteristic of familial life results from this "first revolution"—the discovery or invention of the permanent habitation.[26] Unlike the other animal inhabitants of the state of nature, human beings can make this revolution because they alone can alter the circumstances in which they live. The actions of all other animals are determined instinctually; only humans "perhaps" have no instincts of their own (*Second*, pp. 106, 115). In addition to ("perhaps" instead of) being determined by instinct, human beings can change and develop their behavior, because they are potentially self-determining, by virtue of their "faculty of self-perfection" (*Second*, p. 114). Human perfectibility is the natural faculty enabling humanity to alter its circumstances so that it departs from the state of nature.

The invention of the permanent habitation is itself a departure from the state of nature. A dwelling cannot strictly speaking be deemed natural, because it is not truly necessary; humans previously did without them (*Second*, p. 112). But speaking less strictly, Rousseau can refer to "what is natural in the civil state." This implies that there can be natural responses to what are strictly speaking unnatural situations. The family is an example of such a natural response. Prior to the invention of the permanent habitation, the family is unnatural insofar as mothers can care for their offspring without male assistance, and insofar as males lack any inclination to assist them. Subsequently, men and women begin to live together, motivated in the beginning by some combination of convenience and inertia. Women now bear more children, and thus stand in need of male assistance. But that assistance is now forthcoming, because an effect of permanent cohabitation is the creation of the male desire to assist.

> The first developments of the heart were the effect of a new situation, which united husbands and wives, fathers and children in a common habitation. The habit of living together gave rise to the sweetest sentiments known to men: conjugal love and paternal love (*Second*, pp. 146–47).

As a result of the creation of the permanent domicile, fathers live with children and are now habituated to love them. Maternal love too, it is important to note, is an effect of habituation. "The mother nursed her children at first for her own need; then, habit having endeared them to her, she nourished them afterward for their need" (*Second*, p. 121). Thus for Rousseau, to love children is for both parents a natural (in the sense of automatic) consequence of living with them. Paternal love for children follows no less automatically than does maternal love from the experience of living with children; the only difference between the two loves is that mothers naturally live with their children because they nurse them, and fathers do not. One could say that maternal love is the natural response to a natural circumstance, whereas paternal love (and with it the family) is the natural result of an unnatural circumstance.

The institution of the family is an important point of transition in Rousseau's argument. It signifies the end of that period during which human sexuality was compatible with individual independence. He argues that the sexes are in the most crucial respects equal in the state of nature, that they live together peacefully in the state of nature; he thereby demonstrates that human individuals are not constrained naturally to depend on one another by virtue of their sexuality. By nature, human individuals are of course born sexual creatures; yet by nature they are also born free.

The family puts an end to their freedom. Within its confines, human beings come to depend on one another sexually. This is most obvious in the case of females. Women bear more children, and are more preoccupied with the raising of those children. They are therefore less capable of providing for and protecting themselves and their children, and hence more reliant upon their spouses' assistance. Because of the new situation in which they are placed, women are weaker (more dependent) than was previously the case. In addition, the division of labor which the practice of cohabitation introduces weakens them still further: "It was then that the first difference was established in the way of life of the two sexes, which until this time had been but one. Women became more sedentary and grew accustomed to tend the hut and the children, while the man went to seek their common subsistence" (*Second*, p. 147). The woman remains within the hut while the man ventures forth outside it: the creation of the family brings about the woman's confinement within the family.

If the familial division of labor weakens women, one might expect that it would also have the effect of strengthening men. But Rousseau's argument is of great interest because he denies this. The practice of cohabitation weakens both women and men. "The two sexes . . . began, by their slightly softer life, to lose something of their ferocity and vigor. . . . Each one separately became less suited to combat savage beasts" (*Second*, p. 147). The development of the family occasions the physical dependence of women upon men; but far more importantly it occasions the psychological dependence of each sex upon the other. What individuals of both sexes experience as a result of the institution of the family is of greater importance than are the consequences specific to either sex. Familial life is the cause of the loss not only of female independence, but of all of humanity's individual independence.

But Rousseau does not condemn the family as the agent of the loss of individual independence. On the contrary; although individual independence may have been good for human beings, dependence per se is not necessarily bad for them. Rousseau praises original familial dependence because of the sentiments underlying it. The family is "a little society all the better united because reciprocal affection and freedom [are] its only bonds" (*Second*, p. 147). It is based on conjugal and paternal love, "the sweetest sentiments known to men" (*Second*, pp. 146–47). Familial life weakens individuals, making them depend on one another; but if it renders "each one separately . . . less suited to combat savage beasts," it nevertheless makes it "easier" for them "to assemble in order to resist [the beasts] jointly." The weakened links are jointly as strong as the powerful chain which they compose. Thus the institution of the original family proves that human dependence under certain circumstances can be free, reciprocal, hence worthy of commendation. Rousseau is so far from condemning familial dependence that he regards the period after its institution as historically "the best for man," explicitly to be preferred to "the indolence of the primitive state" which preceded it (*Second*, pp. 150–51).

As we have seen it emerge to this point, conjugal love is a conservative social sentiment. It emerges as the effect of the experience of men and women living with one another, serving to confirm the practice of cohabitation to which they become habituated. Soon, however, another expression of the sentiment of sexual dependence comes into being. Sexual dependence emerges as the cause of the desire to cohabit, no longer simply as the effect of the practice of cohabitation. Having at first confirmed the practices to which men and women were habituated, sexual dependence later causes them to modify their practices.

The Political Implications of Romantic Love

The altered form of sexual dependence can be considered as the first emergence of romantic love.[27] Men now desire to cohabit with specific women before having done so. If conjugal love emerges as the satisfaction taken in what has been experienced, romantic love is the desire for what has not been experienced. Romantic love therefore seeks to change and not to confirm the status quo. It is more easily opposed and subject to frustration than is conjugal love. Like conjugal love, romantic love is "a tender and gentle sentiment"; unlike it, "at the least obstacle [it] becomes an impetuous fury" (*Second*, p. 148). Conjugal love, the expression of familial society, is associated with concord, and romantic love with conflict.

Because it alters the status quo, romantic love is of political importance. It impels men and women to transcend the original family unit, thereby bringing about the total socialization of the human species. For the family as we have described it is so attractive that one must wonder why it is not self-sufficient. This is the question posed by Rousseau in the ninth chapter of his *Essay on the Origin of Languages*. At the time of the development of the original family unit, primitive humans "had the concept of a father, a son, a brother, but not that of man. Their hut contained all of their fellow men. Stranger, beast, monster: these were all one to them. Apart from themselves and their family, the whole universe would count as nothing to them" (*Essay*, p. 45). Conjugal love is so far from guaranteeing the generalized socialization of humanity that it is here seen to combat it. Rousseau then goes on to develop the distinction between conjugal and romantic love, together with its political implications:

> There were families, but there were no nations. There were domestic languages, but there were no popular ones. There were marriages but there was no love at all. Each family was self-sufficient and perpetuated itself exclusively by inbreeding. . . . Instinct held the place of passion; habit held the place of preference. They became husband and wife without ceasing to be brother and sister (*Essay*, p. 33).

Socialization within the family does not explain socialization beyond the family. Unless one assumes (as Rousseau does not) that the incest prohibition is inherent or instinctual, the original family might be a self-sufficient social unit that would actually militate against further socialization. It is quite possible to have families without nations.

Why is the family transcended? In both the *Second Discourse* and the *Essay*, Rousseau suggests two explanations: economic development and romantic love. Rousseau's emphasis on the role played by economics in the formation of civil society is well known: "the true founder of civil society" was "the first person who . . . fenced off a plot of ground" (*Second*, p. 141). The invention of agriculture led to the institution of private property, which led in turn to "the first rules of justice," and ultimately (at the suggestion of the rich) to the creation of "a political establishment" (*Second*, pp. 154, 158–59).

The institution of government would thus have been unthinkable without the institution of private property in land: "agriculture . . . leads to property, government, and laws" (*Essay*, p. 37). But the development of agriculture was itself an effect of the emergence of the family: "until the family was instituted, and men had stable habitation, there was no . . . agriculture" (*Essay*, p. 34).[28] By leading to the introduction of agriculture, the family brings about its own transcendence and the birth of the political community. Even though Rousseau sees the genesis of political institutions as an outgrowth of economic developments, agricultural economics itself is a response to erotic developments: sexuality is the bridge to politics in the sense that the human transformation of sexuality is necessary (though not in itself sufficient) for the emergence of the polity.

Rousseau understands the origin of politics to be psychological as well as institutional in character, however; not only must one account for the emergence of laws and magistrates, one must also explain the origins of interfamilial solidarity and of the urge to dominate others and to win their approval. Economic developments play a role here, too; nevertheless, the role played by romantic love is much more direct and decisive in bringing about these very important psychological transformations than is the case with regard to the introduction of political institutions.

Economic needs provided the historical occasion for the emergence of romantic love: interfamilial society was initially occasioned in warm, arid countries by the need to cooperate in order to sink wells (*Essay*, p. 44). But the important conversations which took place around these wells were erotic and not economic in character. It is around wells that "the first rendezvous of the two sexes [took place]. Girls would come to seek water for the household, young men would come to water their herds. . . . The heart . . . feels a pleasure at not being alone. . . . There at last was the true cradle of nations: from the pure crystal of the fountains flow the first fires of love" (*Essay*, pp. 44–45). In the *Second Discourse* as well it is romantic attachments which are of crucial importance in breaking down the self-sufficiency of the family: "Permanent proximity cannot fail to engender at length some contact between different families. Young people of different sexes live in neighboring huts; the passing intercourse demanded by nature soon leads to another kind no less sweet and more permanent through mutual frequentation" (*Second*, p. 148). According to the *Second Discourse*, the invention of politics in the strict sense follows as a consequence of the invention of private property. In a looser sense, however, political life can be said to have begun with the institution of interfamilial contacts; for these contacts led human beings to "form in each country a particular nation, unified by customs and character, not by regulations and laws but by the same kind of life and foods and by the common influence of climate" (*Second*, p. 148).

Thus particularized or romantic love has the paradoxical effect of generalizing human affections or fully socializing humanity. This paradox can easily be resolved. For the principle of physical love, that "any woman is good for [natural man]," seems to be more general than in fact it is. In fact, the *Essay* teaches us, "any woman" can mean the woman closest at hand—at the stage of familial society, one's sister. If the individual inside the family is no longer self-sufficient, his or her desires can still readily be satisfied within the family. Because the problem of individual insufficiency is so easily solved it is not yet really a problem.

Particularized love implies that the problem of individual insufficiency is felt more acutely. To say that "the heart . . . [now] feels pleasure at not being alone" is to say that it can feel pain at being alone, that it can feel alone even in the midst of brothers and sisters. Perhaps only one specific woman will now satisfy a specific man; but she might now be *any* woman, because she need no longer be the woman closest at hand. The heightened sense of individual insufficiency particularizes love, and provides individuals with a motive for desiring to extend sociability beyond the family.[29] Romantic love is political because it leads to the creation of peoples, because it reflects individual dissatisfaction with life led within the family.

For the same reason romantic love is the source of popular as opposed to domestic languages. Passion, not need, explains the origin of language and hence the origin of society: "In a mild climate with fertile land, it took all the animation of pleasurable feelings to start the people speaking" (*Essay*, p. 46). For people to talk to one another, they must sense a void which others can help to remedy. "In a mild climate with fertile land," they cannot lack material sustenance, with which they can easily provide themselves. They can only feel the desire to be mutually completed by one another. Again we see that romantic love socializes people because it gives evidence of their individual insufficiency.

We now arrive at a root cause of Rousseau's ambivalence toward sexual dependence. We have just emphasized the generalizing effect of romantic love, the role that it plays in bringing political society into being. But Rousseau never denies that romantic love is particularized and particularizing, despite its generalizing effect. Moral love "determines . . . desire and fixes it exclusively on a single object" (*Second*, p. 134). It is an obvious question whether love of this sort is compatible with Rousseau's general and egalitarian morality. In obeying the general will, "as each gives himself to all, he gives himself to no one" (*Social*, I, 6, p. 53). Obedience to the law substitutes "a moral and legitimate equality for whatever physical inequality nature may have placed between men" (*Social*, I, 9, p. 58). Physical and not moral love would seem to correspond to this morality— "any woman is good" for primordial man because, obedient to the dictates of physical love, he makes no distinction among women. By contrast, it is obvious that romantic love is inconceivable without the making of distinctions among potential mates: "People grow accustomed to consider different objects and to make comparisons; imperceptibly they acquire ideas of merit and beauty which produce sentiments of preference" (*Second*, p. 148).

Romantic love thus has two different consequences of political importance. We have seen that it creates the condition of political morality: it fashions a potentially solidary people out of hitherto discrete, self-sufficient, mutually suspicious families. But no sooner does it do so than it threatens the very maintenance of the solidarity whose existence it makes possible. The *Essay* emphasizes the former, positive aspect, and the *Second Discourse* the latter, negative one. Yet the two aspects are necessarily connected; in the end neither is conceivable without the other.

Rousseau contends that love is responsible not only for language, but for the other modes of self-expression which may be regarded as extensions of language—singing, dancing, communal festivities. In short, love is responsible for the performing arts. He traces this same development in both writings, but with strikingly different emphases. Consider first the *Essay*'s description:

> The original festivals developed. Feet skipped with joy, earnest gestures no longer sufficed, being accompanied by an impassioned voice; pleasure and desire mingled and were felt together. There at last was the true cradle of nations (*Essay*, p. 45).

It would be difficult to paint a more attractive picture of communal solidarity developing out of the mutual expression of tender, innocent, sincere romantic sentiments. Love leads to art, love leads to politics; all is in harmony.

But compare the treatment of the same sequence of historical developments in the *Second Discourse*:

> People grew accustomed to assembling in front of the huts or around a large tree; song and dance, true children of love and

leisure, became the amusement or rather the occupation of idle and assembled men and women. Each one began to look at the others and to want to be looked at himself, and public esteem had a value. The one who sang or danced the best, the handsomest, the strongest, the most adroit, or the most eloquent became the most highly considered; and that was the first step toward inequality, and, at the same time, toward vice. From these first preferences were born on one hand vanity and contempt, on the other shame and envy; and the fermentation caused by these new leavens eventually produced compounds fatal to happiness and innocence (*Second*, p. 149).

Here too love leads to art, and love leads to politics. But Rousseau evaluates these same phenomena very differently here. Festivities do not unite peoples, instead they divide individuals. Natural inequalities which had earlier been irrelevant are now used in the erection of a hierarchy of desirability. Precisely what the morality of the general will must overcome (the importance of natural inequalities) is brought into being at the festivities, the "true children of love."

Yet love is no less important as a political phenomenon in this account than it is in the *Essay*. It is just that the political is understood differently here than in the *Essay*. In the *Essay*, the political is equated with national solidarity; love is political because it transcends the family and establishes national solidarity. The *Second Discourse* equates the political with the search for individual pride and preeminence. Here love is political because it lies at the root of "public esteem," of "the idea of consideration" (*Second*, p. 149). Love gives birth to the desire for admiration; and this desire is soon extended from the desire for the admiration of the beloved to the desire for the adulation of the whole community. One could say that the aspiring tyrant simply radicalizes and universalizes the sentiment underlying the behavior of the serenading lover (while failing to reciprocate the love he seeks). Politics is not seen as the harmonious merging of individuals into a people, but as the competition of selfish individuals for public approval, for those third-order needs stemming from public opinion.

The two works point to two different socializing effects of love, positive and negative. Love socializes humans by making them recognize their need to be completed by others. The attractive primeval nation described in the *Essay* is based on the joint and mutual generalization of this recognition. But love also implies the desire to be recognized by others as the desirable agent of their completion. It therefore provides a basis for the exploitation of others. For the desire to be desired by others can take on a life of its own, far surpassing in intensity the desire for others. In the *Essay* love unites us to others because the desire for others and the desire to be desired by others are equal and reciprocal. In the *Second Discourse*, love leads us to exploit others because the desire to be desired by others surpasses the desire for others. Elsewhere Rousseau distinguishes between the phenomena described in the two works by calling reciprocal desire "love" and unreciprocal desire "vanity" (*Emile*, V, p. 430).[30] This distinction is compatible with the presentation of the *Second Discourse*; but the *Second Discourse* explains vanity as a "true child of love." The desire to be desired exists first in love, together with desire proper; it then liberates itself, becoming independent in the form of vanity.[31]

The *Second Discourse* supplements the *Essay* by focusing on desire and also dependence that is not reciprocated. The extreme form of unreciprocated desire is not vanity but jealousy. We saw above that jealousy did not exist in the original state of nature. Now it has come into being, causing the conflicts which did not exist earlier.

> By dint of seeing one another, they can no longer do without seeing one another again. A tender and gentle sentiment is gradually introduced into the soul and at the least obstacle becomes an impetuous fury. Jealousy awakens with love; discord triumphs, and the gentlest of the passions receives sacrifices of human blood (*Second*, pp. 148–49).

As women become more important to men, women become the cause of disputes among men. Generalized sexuality and sexual peace are replaced by particularized sexuality and sexual combat; love is political not only as it unites families and originates languages but also as it divides individuals and occasions wars. Rousseau's Cain could well murder Abel because of jealousy, as the Bible suggests; his jealousy, however, would be excited by the choice of a woman.

To summarize, Rousseau presents two versions of his account of primeval sexuality and its humanization. In the *Second Discourse* (though not in the *Essay*), he argues for the original compatibility of natural sexuality with human independence. The humanization of sexuality is tantamount to the human creation of sexual dependence. The effects of that creation are of greatest interest to us, however. Both versions agree that the humanization of sexuality leads to the full socialization of the human species. My earlier formulation—that humanized sex is a bridge to politics—can be repeated here. National solidarity and individual desire for public preeminence are both political phenomena; Rousseau praises one and condemns the other. Yet both emerge from the humanization of sexuality. Rousseau is ambivalent about humanized sexuality because he is ambivalent about the humanization and politicization of the species.

The Natural Sexuality of Civilized Human Beings

Rousseau's second account of the nature of sexuality is found in *Emile* and the *Letter to D'Alembert*. In these works Rousseau does not explain how the sexual dependence of civilized men and women comes into being (the focus of the *Second Discourse* account), but how it functions. Sexual dependence is understood to be "natural in the civil state," although it is unnatural "in the savage state."

Rousseau argues that sexual relationships between civilized men and women are inherently psychological as well as physical in character—exactly the opposite of his description of natural sex among the savages. In speaking of civilized humans, one cannot "begin by distinguishing between the moral and the physical in the sentiment of love" (*Second*, p. 134). Love is naturally a moral relationship, because it involves the mutual interdependence of the two sexual partners. It is in some sense a political relationship because the interdependence of the partners is expressed in each partner's experience of ruling and being ruled through it.

The treatment of sexual modesty well illustrates the difference between the two accounts. Sexual modesty is not a major theme of the *Second Discourse*. Rousseau argues there that sexual desire is primordially limited, because it is not inflamed by the imagination; humans are naturally continent, one could say. But he also contends that sexuality is random and promiscuous; it is in fact because sexual partners are so readily available that their favors are so lackadaisically sought after. And an important reason for the ready availability of sexual partners is the comparative unimportance of pregnancy in the original state of nature. Women conceive infrequently, can nurse their offspring without great difficulty, and need nurse them for a relatively brief time. The consequences of the sexual act for the two sexes are then surprisingly similar: women are not significantly more inconvenienced than are men.

Rousseau's accounts of sexuality in *Emile* and the *Letter to D'Alembert*, however, emphasize the importance of sexual modesty, and in particular the importance of the difference in the consequences of sexual union for the two sexes. In presenting this alternative account, Rousseau poses a series of rhetorical questions:

> Why should we blush at the needs which nature has given us? Why should we find a motive for shame in an act so indifferent in itself and so beneficial in its effects as the one which leads to the perpetuation of the species? Since the desires are equal on both sides, why should their manifestations be different? Why should one of the sexes deny itself more than the other in the penchants which are common to both? Why should man have different laws on this point than the animals? (*Letter*, p. 83).

Consider the relevance of these questions to the original natural man and woman as portrayed in the *Second Discourse*: humans do not naturally blush, and find no motive for shame; the natural female is not more modest than the male, and the sexual behavior of the human species is not radically different from that of the animals. The sexual modesty discussed by Rousseau in *Emile* and the *Letter* is therefore altogether unnatural by the standard of the *Second Discourse*.

Yet in both *Emile* and the *Letter* Rousseau wishes to defend the natural status of modesty. To do so he asserts the importance of the differentiation between males and females, departing again from the *Second Discourse* account. "In the union of the sexes each contributes equally to the common aim, but not in the same way. . . . [The man] ought to be active and strong; [the woman] passive and weak. One must necessarily will and be able; it suffices that the other put up little resistance" (*Emile*, V, p. 358). It would seem that Rousseau here follows the tradition of emphasizing male strength and female weakness. In fact it is very important to note that he does not; his statements are normative and not simply descriptive. He does not say that sexual acts are successful because men are stronger than women. He says instead that they are successful only *if* men are stronger than women. Men are potentially stronger than women; the problem is to actualize that potential. For woman's desire is permanent, whereas man's desire is temporary.[32] Successful sexual acts require the arousal of the male, which is to say that unsuccessful sexual acts result from his failure to be aroused. Sexual desire is not a psychological problem in the early stages of the state of nature as described in the *Second Discourse*; as we have seen, desire arises infrequently and sporadically, but there is no suggestion that it does not arise mutually in both sexes. But here Rousseau calls the mutuality into question. At this stage of his account, female desire seems to be wholly spontaneous, physical, and natural; man's desire, by contrast, is sporadic and hence uncertain.

The guarantee of sexual success (that is, the sexual act's attainment of its natural end) is, then, male arousal. The sexual act is a social relationship, requiring the cooperation of two individuals. Of the two individuals, the female's performance is guaranteed, but not the male's. Male desire is the weaker of the two, yet the strength of female desire is of no avail without male assistance. The woman therefore depends upon the uncertain performance of the male for the satisfaction of her desire. Paradoxically, the weakness of male desire gives the male priority in the relationship; because he is weak, the female must please him. Since it is only the man who must "will and be able," he need not please his mate. The mutuality of the *Second Discourse* is abandoned at the outset in *Emile*. Rousseau concedes that "this is not the law of love" (which presumably is mutual). "But it is [the law] of nature, prior to love itself" (*Emile*, V,

p. 358). If the problem of love is the arousal of mutual desire on the part of both partners, the problem of nature is the arousal of desire on the part of the male partner.

How then can the female please the male? "She ought to constrain him to find his strength and make use of it. The surest art for animating that strength is to make it necessary by resistance. Then *amour-propre* unites with desire" (*Emile*, V, p. 358). Male desire is weaker, but male physical strength is greater. If the male can triumph in the superiority of his physical strength, the weakness of his desire can be overcome. Successful physical love requires the psychological element of male *amour-propre*, or self-esteem. If female desire is spontaneous and physical, male desire is sporadic, and must therefore be given a psychological boost. In this account the male need for sex is not a second-order need, but from the very outset is a third-order need. (For this reason, Rousseau here is altogether consistent with his most radical statement of the conventionality of sexual desire, which is also found in *Emile*, even though he discusses the natural laws of sexual desire here. Male sexual desire is a product of the imagination, hence a psychological and not a physical need.)[33] Sex is not merely a bridge to the goods based on the esteem of men (or rather of women). The male desires not his partner, but his partner's esteem (and his own self-esteem) as the stronger. He desires to be desired more than he truly desires. Because of its psychological basis, the sexual relationship must seem to the male to be a political relationship; one in which his physical strength gives him title to rule the female. Because his desire is weaker, the male must seem to be the stronger. Female modesty, the resistance to male sexual advances which is then overcome, gives the male the desired appearance of strength.

A variant of the argument on behalf of modesty is to be found in the *Letter to D'Alembert*. Rousseau there defends female modesty on hedonistic grounds: favors granted reluctantly are more eagerly sought after than those granted freely. In *Emile*, female modesty gives men desire; it is a necessary condition of the success of the sexual act. In the *Letter* the argument stresses not simply the possibility but also the pleasurability of sexuality. "The apparent obstacle, which seems to keep this object at a distance, is in reality what brings it nearer. The desires, veiled by shame, become only the more seductive; in hindering them, chasteness inflames them" (*Letter*, p. 84).[34] Inflamed desires are a source of pain and conflict in the *Second Discourse*; here a source of pleasure and delight. Rousseau vindicates the cause of humanized as opposed to animal sexuality in the *Letter*—exactly the opposite of his rhetorical intention in the *Second Discourse*. The instinctual, physical mutuality of desire, made to seem so attractive in the *Second Discourse*, is here subjected to what could be called an "agonizing reappraisal":

If the two sexes had equally made and received the advances, vain importunity would have never been preserved; the passions, ever languishing in a boring freedom, would have never been excited; the sweetest of all the sentiments would hardly have touched the human heart, and its object would have been badly fulfilled (*Letter*, p. 84).

A more thoroughgoing attack on the sexual life of the original state of nature from a strictly hedonistic standpoint would be hard to imagine. Female modesty, absent in the original state of nature, makes sexual encounters more enjoyable for both partners. Sexual pleasure is therefore a benefit bestowed upon human beings by their civilization. The *Letter to D'Alembert* here provides a hedonistic defense of civilized life; yet for all its hedonism, it is remarkably similar to the *Social Contract*'s moral justification of civilized life: for in the latter work too we are told that man "ought ceaselessly to bless the happy moment that tore him away from [the state of nature] forever, and that changed him from a stupid, limited animal into an intelligent being and a man" (*Social*, I, 8, p. 56). Like morality, moral love is impossible in the state of nature, and is a positive aspect of civilized life.

If the male is to desire, then, his partner's favors must seem to him to be difficult to attain. That which is to be explained in the *Second Discourse* (the transformation of sex by chance into sex by choice) is here assumed from the outset. It may be assumed because in this account women manipulate men psychologically. Men appear to rule because of their physical strength, but their rule is largely a matter of appearance alone. In fact sexuality depends on the manipulation by women of men, which leads men to value women's favors more highly. Since men would not desire what they could easily attain, and since the satisfaction of their own desires requires women to arouse men's desires, Rousseau speaks of "the modesty and the shame with which nature armed the weak in order to enslave the strong" (*Emile*, V, p. 358). Just as the weakness of male desire gives men priority, so despite their physical weakness do women achieve a complementary priority. Despite their weakness, women rule by means of the weapon of their modesty, which makes them more desirable. Despite the greater permanence of female desire, women are better able than are men to repress their desire. In part, women do so so that men may better satisfy women's desire. If the desire of each sex can be satisfied only by the ministrations of the other (a key premise of Rousseau's teleological understanding of sexuality), it is obviously in the interest of the more desirous sex to inflame the desire of its less desirous counterpart. That men can satisfy the desire of women at all is a function of women's ability to mask their own desire, and so make themselves more desirable. There is, however, a second reason, unrelated to the satisfaction of sexual desire, which explains why women repress their desire. Because they are able to do so, women have far greater power over men (notwithstanding women's greater physical weakness). Modesty enables women to control men, hence to serve women's political as well as their sexual interests. Modesty serves this purpose by converting the physical weakness of women into strength.

In the *Second Discourse*, we noted, Rousseau denounces the sexual rule of women: he describes love as "an artificial sentiment born of the usage of society, and extolled with much skill and care by women in order to establish their ascendancy and make dominant the sex that ought to obey." We observed that by reason of this denunciation Rousseau emerges as a far severer critic of civilized sexual morality than is Buffon. For Buffon contends that women have benefited society as well as themselves by overcoming the tyrannical domination of men's brute physical superiority.

> It is only among the nations civilized to the point of politeness that women have obtained that equality of condition, which however is so natural and so necessary to the gentleness of society; this politeness in *moeurs* is also their work; they have opposed victorious arms to strength, since by their modesty they have taught us to recognize the empire of beauty, a natural advantage greater than that of strength, but which presupposes the art of making itself valued. . . . A thing's price increases with the difficulty of obtaining its possession. Women have had beauty ever since they have known how to respect themselves enough to refuse themselves to all those who wanted to attack them by other means than by those of sentiment; and once sentiment was born, politeness of *moeurs* had to follow from it.[35]

The Rousseau of the *Second Discourse* opposes Buffon's position, yet the Rousseau of *Emile* follows it faithfully. What women achieve artificially through love in the *Second Discourse* they achieve naturally through their modesty in *Emile*. Once again we see that "what is natural in the civil state" is not "what is natural in the savage state."

The sexual relations of civilized men and women are thus an expression of their respective desires to rule. The modesty of women is the all-important psychological regulator of these relations; it moderates the rule, by alternately compensating both males and females for their respective weaknesses. We have just seen how it compensates women for their inferiority in physical strength, but it compensates men for the weakness of their desire as well. Because of the role of modesty, the sexual relationship embodies the alternating rule of each of the sexes, but the absolute and tyrannical rule of neither.

How does modesty benefit both sexes? "If reserve did not impose on one sex [i.e., women] the moderation which nature imposes on the other, the result would soon be the ruin of both, and mankind would perish by the means established for preserving it" (*Emile*, V, pp. 358–59). Note that male and not female modesty is equated here with nature, contrary to Rousseau's statement above. If physiology is equated with nature (the position of the *Second Discourse*), this is the case; males and not females are biologically continent, limited in desire.[36]

Because female modesty places a psychological limitation on female desire, it compensates both sexes for the nonexistent physiological limitation. The restraint on female desire makes females more desirable, increasing the male desire to satisfy women, and serving the female desire to rule men. At the same time, female modesty also benefits the male sex. Were it not for female modesty the frequency of sexual encounters, occasioned by the insatiability of female desire, would be fatal to men, who "would be tyrannized by women, . . . would finally be their victims, and would see themselves dragged to death without being able to defend themselves" (*Emile*, V, p. 359).[37]

This is a bizarre and remarkable statement; in view of Rousseau's continual emphasis upon male superiority in physical strength, it may seem a particularly surprising argument for Rousseau to make. It is important to note, however, that in Rousseau's view female desirability (unrestrained by female modesty) would effectively negate male superiority in physical strength. Males would be tyrannized by females because they would *want* to be tyrannized by them: men would be women's "victims" because of "the ease with which women arouse men's senses and reawaken in the depths of their hearts the remains of ardors which are almost extinguished" (*Emile*, V, p. 359). For this reason, Rousseau would not have to rely on the very different reasoning which Hobbes presents in *Leviathan*, where he too must explain the vulnerability (in a very different context) of the physically strong before the physically weak: "The weakest has strength to kill the strongest, either by secret machination, or by confederacy with others."[38] Women would not need to make use of stratagems or to unite with other women in order to subjugate men; men would not be "able to defend themselves" because they would not be *eager* to defend themselves. Earlier, we saw that men are sexual because they desire to appear to rule; Rousseau's nightmarish fantasy of sexually insatiable females suggests an alternative vision of men whose sexuality causes them to desire to be enslaved. The relationship between male sexuality and male submission points to a major theme of Rousseau's second teaching—the dangers and disadvantages of sexuality for men. But in any case, Rousseau's immediate purpose in this context is to stress not the dangers of sexuality but instead the success with which female modesty averts them: it ensures both male potency in sexual encounters and male survival despite them. In the absence of female modesty, male desire would be either too weak to suit women's desire, or too strong to suit men's ability to perform.

A comparison to the *Second Discourse* is again illuminating. There too Rousseau speaks of the potentially fatal consequences of the sexual act, but with a completely different emphasis. "Among the passions . . . there is . . . a terrible [one] which . . . in its fury, seems fitted to destroy the human race it is destined to preserve" (*Second*, p. 134; see also p. 149). But the terrible passion does not destroy the human race because primitive sexuality is random, promiscuous, and wholly without a psychological component. According to the *Second Discourse*, only purely biological sexuality is *not* potentially destructive to humanity—precisely the opposite of Rousseau's argument in *Emile*. Jealousy and modesty are both psychological phenomena related to the expression of sexual desire: one is probably inconceivable without the other. Yet the presence of the former ("in the savage state") and the absence of the latter ("in the civil state") are both held to have equally fatal effects upon the human species.

Thus the function of sexual psychology is to reverse, or compensate for the differences in, sexual physiology. Men should be strong and women weak: yet by nature (when nature is equated with biology) female desire is infinite, male desire finite, all-too-finite. The purpose of nature (the success of the procreative act) is achieved through the agency of female modesty, a psychological phenomenon which reverses what nature seemingly ordains by the different physical endowments it bestows upon the two sexes: female desire is weakened, which has the effect of strengthening or inflaming male desire. By a "law . . . of nature" females must please males in order to make men desire; but because men do desire, it is also a law of nature that they depend on women. "The stronger appears to be master, but actually depends on the weaker. This is due not to a frivolous practice of gallantry or to the proud generosity of a protector, but to an invariable law of nature" (*Emile*, V, p. 360). Paradoxically, then, because women must please men so as to make men desire, men must please women so as to persuade women to allow men to satisfy their male desires. No sooner does Rousseau deny the natural need for mutuality of desire in one breath than he asserts it with his next. A "law of nature . . . causes [man] . . . to depend on [woman's] wish, and constrains him to seek to please her in turn, so that she will consent to let him be the stronger" (*Emile*, V, p. 360). The sexual relationship is a political relationship because men and women alternate in it as ruler and ruled. As Hegel observes, it is not always so easy to distinguish the master from the slave.[39]

Historically, sexual dependence leads up to political dependence, and, psychologically, the sexual relationship is akin to a political relationship. These conclusions emerge from this analysis of Rousseau's accounts of natural sexuality. At this point they remain as somewhat formal conclusions, however. I have shown that there is a relationship between politics and sexuality but not how the relationship affects politics and sexuality. To remedy this defect, we must now examine sexual dependence relative to the various political regimes, noting the reciprocal effects that societies and sexual *moeurs* have had upon one another.

3

The Political History
of Sexuality

Civilized sexuality is political in that it enables men and women to rule one another. This conclusion, established in the foregoing survey of the natural history of sexuality, now serves as the premise for a discussion of its political history. Sexual interdependence has a political history because sexual relationships not only resemble political ones but also affect them in important ways.

To say that sexual relations affect the polity is to suggest that women affect the polity. In many respects this is a surprising claim for Rousseau to make, since he clearly does not regard women as citizens. He believes instead that the "power" of women ought to be "exercised solely in conjugal union" (*Second*, p. 89). As we shall see, this means that their power over men ought not to be exercised in extramarital liaisons; but it also means that their power ought not to be exercised as voters or as magistrates.[1] If "love is the realm of women" (*Letter*, p. 47), politics appears to be exclusively the realm of men.

Why does Rousseau endorse the exclusion of women from direct political participation? To begin with, he associates political participation with the capacity and the obligation to bear arms; only those whose bodies enable them to be soldiers can truly be citizens. Male physical strength in itself is no more a title to political than to sexual rule;[2] but it is a necessary precondition to political rule. Brute force does not legitimate a ruler; but in a world of competing sovereignties and domestic insurrections no ruler, however legitimate, can hope to survive without adequate force at his disposal. In sexual relations, "an invariable law of nature" dictates that the stronger depend on the weaker; but in military matters, "the most inviolable of all laws of nature is the law of the strongest" (*Emile*, V, p. 60; *Poland*, XII, p. 80).

Because of external threats, sovereign communities must be large enough to defend themselves. Yet for "internal and absolute" reasons (which ought to take precedence over the fear of external threats), good political communities must be small (*Social*, II, 9, p. 73). Rousseau responds to this dilemma by advocating a republican citizen militia. "The state's true defenders are its individual citizens, no one of whom should be a professional soldier, but each of whom should serve as a soldier as duty requires" (*Poland*, XII, p. 81). "In a republic, men are needed" (*Letter*, p. 101) because republics lack standing armies and depend on comparatively small groups of citizen-soldiers to defend themselves. Thus Rousseau associates republicanism with masculinity. For a republic to survive, its citizen-soldiers, who are likely to be outnumbered on the battlefield, must be willing to risk their lives in its defense.

For biological reasons, the soldiers who are to defend the republic must be male. Because men are physically stronger than are women, it is more reasonable to ask men to die on the battlefield than it is to ask women to do so. Everything else being equal, a male can more plausibly hope to survive a life-or-death encounter than can a woman. The male soldier risking his life is courageous; the female soldier risking hers would be rash.

Men are also needed, Rousseau adds, because women are inconvenienced by pregnancy. "Will a woman abruptly and regularly change her life without peril and risk? Will she be a nurse today and a warrior tomorrow? . . . Will she suddenly go from shade, enclosure, and domestic cares to the harshness of the open air, the labors, the fatigues, and the perils of war?" (*Emile*, V, p. 362).[3] Rousseau contends that the bodily distinction between the sexes is politically relevant because war is politically relevant. Because of war, politics is primarily the realm of men.

Male superiority in combat is one reason for Rousseau's identification of citizenship with masculinity, but it is not his only reason. For Rousseau's defense of citizen courage is not quite as utilitarian as the above argument would suggest. Citizen courage is not merely a necessity which might be rendered superfluous at some future date by the technological development of insuperable defensive weapons. It is instead an admirable quality in itself, reflecting as it does the capacity to subordinate the natural desire for self-preservation in the name of the greater good of one's fellow citizens. Citizen courage is good because it makes republicanism possible; but this proposition is at least as true when reversed, for it is also the case that republicanism is good because it provides for the exercise and display of citizen courage.

When one considers what makes citizen courage possible, one can see why Rousseau might contend that psychology as well as physiology makes men more likely to be citizens than are women.

He could do so because in his view citizenship is by definition unnatural; to be a citizen is to be "denatured" (*Emile*, I, p. 40; cf. *Social*, II, 7, p. 68), because it is to prefer the general will to one's own particular will. The citizen must alienate "all his rights to the whole community" (*Social*, I, 6, p. 53), up to and including the right to life: "When the prince has said, . . . 'It is expedient for the State that you should die,' [the citizen] ought to die" (*Social*, II, 5, p. 64). Paradoxically, because men are naturally more isolated than are women, it might be easier for them to be denatured, or totally to alienate themselves and their rights to the community. The isolated male need alienate only his life; the female, who is naturally more social (if only because of her more immediate ties to her children), would have to alienate not only her life, but her protection of her children's lives as well. On Rousseauian grounds it might therefore be harder for women than for men to generalize their wills, because women are more closely tied to more particular wills than are men.[4]

Because women are excluded from direct political participation, the realm of politics appears to be wholly male, and male political rulers appear to be wholly uninfluenced by their sexuality. But this appearance of the absolute rule of males does not wholly conform to reality. In politics as in sexuality, women can be said to rule to a considerable extent, even though they appear only to be ruled. In politics as in sexuality, one can say that male rule is open and apparent, whereas female rule is hidden and indirect.

We have seen Rousseau's insistence on the importance of the appearance of rule in male sexuality; he contends that men become sexually active because they wish to enjoy what they perceive as their domination over their female partners. "*Amour-propre* unites with [male] desire" (*Emile*, V, p. 358); the male wishes to compare his greater physical strength with that of his beloved, and to triumph in his perception of his superiority. He is sexual because his sexuality enables him to "triumph in . . . victory" (*Emile*, V, p. 358) over her.

The male believes that he triumphs over the female (as is evidenced in the male understanding of sexual union as a "conquest" or a "possession"); but in fact, to a considerable extent the male deceives himself. He thinks that he rules his partner directly; in reality, she manipulates him indirectly. The male may "triumph in . . . victory," but it is a victory "that the [female] has made him win" (*Emile*, V, p. 358). In sexual relations, "the stronger appears to be master but actually depends on the weaker" (*Emile*, V, p. 360).

Thus Rousseau's understanding of sexuality is based upon a distinction between the appearance of male rule and the reality of the joint rule of both sexes. Interestingly enough, this same distinction is to be found in Rousseau's explicitly political teaching. We have seen that, insofar as political rule is a matter of appearance, of manifest impersonal legal and institutional arrangements, Rousseau believes it should be wholly male. Manifest legal and institutional arrangements are undeniably important in Rousseau's view; he does not, however, limit his understanding of politics so as to take account of them alone. Rousseau's understanding is instead far more complex. Although he believes that political rule must be manifest and impersonal to be legitimate, he also believes that it must on occasion be hidden or personal to be effective. Because Rousseau ac-

knowledges the necessity of hidden and personal rule, he can also acknowledge and admire the political power of women (even as he advocates their formal political powerlessness).[5]

In one sense, the intentions of those who rule must be wholly apparent
if their rule is to be legitimate. There must be no distinction between the
appearance and the reality of rule.[6] Thus the first historical form of rule
was morally indefensible, because it ensued from a deception imposed
upon the poor by the rich: the rich "easily invented specious reasons," and
thus "w[o]n over crude, easily seduced men" (*Second*, p. 159). Today as
well, rule is illegitimate because it is deceptive: "Only individual interest
and men's passions reign under [the] name [of law]" (*Emile*, V, p. 473).
"All these grand words of society, of justice, of law, of mutual defense, of
help for the weak . . . are only lures invented by clever politicians . . . to
impose themselves on the simple" (*Fragments*, p. 475). In illegitimate
societies, the appearance of law masks a reality in which some take
advantage of others, in which burdens are not shared equally by fellow
citizens, in which "all" are "guided by secret motives" (*Social*, IV, 1,
p. 109).

Rousseau attempts to correct these deficiencies through the mecha-
nism of the general will, which operates so as to ensure that no one can
take advantage of another. The general will is designed to make rule
legitimate, by making it wholly impersonal and wholly manifest. Citizens
must know that they obey nobody but themselves, and hence that they
obey no one in particular. To achieve these two goals, laws must be made
by all and must apply to all (*Social*, I, 6, p. 53; cf. also Masters' n. 31 on
p. 137, as well as *Social*, II, 6, pp. 66–67). When laws are properly made,
when there is adherence to the general will, rule is legitimate. Then there
is no discrepancy between appearance and reality: "the State . . . has no
tangled contradictory interests; the common good is clearly apparent
everywhere" (*Social*, IV, 1, p. 108).

In another sense, however, political power cannot be altogether manifest, and is never wholly impersonal. This becomes clear at the very
outset of all legitimate societies. The citizens must enact the law themselves; but the laws which they enact must be proposed to them by a
legislator, who must deceive the people (by claiming divine sanction) in
order to persuade them to adopt his legislation (*Social*, II, 7, pp. 69–70).[7]
The people who openly enact the laws are thus unknowingly manipulated
by a particular individual into doing so.

The need for manipulative personal authority does not end with the
emergence of the state. Political leadership is always necessary, and is
most successful when least apparent: "The greatest talent of leaders is to
disguise their power and to make it less odious, and to manage the State so
peacefully that it seems to have no need for managers" (*Political*, p. 215).
Furthermore, the rule of law can never be wholly impersonal and man-

ifest, because written law cannot always answer the most important questions. For this reason, written law must always be supplemented by unwritten law, "the most important" part of the law, which consists of "mores, customs, and especially . . . opinion." Because it is unwritten, it is less than fully apparent, a latent and not a manifest phenomenon. Thus it is "not engraved on marble or bronze, but in the hearts of citizens." The existence and importance of unwritten law demonstrate the limits of manifest rule, which must always be supplemented by hidden rule. Unwritten law "*imperceptibly* substitutes the force of habit for that of authority." Hence "the great legislator attends [to it] *in secret* while *appearing* to limit himself to the particular regulations that are merely the sides of the arch of which mores, slower to arise, form at last the unshakable keystone" (*Social*, II, 12, p. 77, emphasis mine; cf. also *Social*, IV, 7, p. 124).

Personal authority is more effective than impersonal authority because it makes a greater emotional impact upon those subject to it.[8] Informal authority is often more effective than is formal authority, because of the tendency to resist formal authority. This is relevant to Rousseau's conception of the political role of women, because he associates women with personal and particularly with informal rule. This is evident from some of his political metaphors. Although the rule of magistrates must be impersonal, citizens should venerate their state in anthropomorphic terms: they should regard it as "the tender mother who nourishes them" (*Political*, p. 223).[9] Furthermore, the informal authority exerted by public opinion (which is greater than that formally exerted by legal authority) is also feminine in character: "Opinion" is the "queen of the world." It "is not subject to the power of kings; they are themselves her first slaves" (*Letter*, pp. 73–74).

Nor is Rousseau's association of women with control over public opinion wholly metaphorical. It is women who ultimately control the mores and opinions of male citizens. "Men's way of thinking in large measure depends" on women (*Letter*, p. 72). "Do you want to know men? Study women" (*Letter*, p. 82). Rousseau realizes that political authority is not wholly manifest and direct, and associates covert and indirect authority with the rule of women. Because this is so, what is true with regard to sexuality is also true with regard to politics: the reality of feminine power is greater than is its appearance.

Sexual interdependence is therefore politically important in that it enables women to influence what would otherwise appear to be the exclusively masculine political realm. Men govern politically even though in part they are governed sexually. In discussing the political history of sexual interdependence I shall explain the effects of each government upon the other, as they have related very differently to one another at different times.

In this account I shall focus on the two contrasting political societies that most preoccupy Rousseau—the classical republics of antiquity, and the corrupt regimes of modernity. Rousseau's critique of the modern regimes is incomprehensible outside the context of his adulation for republican antiquity. In his own time he sees men who are subjects, who let themselves be governed by others, who are too cowardly and self-interested to take on the responsibility of governing themselves. In antiquity, by contrast, he sees citizens—men who were courageous, unselfish, and dedicated to the common good. Patriotism and republican virtue flourished in classical Greece and Rome, but are almost nowhere to be found in the modern West. Ancient political life ennobled and elevated those who took part in it; at most, modern political life enriches those who are clever enough to know how to manipulate it. "Ancient politicians incessantly talked about morals and virtue, those of our time talk only of business and money" (*First*, p. 51).

Such in brief is the contrast that Rousseau draws between ancient and modern politics. But this contrast can in turn be understood in light of a second contrast—between sexual relations in antiquity and in modernity. For politics, the realm of men, is not sufficient unto itself. It is instead greatly influenced by the relations between men and women that underlie it. One cannot fully understand Rousseau's account of different political societies without incorporating his account of different arrangements of sexual relations.

The praiseworthy politics of the ancient republics seems, at first glance, to have been virtually uninfluenced by their women. "The ancients spent almost their whole lives in the open air, either dispatching their business or taking care of the state's in the public place. . . . In all of this, no women" (*Letter*, p. 101). If the ancients conducted their public life without women, the moderns by contrast seem not to have a true public life because they are thought to be effeminate, or to resemble women. As we shall see, Rousseau frequently describes the decline of political virtue in the modern West in terms of the emasculation or effeminacy of modern men. In this respect he, like other Enlightenment thinkers, follows Machiavelli, who was the first to associate virile republicanism with antiquity, and modernity with monarchy, Christianity, and effeminacy: "It would seem that the world has become effeminate and Heaven disarmed."[10]

We shall see Rousseau claim that the influence of modern women has made modern men effeminate. For this reason he poses the following rhetorical question: "Do you think . . . that, in taking so much effort to increase the ascendancy of women, men will be the better governed for it?" (*Letter*, p. 47).

Rousseau denounces the open ascendancy of modern women, however, only because it has led to the effeminacy of modern men. But it is possible for women to be sexually ascendant (while overtly submitting to the rule of men) without making men effeminate. This is most clearly demonstrated by the example of the republics of classical Greece, wherein women were in reality far more influential than was apparent at first glance. In Rome too Rousseau sees women as the "secret cause" of the republic's political strength.

This comparative historical analysis suggests that in Rousseau's opinion sexual interdependence has always given women influence, and that their influence has had good as well as bad effects on politics. Thus the choice between antiquity and modernity, or between republicanism and political corruption, is not one between the subjection and ascendancy of women. More properly it is one between two different modes of the ascendancy of women—a covert ascendancy (under which men maintain their masculinity) and an overt ascendancy (under which masculinity is attacked and ultimately obliterated). While Rousseau criticizes modern society, in which women cause men to resemble women, we shall see that he also criticizes an ancient society in which men caused women to resemble men. The good society is based instead upon sexual differentiation, entailing the mutual dependence of the two sexes. The question, then, is not whether women shall be ascendant over men, but rather how and to what extent they shall be ascendant.[11]

The Polis and the Family

To this point, by noting Rousseau's emphasis on hidden and indirect political influence, I have refuted one argument which would deny the political importance of women. I have yet to deal with a second argument, however, which denies not the reality of women's political ascendancy but its defensibility: if the family must be seen as a disruptive partial society, and if women are more attached to their families than are men, Rousseau cannot advocate women's political ascendancy. We must therefore consider the relationship between the family and the general will, as it existed in the political community which most closely adhered to the general will—the *polis* or the ancient city.

In the *polis*, citizens were both willing and able to subordinate their particular interests to that of the political community, or rather to identify their interests with that of their community—hence to generalize their wills. Rousseau admires the ancient citizen whose "value is determined by his relation to the whole, which is the social body. . . . Each individual believes himself no longer one but a part of the unity and no longer feels except within the whole" (*Emile*, I, pp. 39–40).

Citizens are not independent integers, but dependent parts of a larger political whole. In this respect they can be said to resemble members of families, who are dependent parts of a larger conjugal whole.

We have seen in chapter 2 that the family is the product of the loss of the primordial sexual independence of human beings. With the creation of political society (which requires that the family be transcended),[12] human beings come to live as dependent parts of two different wholes— the family and political society. It is clear that the *polis* suppresses individual self-interest in the name of communal solidarity. The individual parts are subordinated to the whole. What is less clear is the effect of this subordination on the family, the smaller social whole intermediate between the individual and the *polis*. I previously suggested that the *polis* would have to suppress families, because it would see them as individual parts subordinated to the political whole. A second possibility exists, however: families could be seen as smaller social wholes, which could aid the *polis* by teaching their members to be public-spirited, or to subordinate themselves to both the familial and the political wholes.

We have already seen why Rousseau can and does see the family as a threat to the political solidarity of the ancient city. The danger posed by the family can be said to underlie his comparison between Plato's theoretical vision and Sparta's practical example of the *polis*. Rousseau seems to prefer theory to practice: "Plato only purified the heart of man; Lycurgus denatured it" (*Emile*, I, p. 40). The remark seems like more of a criticism of the Spartan legislator than in fact it is: in the context Rousseau observes that "good social institutions are those that best know how to denature man" (*Emile*, I, p. 40). Nevertheless, it seems clear that it is better to purify than to denature; Rousseau explicitly argues that it is more feasible in practice to purify than to denature (despite the fact, which he acknowledges, that Plato and not Lycurgus was the theorist). He does not, however, explain what he means by "purify" and "denature."

To understand this distinction, we must compare the role of the family in the two regimes. We can do this by considering two anecdotes of Spartan life introduced by Rousseau in this context in order to illustrate the meaning of citizenship in the *polis*. In the first, a Spartan who has been denied political advancement to the Council of Three Hundred rejoices upon discovering that there are so many Spartans more worthy than himself.[13] In the second, a Spartan mother, whose five sons are fighting in the army, asks for news of the battle. She is told that her sons have been killed. She is enraged, and says that that was not what she asked. She is then told that Sparta won the battle, and thereupon runs to the temple to thank the gods. The first story, Rousseau says, illustrates the male, the second the female, citizen.

The second story illustrates Spartan denaturing better than the first. For on Rousseau's grounds, the Spartan male's political ambition is no more natural than is his political allegiance to Sparta. His case is surprising only in that the less selfish of his two unnatural sentiments predominates. But the Spartan mother does subordinate a natural sentiment in the name of her political allegiance. For Rousseau contends that familial attachment is more natural (though not itself unambiguously natural) than is political allegiance. Sparta maintains the particular family as a social institution; the mother knows that the slain soldiers are *her* children. Women were allowed to exert political influence in Sparta only because they were able to overcome their allegiance to their particular families. Nevertheless, they were allowed to do so, and the institution of the family continued to exist in Sparta.

Thus Sparta denatured its men (and in particular its women) in that it subordinated the family to the *polis*.[14] Rousseau's contention that Plato's *Republic* purifies rather than denatures can also be understood with reference to the family. For the *Republic*, unlike Sparta, generalizes rather than subordinates the familial attachment. The best regime in the *Republic* creates an artificial collective family. Fellow citizens (more accurately, fellow guardians) are to regard one another as fellow family members. This is the purpose of its institution of the communism of women and children. "With everyone [a guardian] happens to meet, he'll hold that he's meeting a brother, or a sister, or a father, or a mother, or a son, or a daughter or their descendants or ancestors."[15] The denatured Spartan mother rejoices at the death of her children; the purified male or female guardians of Plato's *Republic* are to fight exceptionally hard because they are fighting in defense of their "children."[16]

Loyalty to the *polis* is threatened by attachment to one's own family. The comparison between purification and denaturing seems to suggest that Rousseau prefers Plato's generalization of the family to Lycurgus's subordination of it. Rousseau's sympathy for the Platonic response is confirmed by a passage in his *Political Economy* that clearly reflects Plato's argument in the *Republic*.

> Public [as opposed to familial] education, under rules prescribed by the government . . . , is . . . one of the fundamental maxims of popular or legitimate government. If children are raised in common in the midst of equality, . . . if they are surrounded by examples and objects that constantly remind them of the tender mother who nourishes them, her love for them, the inestimable benefits they receive from her, and what they owe in return, there can be no doubt that they will learn from this to love one another as brothers, . . . and one day to become the defenders and fathers of the homeland whose children they will have been for so long (*Political*, p. 223).

Under this arrangement, the fathers "will have in common, under the name citizens, the same authority over their children that they exercised separately under the name *fathers*, and will be no less well obeyed when they speak in the name of the law than they were when they spoke in the name of nature" (*Political*, p. 223). Affection for the family ceases to threaten loyalty to the polity if the family can in some way be generalized or expanded so as to be confounded with the polity.[17]

Rousseau does not prefer Plato's *Republic* because Sparta lacks public education; he specifically cites Sparta as one of the few places where the beneficial effects of public education were to be seen, where "even in the family the republic commands in preference to the father" (*Fragments*, p. 488). Both Plato's *Republic* and Lycurgus's Sparta elevate political over familial authority, but Plato does so more radically, and so he purifies the human heart; whereas the more conservative Lycurgus more or less maintained the usual family unit, yet insisted (and what is remarkable, succeeded in his insistence) that the Spartans rejoice at the death of their next of kin, provided that through their death the city was victorious.[18] For this reason, Rousseau "would find [Lycurgus's regulations] far more chimerical" than Plato's—were it not for the fact that they were actually successfully implemented (*Emile*, V, p. 40).

Thus far we have seen Rousseau point to the ways in which the family endangers the ancient city. But it is extremely significant that he also indicates that the ancient city depends upon the family. For this reason, one can say that with respect to the family Rousseau ultimately prefers Lycurgus's less consistent conservatism to Plato's thoroughly consistent radicalism. In the end it is better to denature than to purify, better to retain a modified version of the individual family than to abolish it altogether. In part this is because the republic is too weak to generalize the particular family out of existence; in part it is because the republic is based upon the individual's willingness to subordinate his or her self to others— and only the family provides any sort of natural basis for such self-subordination. The male citizen is denatured, in that his loyalty to his particular family must not be absolute; he must be willing to die for the city rather than flee and live with his family. But the male citizen is not purified, in that his loyalty to his particular family is not generalized and hence eliminated; he is willing to fight for and defend his city, in part because in doing so he also fights for and defends his particular family.

It is desirable from a political standpoint to retain the particular family. This becomes apparent from Rousseau's discussion of Plato, whose advocacy of the destruction of the particular family unit Rousseau criticizes—although he also says that those who attack the *Republic*'s "alleged community of women . . . prove that [they] have never read him" (*Emile*, V, pp. 362–63).[19] Rousseau's criticism can be understood in terms of his attack upon what seems today to be Plato's far less radical earlier proposal in Book V of the *Republic*: the institution of identical education and employment of both sexes. It is because of his abolition of the family, Rousseau argues, that Plato is compelled to advocate this proposal.[20] Because the women of the *Republic* do not nurture children, do not perform the one set of tasks for which as women they are particularly fitted, "no longer knowing what to do with women, [Plato] found himself forced to make them men." The fault which Rousseau finds in Plato's plan, then, is

> that civil promiscuity which throughout confounds the two sexes in the same employments and in the same labors and which cannot fail to engender the most intolerable abuses. . . . [Rousseau deplores] that subversion of the sweetest sentiments of nature, sacrificed to an artificial sentiment which can only be maintained by them—as though there were no need for a natural base on which to form conventional ties; as though the love of one's nearest were not the principle of the love one owes the state; as though it were not by means of the small fatherland which is the family that the heart attaches itself to the large one; as though it were not the good son, the good husband, and the good father who make the good citizen! (*Emile*, V, pp. 362–63).[21]

Rousseau argues that the political interdependence of citizens in a republic emerges as an extension of the more natural conjugal interdependence of the family. Sexual division of labor within the family weakens men by making them dependent upon women. But at the same time it strengthens them, by making them aware of the dependence of their women upon them. A man will hunt more energetically, if need be fight more fiercely, because he provides for and defends two or more people, instead of just himself. In part because they now search for "their common subsistence," men are more active after the sexual division of labor than they were during "the indolence of the primitive state" (*Second*, pp. 147, 150–51).

Thus men become stronger, or more effective providers and defenders, when they sense the comparative weakness of the women dependent upon them.[22] The weakness of their dependent women makes them the strong men who are needed in a republic. Men fight to protect their republic, for which they feel an artificial political attachment, because in so doing they are fighting to protect their families, for which they feel a more natural conjugal attachment. Since men are stronger and more public-spirited when they fight in defense of weaker women, it follows that Plato errs greatly in attempting "to make [women] into men." "In a republic, men are needed"; one ensures that they exist by maintaining and heightening the distinction between the sexes, by sharply differentiating women from men.

Thus the male republican citizen is also a good family man; he is "the good son, the good husband, and the good father." This is not to claim that the ancient republic is a mere product of the family, exerting no reciprocal control upon it. On the contrary; it is proper for the republic to supervise the family. The state may define or regulate by law what it is to be a good father; indeed such legal assistance may be useful as a supplement to natural inclination in order to make fathers good.[23] Republican government may be incompatible with the absolute power of heads of families; it may require the substitution of public education for education within the family (though we shall soon see that neither of these statements is unqualifiedly correct); but it seems that it does not require, nor ought it to attempt, the destruction of the particular or natural family.

To say that patriotism emerges as an extention of conjugal affection is not to say that the republic itself may be understood as an extension or generalization of the family. This is another respect in which Rousseau criticizes Plato. For Rousseau's extended metaphor comparing familial to political attachment, quoted above, is uncharacteristic even of the *Political Economy* in which it appears. In the metaphor Rousseau attempts to perform the difficult if not impossible task of providing a republican version of the analogy comparing the state to a family. That analogy had been typically employed by monarchists, such as Robert Filmer: since there is but one father in the family, who rules, so ought there to be but one ruler in the state—the monarch. Rousseau's explicit rejection of Filmer's analogy could hardly be worded more strongly: "Since the State has nothing in common with the family except the obligation of their leaders to make each of them happy, the same rules of conduct could not be suited to both" (*Political*, p. 211). He then refers to "the odious system that Sir Filmer tried to establish in a work entitled *Patriarcha*." Rousseau also makes the irrelevance of the familial analogy clear at the very outset of the *Social Contract*:

> The entire difference is that in the family, the father's love for his children rewards him for the care he provides; whereas in the State, the pleasure of commanding substitutes for this love, which the leader does not have for his people (*Social*, I, 2, p. 47).[24]

Familial affection cannot be generalized; one loves one's own children, but one cannot love all children. For this reason the republic is wrongly seen as an extended family. Even in his own metaphor, Rousseau claims no more than that the citizens learn to love their country (not their country's magistrates) as a mother. He does not claim that the magistrates can or should regard the citizens as their children.

The Political Power of the Women of Sparta

Citizen-soldiers may be willing to die for their country because they see it as their "tender mother." But they also die for it because they are protecting the women who really are their "tender mothers," and their wives, and their daughters. This is the source of the power of Spartan women over their men, and the reason for the political utility of that power. The Spartan mother rejoiced at the death of her sons in battle; we can guess that they were willing to die, or to perform as "good citizens," in part because they were "good sons." Rousseau claims that "the fate of [the female] sex will always be to govern [the male]. It is fortunate when [their] chaste power, exercised solely in conjugal union, makes itself felt only for the glory of the State and the public happiness! Thus did women command at Sparta" (*Second*, p. 89).[25] He speaks of "the ambition of the women of Sparta, which was to command men" (*Emile*, V, p. 393). Their ambition is most dramatically satisfied when their men die in battle on their behalf. The Spartan mother could rejoice not only because Sparta emerged victorious in the battle but also because her sons were sufficiently good sons to be willing to die in it for her. A Spartan wife in similar circumstances could take the same bittersweet satisfaction. "The woman who is at once decent, lovable, and self-controlled, who forces those about her to respect her, who has reserve and modesty, who, in a word, sustains love by means of esteem, sends her lovers with a nod to the end of the world, to combat, to death, to anything she pleases. This seems to me to be a noble empire, and one well worth the price of its purchase" (*Emile*, V, p. 393). Men are stronger than women; but if the men exercise their strength at the behest of women (as they did in Sparta), then even in politics, no less than in sex, "the stronger appears to be master but actually depends on the weaker." Sexual differentiation in Sparta thus benefited both sexes and the common good. The men were more manly, or fought more courageously, because they felt they were protecting the weaker women dependent upon them; the women could feel that the men in turn depended on them, since the men fought in their behalf and were willing to die in their defense. Women commanded in Sparta by virtue of the fact that they did not defend themselves there, but were defended by others. One commands by getting others to serve one, instead of having to serve oneself.

Rousseau is not the first to claim that women governed Sparta; Aristotle makes this the basis of his critique of the Spartan constitution.

> All martial races are prone to passionate attachments either to men or to women. It was attachments of the latter sort which were common at Sparta; and the result was that, in the days of her hegemony, affairs largely fell into the hands of women. But what is the difference between governors being governed by women and women being actually governors? The results are the same. . . . The women of Sparta have had a most mischievous influence.[26]

Rousseau accepts the fact of female domination over Sparta; what he rejects is Aristotle's criticism following that fact. For Rousseau believes that there is a considerable difference "between governors being governed by women and women being actually governors." Men and not women must govern, but men are likely to govern more effectively if doing so will gratify their female governors. Rousseau's defense of the indirect government of Spartan women is based upon a judgment of Plutarch's as to the value of their participation in communal celebrations: by praising the courageous and mocking the cowardly, the young Spartan women "inspired the younger sort with an emulation of . . . glory. Those that were thus commended went away proud, elated, and gratified with their honor among the maidens; and those who were rallied were as sensibly touched with it as if they had been formally reprimanded." The rule of the Spartan maidens was unofficial, in that they wholly lacked all power "formally" to reprimand anyone. Nevertheless, their power was great, because they informally controlled public opinion, thus embodying the unwritten law which is politically predominant. Their actions as judges "gave [the Spartan maidens] some taste of higher feelings, admitted as they thus were to the field of noble action and glory. . . . Hence it was natural for them to think . . . that the women of Lacedaemon were the only women in the world who could rule men."[27]

Rousseau praises the effect that the Spartan celebrations had on both sexes. The processions encouraged heterosexual desire among the Spartan males: the maidens "present[ed] to the depraved senses of the Greeks a charming spectacle fit to counterbalance the bad effect of their indecent gymnastic" (*Emile*, V, p. 366). In addition, the processions strengthened the young women's bodies, and taught them "the continual desire to please" men "without ever endangering [the women's] morals" (*Emile*, V, p. 365).[28] Thus the mutual dependence of the two sexes was reinforced. In order for the two sexes to attract one another, and to depend on one another, they had to be unlike one another; Rousseau contends that the sexes attract one another as opposites (*Emile*, V, p. 364). Men are most attractive to women as well as most useful to the republic when they are most unlike women. In order to reinforce the distinction and hence the attraction between the sexes, young men and women were not permitted to spend much time together. Men desire women more when women are modest or not easily attainable; sexual familiarity breeds contempt (*Letter*, pp. 84, 104). The Spartan maidens danced in the processions in the nude, as we are told by Plutarch (though not in this passage by Rousseau),[29] yet their morals were not endangered, because the "young girls appeared often in public, not mixed in with the boys but gathered together among themselves."

Men and women lived apart, or lived different lives. This remained true of the Spartans after they were married. While the men acted publicly as soldier-citizens, "shut up in their houses, [the Spartan women] limited all their cares to their households and their families" (*Emile*, V, p. 366). Like the Spartan mother of Rousseau's story, and unlike the female guardians of Plato's *Republic*, they sent their sons and husbands off to war without going to war themselves. Spartan women lived privately and encouraged their men to act publicly. The beneficial influence of Spartan women depended, then, upon their differing from Spartan men. The desire to please women is an important basis for the male desire to excel, and it requires that women not resemble men. "From these mothers were born the healthiest, the most robust, the most well-built men in the world. And in spite of the ill repute of some islands, it is an unchanging fact that of all of the peoples of the world—without excepting even the Romans—none is cited where the women were both purer and more lovable, and where they better combined morals with beauty than in ancient Greece" (*Emile*, V, p. 366).[30]

The paradox of Sparta, then, is that the republican virtue of its male citizens existed not because they were insensible to erotic and familial attachments, but because of the legislator's success in manipulating and redirecting those attachments. "In a republic, men are needed," and the Spartans were undoubtedly the sort of men a republic needs; but the existence of such men is in no way incompatible with the continued (and in some way even heightened) influence and importance of women.

The Political Power of the Women of Rome

Republican Rome is Rousseau's other example of ancient civic virtue. Familial life there was more autonomous, less regulated by government than in Sparta. This is because *moeurs* were of greater importance than the laws in Rome, whereas in Sparta laws were the source of *moeurs* (*Fragments*, p. 488). The Romans, it appears, were less denatured than their Spartan counterparts, because the duties fulfilled by public magistrates in Sparta were fulfilled privately in Rome, within each family, by its father.

> The Romans' virtue, engendered by a horror of tyranny and the crimes of tyrants and by innate patriotism, turned all their homes into as many schools for citizens; . . . the father—more feared than magistrates—was the censor of mores and avenger of the law in his domestic tribunal (*Political*, p. 224).

Since Rousseau speaks of "the unlimited power of fathers" (*Political*, p. 224), one might think that the greater autonomy accorded to families paradoxically implied a reduction in the influence and importance of women. Again, this is not the case. For in this respect Rousseau makes no distinction between Rome and Sparta. If anything, Roman women were still more important than their Spartan counterparts.

> All the great revolutions there came from women. Due to a woman Rome acquired liberty, due to a woman the plebeians obtained the consulate; due to a woman the tyranny of the Decemvirs was ended; due to women Rome, when besieged, was saved from the hands of an outlaw (*Emile*, V, p. 390).

This passage appears to be adapted from one of two unpublished essays by Rousseau on women which exist in fragmentary form: the title *Sur Les Femmes* has been assigned the first, and the second is the *Essai Sur Les Événements Importants Dont Les Femmes Ont Été La Cause Secrète*. It is worth examining the two brief essays (together they come to only five pages), because the contrast between them confirms our understanding of Rousseau's conception of the important and positive role played by women in antiquity.

Sur Les Femmes is like no other work of Rousseau's about women. It seems to indicate the existence of an earlier, feminist Rousseau,[31] who stresses the injustices done to women, the legal restrictions limiting their freedom. Rousseau argues for the total equality of men and women in the essay: women have been "models as perfect [as men] in all forms of civic and moral virtues." Perhaps a greater number of illustrious men could be cited, but Rousseau is unimpressed by the quantitative difference, because until now the competition between the sexes has been an unfair one: "Proportionately, women could have given greater examples of greatness of soul and love of virtue and in greater number than men have ever done, if our injustice had not deprived them along with their liberty of all occasions to manifest them to the eyes of the world" (*Femmes*, p. 1255).

Thus the first fragment emphasizes women's historic inability to exercise their power openly. As its title suggests, the second fragment complements it perfectly by stressing women's historical success at exercising their power secretly. Because they have not been allowed to act openly, we may assume, women have come to be adept at acting surreptitiously. Their influence has been great, though rarely avowed or suspected. Rousseau discusses the importance of women in the context of a theory of human motivation, or of a philosophy of history.

> One honors men too much or sometimes perhaps not enough by ascribing the majority of the brilliant actions which have an impact upon history to their ambition, courage, love of glory, vengeance, or generosity; often they have no other cause than the passions, which, while being ostensibly less noticeable, are certainly only better at

producing the most prodigious effects. The vulgar assuredly do not suspect that they have as much of an influence on great men as in fact they do (*Événements*, pp. 1257–58).[32]

The true causes of great historical events are often not political principles or even political passions such as ambition, courage, or love of glory. Instead they are erotic passions.

Roman women figure prominently in both essays. In the first, Rousseau compares Lucretia to Cato: "The one died for the loss of his liberty, the other for that of her honor" (*Femmes*, p. 1255). In the second (as in the passage on women and revolutions in *Emile*) he mentions the "establishment of the Roman republic, the rescue of Rome by the mother of Coriolanus, . . . the erection of a plebeian consulate" as political effects whose secret causes were women (*Événements*, p. 1259).

Lucretia is an especially interesting example for our purposes, since she is the subject of still another incomplete and unpublished (though somewhat lengthier) fragment of Rousseau's, his tragedy *La Mort de Lucrèce*. This is a work which dates from 1754, or from Rousseau's maturity. He discusses the abandoned project in his *Confessions*: "I projected . . . a tragedy in prose, the subject of which was nothing less than Lucretia, by which I hoped to crush the scoffers, although I ventured to introduce this unfortunate woman on the stage again at a time when she was no longer possible at any French theater" (*Confessions*, VIII, p. 407). We have all of the first act, some of the second, and a few isolated fragments of the work—hardly enough with which to attempt a systematic analysis, but enough to provide us with at least the raw material for a view of one of history's most influential and virtuous women, as seen by Rousseau.

Lucretia, as we noted, is referred to as an exemplar of female civic virtue in the fragment *Sur Les Femmes*. Rousseau there attacks the constraints which prevent women from manifesting their virtue publicly:

> Women [are] deprived of their liberty by the tyranny of men, who are masters of everything, for crowns, offices, posts of responsibility, the command of armies, all is in their hands; they have gotten hold of it from the beginning of time by what natural right I know not, which I have never been able to understand, and which could have no other foundation than greater strength (*Femmes*, p. 1254).

So far as I know, this criticism of the traditional restraints upon the political activity of women is unique in Rousseau. Instead of attacking the apparent restraints upon women, Rousseau elsewhere emphasizes the hidden power of women. In other words, he responds to the feminist accusations against men contained in *Sur Les Femmes* by pointing to the importance of feminine influence on men as it is demonstrated in the

Essai Sur Les Événements. If women openly exercise less power than do men, surreptitiously they may exercise more because of their influence upon men. The legal injustices suffered by women, which restrict their public activities, are thought to be of lesser importance since women have succeeded in circumventing them. Nor does Rousseau criticize women for this. In the first fragment he attacks the restrictions under which women suffer, but in the other he simply states as a fact (without pronouncing either praise or blame) their evasion of the restrictions.[33]

Thus what we have seen in the case of Sparta is confirmed by the *Essai*'s theoretical argument. Rousseau contends that women are, or should be, public by virtue of being private; they have, or should have, a salutary effect on public life through their influence over men and their devotion to their families. It is interesting to note that this is the position of Rousseau's Lucretia as well. The woman whose virtue is vaunted in *Sur Les Femmes* as proof of the injustice of restricting women to private life speaks in *La Mort de Lucrèce* in defense of restricting women to private life! Far from being the model of the public woman, the female counterpart to Cato, she willingly restricts herself to a domestic life at the outset of the tragedy. The wife of Collatinus, but the object of the infatuation of Sextus, son of the Roman king, she chooses to remain at home. Her confidante Paulina (an agent of Sextus's) contends that she "imprisons" herself in her home, and "deprives . . . the Roman people of the example of her virtues." Lucretia responds:

> Do you call the sweetness of living peaceably in the bosom of one's family a prison? As for me, I have no need of any other society for my happiness nor esteem for my glory than that of my husband, my father, and my children. . . . I have always believed that the woman who is most worthy of esteem is she of whom one speaks the least, even to praise her. May the Gods preserve my name from ever becoming famous: this deadly renown is purchased by our sex only at the expense of happiness or innocence (*Lucrèce*, p. 1024).

Lucretia, the perfect ancient woman, is a private woman devoted to caring for her family, hardly a suffragette. But Rousseau does not think that the privacy which he declares to be appropriate for women is necessarily a mark of their inferiority. Rousseau rejects the feminism that he earlier advocated in *Sur Les Femmes* not because he believes in the inequality of the sexes, but because he believes in the social utility of differentiating between the ways of life of the two equal sexes.[34] In Lucretia's own case it is perfectly apparent that she is her husband's superior. In a fragment of a later portion of the play, Brutus, the tragedy's male hero, reproaches Lucretia's father: "Victim of prejudice, you have preferred to confide in your son-in-law and not your daughter, without realizing that he is only a woman, and that she is more than a man" (*Lucrèce*, p. 1043). It is a prejudice to assume the superiority of all males to all females, and accordingly a source of error. Lucretia is more able than Collatinus, whom Brutus describes elsewhere as "ambitious, weak, and maladroit" (*Lucrèce*, p. 1042). Nevertheless, despite her superiority, her life is a private one. The capacity to act publicly is still thought to be reserved in principle to men. For this reason peoples who cannot dispense with monarchy, according to Brutus, are "effeminate" (*Lucrèce*, p. 1041). Again we see that republican self-government heightens the distinction between the sexes. Rousseau's Brutus agrees with Rousseau himself: "In a republic, men are needed." Rousseau's tragedy celebrates the virtue of a woman, one whom Rousseau elsewhere describes as a "perfect model of civic virtue." But at least in the portions of the tragedy that we possess, Lucretia does not appear as a female Cato. Her virtue is predominantly personal (fidelity to her husband) and not political (devotion to a republican ideal). Civic virtue, as it appears in Rousseau's play in praise of the "perfect [female] model of civic virtue," is preeminently a masculine preserve. What we learn of Lucretia confirms what we discovered of the women of Sparta: women were of great political importance in antiquity, but did not occupy or seek to occupy great political positions. Women were a major influence upon men in antiquity, and an important motivating force upon them, but this was because they did not seek to resemble men, or to have men resemble them.

The influence of women in antiquity is aptly characterized by the adjective used by Rousseau in the title of his early essay—women were the "secret" cause of public events. "The ancients . . . had as their maxim that the land where *moeurs* were purest was the one where they spoke the least of women, and that the best woman was the one about whom the least was said" (*Letter*, p. 48).[35]

Women benefit the republic by serving as the secret cause impelling men to act in public. In addition, they benefit themselves. Their weakness is compensated for by the masculine strength at their disposal. "Woman, who is weak . . . , estimates and judges the forces she can put to work to make up for her weakness, and those forces are men's passions. Her science of mechanics is more powerful than ours. . . . She must have the art to make us want to do everything which her sex cannot do by itself" (*Emile*, V, p. 387). But the harmony between the public interest and feminine self-interest is a tenuous one. For it is not obvious that women must impel men to act only as the republic would have them act. It is also conceivable that men's erotic passions could threaten rather than support their patriotic sentiments. Erotic attachments are extremely powerful, but not necessarily or perhaps totally subordinated to the public good. Women can also motivate men to act selfishly. The danger that women's influence upon men might possibly have posed to the republic suggests another reason why women were allowed to function only as a secret cause, as indicated in the following story:

> When the patrician Manilius was driven from the senate of Rome for having kissed his wife in the presence of his daughter, considering this action only in itself, what had he done that was reprehensible? Nothing, unquestionably; the kiss even gave expression to a laudable sentiment. But the chaste flames of the mother could inspire impure ones in the daughter (*Letter*, p. 52).

The moral standards of the community may be threatened even by legitimate erotic attachments. The community's response to the threat is not to outlaw or (as in the *Republic*) to generalize but instead to insist upon the privatization of erotic attachments. It is not to be expected (nor is it to be desired) that men not depend on women. Nevertheless, the danger always exists that women might cause their men to turn from public to exclusively private concerns. For this reason, men's dependence on women must be private and not public (and women's rule over men must be informal and indirect).

Rousseau wishes to argue that the political attachments of the ancient republicans were in some sense stronger than erotic ones. "Love of the homeland, a hundred times more ardent and delightful than that of a mistress, likewise cannot be imagined except by being felt" (*Political*, p. 219). But as we have seen, Rousseau also contends that the love of one's country is in some sense the extension of the love of one's wife (if not one's mistress). This implies that erotic attachments are in fact more fundamental (even if less delightful) than political attachments. Rousseau is perfectly explicit on this point.

> The love of humanity and of one's own country are the sentiments the depiction of which most touches those who are imbued with them, but when these two passions are extinguished, there remains only love, properly so called, to take their place, because its charm is more natural and is more difficult to erase from the heart than all the others (*Letter*, p. 117).

Despite the more natural charm of "love, properly so called," the political attachments existing in antiquity prevented erotic attachments from achieving the full autonomy or total sway over human hearts which might otherwise have occurred. Thus it was because of the existence of political concerns that chastity was both conceivable and honorable in antiquity. "Among the pagans this . . . virtue was universally honored, regarded as appropriate for great men, and admired in their most illustrious heroes. I can name three of them who . . . all have given memorable examples of continence: Cyrus, Alexander, and the young Scipio" (*Dernière*, p. 75n).[36]

The same republican dedication that is made possible by erotic attachments also serves to limit or restrain erotic attachments.

To summarize, we may say that the republics of antiquity did not destroy erotic and familial attachments; they supplemented them with political attachments. They did not do more because, as Rousseau contends, political attachments cannot exist without the prior existence of erotic and familial attachments. But at the same time, their political attachments enabled and required Spartans and Romans to suppress and subordinate their erotic attachments. Because "love . . . of one's country" is less natural than "love, properly so called," to do so they had to be somewhat denatured. But because love of one's country is possible only as the artificial extension of the love of one's family, they could not be totally denatured. Thus the republics of antiquity embodied an uneasy compromise or shaky equilibrium between tolerating selfish human nature and denaturing it. The key to the compromise was women operating as the "secret cause," as the private and potentially subversive motivators of patriotic actions. Women were more important in the politics of antiquity than was publicly apparent; but as soon as women came to be publicly apparent, politics was no longer the politics of antiquity. The public life of males in antiquity, as Rousseau reconstructs it, depended in large part upon the private life of females.

The Sexual Disorders of Modernity

Both politics and sexual relations are very different in modern times, when the politico-erotic equilibrium of antiquity is destroyed. In modern times ancient civic virtue no longer exists.[37] Modern political degeneracy is shown in the subject matter of modern drama: "The love interest has been reinforced . . . in tragedy to take the place of situations drawn from political concerns we no longer have" (*Letter*, p. 47).

In antiquity, "the love interest" was kept private, because of the predominance of public "political concerns." Now that true political concerns no longer exist, nothing remains to subordinate the love interest. As a result, the love interest has become open or public. Women's predominance is now apparent, and they no longer function as the "secret cause." "With us [as opposed to the ancients], . . . the most esteemed woman is the one with the greatest renown, about whom the most is said, who is the most often seen in society, . . . who most imperiously sets the tone, who judges, resolves, decides, pronounces, assigns talents, merit, and virtue their degrees and places" (*Letter*, p. 49). Rousseau argues that the open predominance of women leads to the weakening of the men whom they influence, making men unfit to fulfill their political responsibilities. "This weaker sex, not in the position to take on our way of life, which is too hard for it, forces us to take on its way, too soft for us; and, no longer wishing to tolerate separation, unable to make themselves into men, the women make us into women" (*Letter*, p. 100).

Women in modernity retain their power; as "the natural judges of men's merit" (*Emile*, V, p. 390), they continue to be able to shape men, to fashion men as they please. Unlike the women of antiquity, however, the women of Rousseau's time exercise their power openly, in order to lessen the differentiation between the sexes, as opposed to heightening it. Women now lead men more closely to resemble women; this exercise of feminine power, Rousseau argues, has baleful consequences for society as a whole, and ultimately for women themselves.

Rousseau's claim that the women of his day predominated is not a product of his paranoia or his excessive imagination. On the contrary, the influence of the women of the eighteenth-century French aristocracy and *haute bourgeoisie* upon the worlds of politics and letters is a matter of historical fact. Vera Lee's *The Reign of Women in Eighteenth-Century France* is a study of this phenomenon. The work notes the capacity of women in high court circles to make and unmake the careers of ambitious states- men, and the role of salon directresses as "judges, arbiters of taste in drama and poetry and mediators in the realm of ideas and ideologies."[38] Their predominance was, to be sure, "based on the famous difference: [their] femininity and [their] ability to exploit it to the fullest."[39] Rousseau would not deny that the women of eighteenth-century Paris continued to be extremely feminine; he would however assert that they used their power to make men less masculine. He would therefore agree that their power was based upon their "femininity," but would add that they un- wisely undercut their power by making men less masculine—or by lessen- ing if not altogether obliterating "the famous difference." Thus Rousseau acknowledges the eighteenth-century "reign of women," but as we shall see he also implies that it was to be short-lived.

What led to the collapse of the sexual regime of antiquity and its replacement by the modern reign of women? Rousseau's explanation begins with the barbarian invasions of Rome. The invaders destroyed the rigid separation and differentiation characteristic of the lives of the two sexes in republican antiquity.

> Everything is changed. Since [antiquity], hordes of barbarians, dragging their women with them in their armies, have inundated Europe; the licentiousness of camps, combined with the natural coldness of the northern climates, which makes reserve less neces- sary, introduced another way of life which was encouraged by the books of chivalry, in which beautiful ladies spent their lives in getting themselves honorably and decently kidnapped by men (*Let- ter*, p. 89).

Beginning with the invasions, men and women spent more time in one another's company. As a result, the division of labor between the sexes was less rigid than was the case either in the original family (when women would "tend the hut" while men "went to seek their common subsistence" [*Second*, p. 147]) or in the classical republics. But Rousseau denies that barbarian cohabitation led directly to the weakening or effeminacy of the male sex. As Plato's *Republic* contends, cohabitation of the sexes might instead lead women to take on masculine characteristics. Rousseau indicates that this is what happened at first. "If the barbarians . . . lived with women, they did not, for all that, live like them. It was they who had the courage to live like the men, just as the Spartan women did. The woman made herself robust, and the man was not enervated" (*Letter*, p. 103).[40] Elsewhere Rousseau makes it seem as though the barbarians actually had a healthier domestic life than did the Romans of the imperial period; it was the decadent Romans, after all, and not the vigorous barbarians, who passed their time away from their families by attending the theater (*Letter*, p. 16).

The moderns, then, are not simply the heirs of the barbarians, but rather their corrupted heirs. The moderns are effeminate, which is to say that they have lost the vigor of the barbarians, who were not weakened by their practice of cohabitation. Rousseau does not explain what caused this lack of vigor. On this point one could rightly link Rousseau with Machiavelli, who proposed "our [Christian] religion," or at any rate its "false interpretation," as the cause of the effeminacy of modern man.[41] Nor are Machiavelli and Rousseau alone in equating Christianity with effeminacy. Much of the anti-Christian animus of the Enlightenment can be understood in terms of this equation. Montesquieu speaks critically of the Christian emperor Justinian, because of the "unexampled" power that his wife exerted over him: "By incessantly intruding the passions and fancies of her sex into public affairs, she corrupted the greatest victories and successes."[42] He comments on the liberty enjoyed by women in the Christian monarchies of the modern West, noting that it is almost the only liberty to be found there. The liberty of women seems for Montesquieu to connote the enslavement of men: the women of the monarchies have "little souls," but manage to weaken men as a result of the women's "art" of "interesting great [souls]."[43] Shaftesbury speaks not of the men and women who are Christians but of Christianity itself, describing it as a religion of "effeminacy and superstition."[44] Thus Rousseau follows several other thinkers who see a connection between the rise of Christianity and the decline of citizenship and republican virtue. Rousseau, as we have seen, identifies republican virtue with masculinity; to the extent that Christianity weakens or destroys republicanism, he is no doubt correct to say that it makes modern man effeminate.

It is perhaps more revealing, however, to consider Rousseau's discussion of the Christian, as contrasted with classical, teaching on sexuality. We saw above that the classical tradition regarded chastity as a virtue appropriate to great political men. Their chastity was possible, we may assume, because it served their political ambition. Christianity retains chastity as a virtue, while transforming and greatly elevating it. But at the same time Christianity destroys the political utility of pagan chastity by rejecting political ambition as a vice, and substituting an otherworldly, religious attachment as the motive for chastity. Rousseau contends that Christianity's denigration of the political has made chastity ridiculous in modern times. "One has difficulty in conceiving how, in such a pure Religion, chastity could have become a base and monastic virtue capable of making ridiculous every man and I would almost say every woman who would dare to pride his or her self on it" (*Dernière*, p. 75n).[45]

Christian praise of chastity has also had disastrous consequences for marital life. For all that a few celebrated ancient heroes were renowned for their chastity, ancient republicanism was fundamentally based upon familial life. Generally speaking, "the good husband" was "the good citizen." For all the tension between them, the republic and the family were also mutually supporting social institutions. In the name of allegiance to the city of God, however, Christianity is uncomfortable with both the republic and the family. In the *Social Contract*, Rousseau discusses Christianity's destruction of republicanism: "I am mistaken when I speak of a Christian republic; these two words are mutually exclusive. Christianity preaches nothing but servitude and dependence" (*Social*, IV, 8, p. 130). And in *Emile* he speaks of the Christian depreciation of the married state: "By exaggerating all duties, Christianity makes them impracticable and vain. . . . There is no other religion in which marriage is subjected to so many severe duties and none in which so holy an obligation is so despised" (*Emile*, V, p. 374).[46]

The influence of Christianity thus helps to explain the weakness of domestic life in the modern West, and the consequent greater interest in extramarital romantic love. Leaving aside the cult of the Virgin, one may say that Christianity does not explicitly preach the romantic ideal or the modern ascendancy of woman as the object of love; one can however argue that chivalric literature and the tradition of gallantry emerge as a reaction against the Christian ascetic denigration of marriage.[47] "So much has been done to prevent women from being lovable that husbands have become indifferent" (*Emile*, V, p. 374). And husbands indifferent to their wives are excessively devoted to their mistresses. The ancient republicans experienced "love of the homeland, a hundred times more ardent and delightful than that of a mistress." Love of country and love of spouses combined to exclude love of mistresses. The ancients were not only better citizens but also better family men than are the moderns. "It is certain that domestic peace was, in general, better established and that greater harmony prevailed between man and wife than is the case today" (*Letter*, p. 89). Christianity has denigrated both love of country and love of spouses in the name of love of God; the effectual truth of the denigration, however, has been to promote the love of mistresses.

Love of mistresses is in principle less desirable from a political standpoint than is the love of spouses. Insofar as the liaison with a mistress is more casual and fleeting, dependence upon her is more superficial than is marital dependence. Furthermore, insofar as the extramarital liaison is intended precisely not to produce offspring, the male has fewer objects of his love to impel him courageously and public-spiritedly to overcome his more narrowly self-interested passions. It is not by accident, or because he is a prude, that Rousseau prefers love of spouses to love of mistresses, and links the former but not the latter to love of country. Christianity's destruction of the commonwealth might in this respect be said partially to follow from its devaluation of the family.

Modern men and social institutions are weaker than their ancient counterparts. Rousseau points to the sexual root of their weakness by speaking of modern effeminacy. Modern men are weak because they have come to resemble women. The predominance of women has led to the eradication of the differentiation between the sexes. One can see this notion in Rousseau's attack upon the prevailing system of education.

> In order to restrain [young men] with the women whom they are destined to divert, care is taken to raise the children exactly like the women; they are protected from the sun, the wind, the rain, and the dust so that they will never be able to bear any of them. . . . All that distinguishes them from the women is that, since nature has refused them women's graces, they substitute for them ridiculousness (*Letter*, p. 112).

He refers to the recipients of this education as "young ladies in jerkins, . . . rather maladroitly counterfeiting men."

But Rousseau's chief use of the concept of effeminacy is, as might be expected, a metaphorical one; as Machiavelli had earlier, he uses the term to indicate the weakness of modern civilized men. The life of reason, the philosophic spirit, weakens modern man: "Study of the sciences is much more apt to soften and enervate [*efféminer*] courage than to strengthen and animate it" (*First*, p. 55). Reason and effeminacy are equated with self-interest as opposed to public spirit: "Irreligion—the reasoning and philosophic spirit in general—causes attachment to life, makes souls effeminate and degraded, concentrates all the passions in the baseness of private interest, in the abjectness of the human *I*, and thus quietly saps the true foundations of every society" (*Emile*, IV, p. 312n; the emphasis appears in the translation). But if modern self-interest is effeminate, so too is modern sociability, no doubt because it deviates from the principles of true citizenship. "In becoming sociable and a slave he becomes weak, fearful, servile; and his soft and effeminate way of life completes the enervation of both his strength and his courage" (*Second*, p. 111). Just as Rousseau links masculinity with the capacity courageously to risk one's life in defense of others dependent upon one, so does he associate effeminacy with the cowardly, self-interested, and calculating concern with one's own welfare alone. Those who are masculine depend upon those who are feminine (who in turn depend upon them); those who are effeminate aspire to self-sufficiency, and refuse to exert themselves on behalf of others because they refuse to acknowledge their necessary and reciprocal dependence on others.

The women of antiquity encouraged their men to acquire and practice the virtues of the citizen—courage and public-spiritedness. These same virtues are absent in modern men because modern men are so similar to modern women. The hidden predominance of women in antiquity, we have seen, produced mutual dependence of the sexes, based on their differences, which led to the flowering of civic virtue. The open predominance of women in modernity brings similarity of the sexes and the consequent absence of civic virtue.

Rousseau criticizes modernity, then, by saying that "unable to make themselves into men, the women make us into women."[48] Clearly this is the mirror image of Rousseau's criticism of Plato's *Republic*. In the *Republic*, women are turned into men; in modernity, men are turned into women. Rousseau opposes both conversions in the name of his own conception of the importance of maintaining the distinctions between the two sexes. If anything, however, he criticizes modern practice far more severely than he does Platonic theory. Platonic unisex is based on a calculated and comprehensible (though for Rousseau clearly mistaken) subversion of the family for the good of the ideal of citizenship. Modern men, by comparison, are not citizens, but we have seen that this is not because of the strength of the family as a competing social institution. If modern men are too private to be good citizens, modern women are too public to be devoted to their families. Ancient practice (unlike Platonic theory) rested on a compromise between familial and political allegiance. The ancients were torn between allegiances, at times mutually conflicting, to two praiseworthy social institutions. Modern practice eliminates the tension by destroying the one and severely weakening the other of the two institutions. It would be an understatement to say that Rousseau does not regard it as an improvement upon Plato.

The modern convergence of the ways of life of men and women hurts both sexes. Men "lose [their] *moeurs* and [their] constitution" (*Letter*, p. 100). It is not surprising that women too "lose . . . their *moeurs*" (*Letter*,

p. 100). But it may be more surprising that the convergence is held to be against women's interests as well as their morals. This is because (as we observed earlier) sexual familiarity breeds contempt. Love of women and respect for women require that the separation of men from women be the rule, not the exception. Because of men's familiarity with women, women

> are flattered without being loved; they are served without being honored; they are surrounded by agreeable persons but they have no lovers; and the worst is that the former, without having the sentiments of the latter, usurp nonetheless all the rights. The society of the two sexes, having become too usual and too easy, has produced these two effects, and it is thus that the general spirit of gallantry stifles both genius and love (*Letter*, p. 104).

Ironically, the open predominance of women makes men less dependent upon them. Sexual similarity is not so much the product as the negation of sexual interdependence, because true sexual interdependence rests on the differentiation between the sexes. Thus Rousseau suggests that the reign of women may be brief because self-destructive, depending as it does upon that distinction between the sexes which women are in the process of deemphasizing. To make men less masculine is therefore regrettable from the standpoint of the female sex in addition to that of political society, and for the same reason: both the female sex and political society require men prepared to sacrifice themselves for others. That they will do so is likely only if they feel stronger than those in whose behalf they sacrifice themselves, which they can do only if they feel different from them. Woman can use "men's passions" to supplement "her weakness" only if man perceives that woman is in some way weaker than he is and different from him.

It is noteworthy that Rousseau criticizes "the general spirit of gallantry" because it "stifles . . . genius." As we saw in the preceding chapter, the human faculty of imitation originates as a result of contact between the sexes. It is a product of each sex's desire to please the other.[49] It now develops, however, that works of art are trivialized if they reflect nothing but the desire of male imitators to gratify and please female auditors. Rousseau contends that there is something inherently masculine about great works of art, something which depends upon a differentiation between the principles of the two sexes (*Letter*, p. 103; see also the criticism of Voltaire in *First*, p. 53). When this differentiation is destroyed, when art is reduced to an exercise in flattering femininity and is no longer also an expression of masculinity, art loses its claim to greatness. One would have thought that for Rousseau the artistic endeavor would be inherently effeminate, but this is not altogether so. Instead, the great artist, as he here emerges, is surprisingly akin to the ancient citizen—he depends on women, but his dependence must be less than totally apparent. In art as in politics, masculine greatness is dependent upon femininity, but seemingly is destroyed by effeminacy.[50]

Rousseau's Sexual Prescription for Modernity

How does Rousseau suggest that modernity respond to its sexual disorders? The principle behind all his suggestions is clear. He favors the separation of the sexes, so as to encourage their differentiation and their mutual dependence. "Let us follow the indications of nature, let us consult the good of society; we shall find that the two sexes ought to come together sometimes and to live separately ordinarily" (*Letter*, p. 100). In light of "the indications of nature," his proposed plan of education is intended to preserve and clarify distinctions between the sexes. "I am leaving prodigies aside. Emile is no prodigy, and Sophie is not one either. Emile is a man and Sophie is a woman; therein consists all their glory. In the confounding of the sexes that reigns among us, someone is almost a prodigy for belonging to his own sex" (*Emile*, V, p. 393).

More specifically, the practical consequence (perhaps the sole practical consequence) that Rousseau's discussions of women are intended to have is to shore up the foundering institutions of marital and familial life. At the beginning of *Emile*, this is made clear.

> Let mothers deign to nurse their children, morals will reform themselves, nature's sentiments will be awakened in every heart, the state will be repeopled. This first point, this point alone, will bring everything back together. The attraction of domestic life is the best counterpoison for bad morals. . . . When the family is lively and animated, the domestic cares constitute the dearest occupation of the wife and the sweetest enjoyment of the husband. Thus, from the correction of this single abuse would soon result a general reform; nature would soon have reclaimed all its rights. Let women once again be mothers, men will soon become fathers and husbands again (*Emile*, I, p. 46).[51]

A reborn sexual division of labor within the family is held to be the basis of moral reformation throughout society as a whole.

Rousseau's concern to accentuate the sexual division also leads him to support the perpetuation of the Genevan circles, or men's clubs, and the corresponding societies for women (*Letter*, pp. 98–99, 104–10). By segregating the sexes, these social institutions prevent the mutual corruption of the sexes. Rousseau does not deny that the men trade "licentious remarks" among themselves, or that the "absent husbands" are criticized by the assembled women (*Letter*, pp. 105, 106). But these are minor disadvantages compared to what would ensue should the sexes socialize more easily: "This language . . . is still preferable to the more studied style with which the two sexes mutually seduce one another and familiarize themselves with all vice" (*Letter*, p. 105).

The segregation of the sexes is meant to apply primarily after and apart from marriage. For that reason, it is not total. All men are supposed to live with (though not in the same manner as) their wives, so as to ensure that no man will live with another's wife. Rousseau certainly believes that government should encourage marriage. In fact he proposes that communal festivities be established in Geneva so as to enable marriageable young men and women to meet one another more easily (*Letter*, pp. 127–31). Rousseau writes the *Letter to D'Alembert* in defense of Calvinist Geneva; he begins by praising Geneva's "philosophic and pacific theologians," and later refers approvingly to the "ecclesiastical writers" who have criticized theatrical representations of romantic love (*Letter*, pp. 14, 51). For these reasons Rousseau's criticisms of the theater have been said to be "radically Puritan"; the *Letter* has been called Rousseau's "veritable . . . Protestant 'profession of faith.'"[52] Nevertheless, insofar as the social arrangements of republican Geneva are intended to segregate the sexes after marriage but further unity within marriage, they seem to Rousseau to be primarily classical rather than Puritan in inspiration: he remarks that the circles "still preserve some image of ancient *moeurs* among us" (*Letter*, pp. 104–05).[53]

Rousseau so strongly favors the mutual dependence of the sexes that he is led to depict favorably even romantic love. In the *Letter to D'Alembert* he castigates the "spirit of gallantry" for "stifl[ing] . . . love," even though earlier in that work he criticizes the poets for failing to "teach the young to distrust the illusions of love, to flee the error of a blind penchant which always believes that it founds itself on esteem" (*Letter*, p. 56). It now becomes apparent that Rousseau's aim is less total than his criticism of love would suggest. He attacks modernity as severely as he does, in fact, precisely because it no longer believes in the illusions of love; as we shall see, it is at least partially correct to say that Rousseau aims to resurrect those illusions as well as to bury them. When women were esteemed, however much that esteem may have been the product of an illusion, they were potentially a moral force within society. The decay of the chivalric ideal indicates the progressive immorality of modern society.

Where is the true lover who is not ready to immolate himself for his beloved, and where is the sensual and coarse passion in a man who is willing to die? We make fun of the paladins. That is because they knew love, and we no longer know anything but debauchery. When these romantic maxims began to become ridiculous, the change was less the work of reason than of bad morals (*Emile*, V, p. 391).[54]

Thus Rousseau is prepared to praise romantic love qualifiedly, because it is more moral, at least, than the self-interest and utilitarian calculation typical of modern times. Love is an illusion which is regrettably destroyed if the sexes come to be too similar to one another, or even if they get to know one another too well. Men and women must ordinarily be separated from one another if men are to think women sufficiently unlike them to idolize women, to consecrate themselves to their service, and to sacrifice themselves in their behalf. We have seen that romantic love is less exalted and praiseworthy than philanthropy or patriotism. Nonetheless, in the context of modern egoism, romantic love appears to be comparatively laudable. "The most vicious of men is he who isolates himself the most, who most concentrates his heart in himself; the best is he who shares his affections equally with all his kind. It is much better to love a mistress than to love oneself alone in all the world" (*Letter*, p. 117).

Rousseau's preferences are clear: it is better to love one's country than one's mistress, but even so it is better to love a mistress than oneself alone. Society requires the mutual interdependence of its members. Hence the self-absorbed egoist is the most antisocial of all human beings. Since "love, properly so called" is "more natural and more difficult to erase from the heart" than all other social attachments, it can at least serve as the most powerful ultimate obstacle to unrestrained egoism. Heterosexual love thus provides the most natural basis for human sociability. It may remain more narrowly self-centered than other forms of social dependence, but at least it represents a beginning point, leading humans from self-absorption to the involvement with and concern for others that society demands.

This is only a qualified defense of romantic love, to be sure. It remains true that "whoever tenderly loves his parents, his friends, his country and humankind, degrades himself by a dissolute attachment which soon does damage to all the others and is without fail preferred to them" (*Letter*, p. 117). Even so, one may say of Rousseau's view of romantic love what has been said of his view of science—that it is "bad for a good society and good for a bad society."[55] "There are countries where the *moeurs* are so bad that they would be only too happy to be able to raise themselves back up to the level of love" (*Letter*, p. 118). It is far better to have men love women than for men to resemble women, and ultimately it is only insofar as men do not resemble women that they can love them.

We can conclude our sketch of the mature Rousseau's theory of the sexual disorders of modernity by noting how much of his theory is already evident in one of his earliest works, the comedy *Narcisse*. Rousseau conceived of the idea of writing the play in 1729, when he was seventeen. The date of its composition is uncertain, although we know that it predates 1732. It is the only one of Rousseau's theatrical works to have been performed (it was given two performances by the *Comédie Française* in

1752) and published at his own request in his lifetime.[56] With some hesitation, Rousseau considered *Narcisse* as a work that was worthy of him. "As there can be no doubt that the piece . . . would bear reading, I had it printed" (*Confessions*, VIII, p. 400).[57]

Narcisse is the story of a young man, Valère, whose sister, Lucinde, attempts to teach him that he is excessively vain about his good looks. She does so by placing a portrait of him, in which he is dressed as a young woman, in his bedroom. All of this takes place on the day during which Valère intends to marry his fiancée Angelique. But instead of seeing the point of the picture, Valère falls in love with the woman portrayed in the picture, not realizing that he is she; and he seeks to postpone his marriage until he can meet her. Angelique, who knows of Lucinde's scheme, determines to cure Valère of his folly, or else to renounce her engagement. Angelique forces Valère to choose between the subject of the portrait and her as his love. He chooses Angelique, who then explains to him that it was he himself in disguise, of whom he was enamored. Valère acknowledges the problem of his vanity, resolves to overcome it, and the couple are married, fully expecting to live happily ever after.

Narcisse, then, is the story of an effeminate young man. The play is often explicit on this point. "Valère is, by his delicacy and the affectation of his finery, a sort of woman hidden under the clothes of a man" (*Narcisse*, p. 977). Lucinde's attendant Marton remarks that Valère in this respect is representative of his age, in which confusion of sexual identity abounds. "Since women today try to resemble men, is it not fitting that the latter meet them halfway, and try to improve in charm as much as the women do in solidity?" (*Narcisse*, p. 977). Lucinde is prepared to concede the advisability of women becoming less frivolous, but disapproves of the male sex's adoption of feminine characteristics: "Do they hope to please women better by striving to resemble them?" (*Narcisse*, p. 978). To which Marton rejoins: "Women hate one another too mutually to love what resembles them" (*Narcisse*, p. 978). After Valère has renounced the portrait for Angelique's love, she remarks that "He was a woman until now; but I hope that henceforth he will be a man, superior to the petty weaknesses which degrade his sex and character" (*Narcisse*, p. 1015). Valère, who because of his infatuation had earlier been reluctant to marry, now is eager to do so: "It can be sweet to lose [liberty] under the laws of [marital] duty" (*Narcisse*, p. 1018). The play concludes with Valère's declaration to Angelique: "You have healed me of a ridicule which was the shame of my youth, and henceforth I am going to demonstrate with you that when one loves well, one no longer muses about oneself" (*Narcisse*, p. 1018).

Thus the play presents an argument in favor of romantic love and sexual interdependence, as an alternative superior to self-absorption or (to use the obvious word) narcissism. The lover is morally superior to the narcissist because he muses about others and not himself. In order to love, he must not be effeminate; that is, he must lack the characteristics of the female if he is to feel the need of a female in order to complete himself. Because the moderns are effeminate, they cannot truly love. Because they are effeminate, they are vain. To say this is not to say that women as a whole are more vain or self-interested than are men; the criticism of effeminacy is not a criticism of femininity. Instead, those who are effeminate are vain because they combine the characteristics of both sexes; they are asocial and self-absorbed because their androgyny makes them sexually independent.

Angelique cures Valère of his narcissism in the play. A woman, she teaches him to depend on women and no longer to achieve an illusory independence of others by resembling a woman.[58] Because he is healed, Valère becomes eager to enter marriage, a sound social relationship. He decides to give up the solitary liberty of the unmarried man and assume the duties to others that the marital state imposes. In short, a woman cleverly manipulates a man so as to make him dependent upon her, hence a social being, and no longer effeminate and self-absorbed.[59]

Because of the prominence of Angelique and Lucinde, *Narcisse* is a play very much like those Rousseau attacks in the *Letter to D'Alembert*: "A natural effect of this sort of play is to extend the empire of the fair sex, to make women and girls the preceptors of the public, and to give them the same power over the audience that they have over their lovers" (*Letter*, p. 47). Nevertheless, in the context of an immoral society (recall that the play was performed in Paris, not Geneva) it can be considered a moral work of art. "It is much better to love a mistress than to love oneself alone in all the world." This is Rousseau's qualified defense of love in the *Letter*, and the explicit moral lesson that he leads us to draw from reading or seeing *Narcisse*.

At the same time that Rousseau was drafting *Narcisse*, it is likely that he was also sketching the fragmentary early essays on women discussed above.[60] This conjunction is of considerable interest. In the essay *Sur Les Femmes*, Rousseau criticizes males for having artificially and arbitrarily maintained sexual distinctions between men and women. In *Narcisse*, by contrast, he criticizes them for obliterating the sexual distinctions between men and women. In *Narcisse*, as in the *Essai Sur Les Événements*, he is quite appreciative of the influence of women; but, as in that essay, the influence which he discusses is really a "secret cause." Valère is taught by Angelique and Lucinde, but he is taught by them to differ from them and not to resemble them. In *Narcisse*, as in the works of his maturity, Rousseau proposes not to eliminate the dependence of men upon women, but to confirm it by heightening the differences between the sexes. For society benefits from the mutual dependence of men and women. Sexual interdependence is the most natural indication of our need to regard ourselves not as wholes, but as parts of a larger social whole. For this reason sexual interdependence could underlie the republican politics of antiquity, and sexual similarity can foster narcissistic self-absorption (by negating interdependence) in modernity. We have seen that sexual interdependence serves society's interests; it now remains for us to examine sexual interdependence from the standpoint of the individual.

∽ 4 ∽

Sexual Dependence
and the Individual

Up to now we have seen Rousseau argue that sexuality can benefit society by making men and women regard themselves as dependent parts, in need of one another for their joint completion. Rousseau contends that the man who recognizes his dependence on women can also be the citizen who recognizes his dependence upon society. The effeminate man, by contrast, cannot be a citizen and so threatens the social order. For he claims to incorporate both masculinity and femininity within himself, therefore not to depend sexually upon either man or woman, and hence to be complete as an individual. For this reason a society composed of effeminate individuals must be deficient.

This is the perspective from which Rousseau evaluates ancient and modern societies. But sexual interdependence affects individuals as well as societies, and Rousseau accordingly considers it from the individual's standpoint as well as from society's. Sexuality may benefit society by making men and women depend on one another; it is less obvious that it benefits the individuals in question. For the *Second Discourse* suggests that men and women were perhaps better off without sexual interdependence (*Second*, pp. 120–21, 135), and certainly better off without the social and political dependence to which it led (*Second*, pp. 127, 160, 179, and especially 192–203).

Men's specific dependence upon women originally made possible and should always motivate their more general social and political dependence. To the extent that Rousseau opposes social and political dependence as a restriction upon individual integrity or independence, he must also oppose the dependence of male individuals upon females.[1] We saw in the preceding chapter that the influence of women has made modern men too self-absorbed, or too independent. A sound political order is no longer possible because women have caused men to resemble women. In this chapter, however, we shall see Rousseau make a very different criticism: the trouble with women is not that they threaten the maintenance of the just political order, but that they necessitate the social relations characteristic of all social and political order. In other words, the criticism of women, surprisingly enough, now may be that they are in some sense too political, and no longer that they cause men not to be political enough.[2]

How exactly is the sexual dependence of men upon women translated into a more general social and political dependence? To what extent is it either possible or desirable for individual men to overcome sexual dependence, to be independent of both sexuality and society? I shall answer these questions by examining Rousseau's presentation of two individuals—Rousseau himself, as he appears in the autobiographical writings, and Emile, the fictional subject of Rousseau's educational program.

There are good reasons for comparing Rousseau and Emile. In one respect, they appear as opposites: Rousseau describes himself as a prodigy, whereas Emile has "only a common mind," and is an *homme vulgaire* (*Emile*, I, p. 52, and *Confessions*, I, p. 6 and II, p. 63; see also *Emile*, II, p. 105, and V, p. 393). Yet they appear to be similar as well: for Rousseau equates both Emile and himself with natural man (*Dialogues*, II, p. 847, and *Emile*, V, pp. 363 and 410). Two natural men can therefore differ very greatly from one another. The difference between them can be understood in terms of Rousseau's distinction between "what is natural in the savage state [and] what is natural in the civil state" (*Emile*, V, p. 406). Emile is undoubtedly a natural man who is prepared to live in "the civil state"; as such, he never overcomes his dependence upon women. Rousseau himself, however, more nearly resembles a transformed version of the natural man who lived "in the savage state." Like savage man, Rousseau is in a sense independent both of women and society; yet his independence is precarious, and achieved only with the greatest difficulty. Thus for men with "common mind[s]," even natural men, dependence upon women is unavoidable. But for exceptional men such as Rousseau, total independence, even independence of sexuality, can perhaps appear as a reasonable goal. Emile is a natural man who is socialized because of his sexuality, whereas Rousseau is a natural man who manages to withdraw from society in spite of his sexuality. Sexuality is a physical force, but it can have such different consequences for different individuals because it is more than just a physical force; the sexuality of civilized beings (as opposed to that of inhabitants of the state of nature) is transformed, magnified, and complicated by their imaginations. Emile and Rousseau differ from one another not primarily in their bodies, but in their imaginations. The imagination is the decisive variable in the impact of sexuality upon civilized humans; for this reason it will be the focus of our discussion.

Emile, who has "a common mind," is a "natural man." But Rousseau says that his "object is . . . not to make him a savage and to relegate him to the depths of the woods." Emile should be able to be "enclosed in a social whirlpool" without adopting "either the passions or the opinions of men" (*Emile*, IV, p. 255).[3] Brought up to live in society (though not to conform to it), Emile is also brought up to depend upon women. This is suggested at the outset of *Emile*, in Rousseau's definition of natural man. "Natural man is entirely for himself. He is numerical unity, the absolute whole which is relative only to itself." Thus far the definition is what we should expect; natural man, like his savage counterpart in the *Second Discourse*, is an independent integer, whom Rousseau contrasts with "civil man, [who] is only a fractional unity dependent on the denominator; his value is determined by his relation to the whole, which is the social body." But Rousseau's definition of natural man continues, so that it can apply to "the civil state" as opposed to the "the savage state." As we might expect, natural man is described as a "numerical unity, the absolute whole." Rousseau then adds an important qualifier; natural man is an absolute whole which is "relative [not] only to itself [but also to] its kind" (*Emile*, I, pp. 39–40).

The Childhood of Emile: Natural Asociality

Thus Emile's naturalness is compatible with his sociality. Yet he becomes social only when he attains puberty; Emile's sociality is caused by his sexuality. Before his adolescence, Emile is asocial or independent. Rousseau explains that this is so because the young child must depend only on things, not on other humans. "Dependence on things, since it has no morality, is in no way detrimental to freedom and engenders no vices. Dependence on men, since it is without order, engenders all the vices, and by it, master and slave are mutually corrupted" (*Emile*, II, p. 85). If the child is subjected to human authority at an early age, he will either be forced to submit to the superior strength of his elders or else he will succeed in playing upon his weakness in order to get his elders to submit themselves to him. The relationship between adult and child is inherently one between master and slave (although the two may alternate playing each role). It is never a moral relationship. This is so, Rousseau contends, because a young child can never regard the will of another as though it were an end in itself; it is always either an obstacle to be overcome or a means to be employed for his own ends. The solution to this difficulty is for the child to be totally unaware of other human wills. "Let him see . . . necessity in things, never in the caprice of men." Rousseau adds that a child regards as a caprice any will "which clashes with his whims" (*Emile*, II, p. 91).

At this stage the child is to be unaware of his dependence upon other, mutable human wills, because he is to equate it with dependence on immutable, inanimate objects. This equation is possible because what the child really needs are in fact those immutable objects alone, for example, food. Human assistance is the means to the child's necessary ends, but the assisting humans themselves are separable and distinct from those ends.

The child is taught to desire the ends and not the assistance except as it is instrumental to the ends; thus he "receives . . . services as a sort of humiliation and longs for the moment when he can do without them and have the honor of serving himself" (*Emile*, II, pp. 85–86). Thus as far as the child is concerned, he depends on other humans only insofar as he is unable to procure the necessary things himself.

Humans inherently reject and rebel against obedience to the arbitrary wills of others (*Emile*, I, p. 66). This is the psychological basis of Rousseau's educational program for young children. It is also the psychological basis for the whole of his political philosophy. He makes this connection himself in discussing his educational program. "If the laws of nations could, like those of nature, have an inflexibility that no human force could ever conquer, dependence on men would then become dependence on things again; in the republic all of the advantages of the natural state would be united with those of the civil state" (*Emile*, II, p. 85).

It is pointless to resist a natural force, hence it is never resisted. "It is in the nature of man to endure patiently the necessity of things but not the ill will of others. The phrase 'There is no more' is a response against which no child has ever rebelled unless he believed that it was a lie" (*Emile*, II, p. 91). The young Emile, who is altogether apolitical, therefore resembles the highly political citizen of the state of the *Social Contract*: both the citizen and the well-raised child are trained to act as if they were subject only to "the necessity of things," and not to "others," as if their superiors were natural forces, not magistrates or tutors.[4] Each is to see his respective world as if it were a world devoid of particular human wills, even though such a picture of the world is not wholly true; for magistrates and tutors after all are humans, not natural forces. Thus both the child and the citizen are to be taught to imagine the world in a certain way, but to be unable to imagine it differently. The magistrate and the tutor are imagined to be different than they really are. The imagination of both young children and mature citizens must be limited, because a limited imagination prepares its possessor to obey authority. In both politics and pedagogy, authority is wielded most effectively when it is least apparent to those who obey it.[5]

Although the young Emile's imagination is limited, the world as he sees it is nevertheless imaginary. Emile must have a false conception of the world precisely in order to restrict the activity of his imagination. Thus Emile's ignorance of the existence of human wills is to lead him to imagine that angry men are physically ill (*Emile*, II, p. 96). "Only objects suitable for him to see meet his first glances" (*Emile*, II, p. 95). The world that Emile imagines is an immutable world. It is imaginary because he cannot imagine that human wills could alter it.

It is necessary that the child not imagine human will ruling the world because human will is mutable; if he did imagine a world with human wills, he could imagine his own will ruling the world. "The child who has only to want in order to get believes himself to be owner of the universe; he regards all men as his slaves" (*Emile*, II, p. 87). If we think that we can get more, we desire more, and we desire more than we can possibly get. The imagination leads us to suppose that we can get more, so it must be suppressed. "It is imagination which extends for us the measure of the possible, whether for good or bad, and which consequently excites and nourishes the desires by the hope of satisfying them" (*Emile*, II, p. 81). But Emile's image of the world restricts the world by removing from it any "measure of the possible."

"The real world has its limits; the imaginary world is infinite. Unable to enlarge the one, let us restrict the other, for it is from the difference between the two alone that are born all the pains which make us truly unhappy" (*Emile*, II, p. 81). In the name of reality's limits, Emile is taught to imagine a world that is unreal because devoid of human wills. He is unable to imagine the world differing from his conception of it, and he is also unable to imagine himself differing from what he is. "The foundation of imitation among us comes from the desire to be transported out of ourselves. If I succeed in my enterprise, Emile surely will not have this desire" (*Emile*, II, p. 104). What is most important, however, is that the young Emile not imagine himself dominating others. Even when Emile begins to exercise his imagination, to imitate others, he imitates an asocial other. In "the first exercise . . . given to his imagination," Emile is taught to imitate "Robinson Crusoe on his island, deprived of the assistance of his kind. . . . This state, I agree, is not that of social man." Emile is imaginatively transported into "the place of an isolated man" (*Emile*, III, pp. 184–85). Emile is to imagine himself as a Robinson Crusoe—but one with neither a man nor to be sure a girl Friday.

In summation, the child is small, weak, in need of the assistance of others. Yet because he would not know how to be grateful for the assistance of others, the tutor must see that he is unaware of it. Thus although he receives their assistance, he does not desire it. He certainly does not conceive that other humans subordinate their wills to his. Rousseau's picture of the child is then highly paradoxical. In fact the child is a very social creature, dependent on other humans for his survival. In thought, however, he is largely unconscious of his dependence on them. He thinks that he depends only on things, whereas in fact he depends on other humans for those things. But Rousseau is primarily concerned with the child's world of thought, not the world of reality. For the world of reality that he inhabits will change; as he becomes older and stronger, he will need to depend increasingly less on others to provide him the things needed for his sustenance. But his world of thought will not change; once the child learns to enjoy bending others to his will, he will never cease to enjoy it.

As soon as [children] can consider the people who surround them as instruments depending on them to be set in motion, they make use of those people to follow their inclination and to supplement their own weakness. . . . It does not require long experience to sense how pleasant it is to act with the hands of others and to need only to stir one's tongue to make the universe move (*Emile*, I, pp. 67–68).

The child cannot truly be solitary; he can however think that he is solitary, and Rousseau argues that he will do so if he is properly raised. No child is either dependent or independent but thinking makes him so.

The Adolescence of Emile: Natural Interdependence

In this sense the child who is raised naturally is solitary. "The child raised according to his age is alone. . . . He does not feel himself to be of any sex, of any species. Man and woman are equally alien to him. . . . It is not an artful untruth which is imparted to him by this method; it is nature's ignorance" (*Emile*, IV, p. 219). But puberty brings his solitude to an end, because sexuality entails the natural interdependence of men and women. Earlier Emile depended on other humans (principally his tutor and nurse) instrumentally; they served as human means to his desired nonhuman end. Now, however, with the onset of sexual maturation, the adolescent's need for another human is not instrumental but essential. The child can treat others as a means to his own end, in fact can behave no differently toward others; but a child can be rendered unaware of his dealings with others, since he does not need them but only the things they provide him. Beginning with his adolescence, however, the child must associate with other humans. The master-slave relationship can no longer be avoided through the seeming avoidance of human relationships altogether. Instead, a different sort of relationship must be constructed and entered into. Because sexuality makes human relationships inevitable, and because master-slave relationships are the simplest, most obvious of human relationships, sexuality presents an obvious danger to moral development; hence Rousseau refers to the moment of sexual maturation as the "moment of crisis," which has "far-reaching influences" (*Emile*, IV, p. 211). Because the moment is so critical, Rousseau advocates postponing it, insofar as this is possible. He recounts a specific method employed in another's education (though not, it seems, in Emile's) to postpone the onset of sexual desire: the young man in question is taken to a hospital ward to observe the suffering of victims of venereal disease (*Emile*, IV, pp. 231–32). Even if this example is extreme, Rousseau in principle advocates "put[ting young people's] nascent imaginations off the track with objects which, far from inflaming, repress the activity of their senses"

(*Emile*, IV, pp. 230–31). The imagination is employed to discourage sexual dependence (just as it was earlier employed to discourage social dependence through the image of Robinson Crusoe).

Sexual initiation should be postponed because precocious sexual activity encourages men to exploit both men and women.

> I have always seen that young men who are corrupted early and given over to women and debauchery are inhuman and cruel. The heat of their temperaments made them impatient, vindictive, and wild. Their imaginations, filled by a single object, rejected all the rest. They knew neither pity nor mercy. They would have sacrificed fathers, mothers, and the whole universe to the least of their pleasures (*Emile*, IV, p. 220).

Rousseau criticizes the unhealthy moral consequences of sexual precocity but argues that these dangers are avoidable. The adolescent male need not be a sexual predator; instead he can be humane (which the preadolescent could not have been), because sexual maturation involves the birth of desire. For the object of his desire is at first very unclear to the desirer, who "desires without knowing what" (*Emile*, IV, p. 220). This amorphous quality of newly awakened sexual desire provides a great challenge to the educator of adolescents. Sexual energy makes human relationships both possible and necessary; but because it is so amorphous, it can be sublimated or redirected so as to make many different kinds of relationships possible. Thus the challenge facing the educator is at first to redirect sexual energy with the aim of leading his charge into harmonious social relationships with others—and only later to allow him to find a more natural, directly sexual outlet for it.

An example given by Rousseau helps to clarify this process of sublimation. He argues that properly raised adolescents are interested in friendship before coming to be interested in sexual love. "The first sentiment of which a carefully raised young man is capable is not love; it is friendship. The first act of his nascent imagination is to teach him that he has fellows; and the species affects him before the female sex" (*Emile*, IV, p. 220). But he further argues that the interest in friendship stems from a redirection of sexual energy. Even though "the species affects him before the female sex," it is only "from the need for a mistress [that there] is soon born the need for a friend" (*Emile*, IV, p. 215). Before he is sexually active, the adolescent acquires the capacity to pity others, to befriend others, to act with humanity; but that capacity itself is an effect of the channeling or sublimation of his sexual energy. Humanitarian sentiment, the psychological motive for moral behavior, appears only when the adolescent is sexually mature, but also only if he is not yet sexually active. Rousseau makes Emile moral by delaying his first sexual experience; thus he "delay[s] the progress of nature to the advantage of reason" (*Emile*, IV, p. 316).

It is morally advantageous to postpone the adolescent's sexual awakening, which may be put off until he is twenty or even older (*Emile*, IV, p. 317). But the "happy period" of Emile's "first innocence" necessarily draws to a close (*Emile*, IV, p. 317). The species may affect him before the female sex, but eventually the female sex must affect him as well. Sexual desire cannot forever be sublimated.

Emile's sexual awakening can be relatively late because his sexual imagination remains inactive; the early and unnatural activity of the sexual imagination is responsible for sexual precocity. For this reason, the tutor has actually not "delay[ed] the progress of nature to the advantage of reason." Rousseau now declares that he has "only prevented imagination from accelerating [the progress of nature]" (*Emile*, IV, p. 316). At this point, however, the tutor employs a different strategy. He no longer prevents Emile's imagination from focussing on sexual objects, so as to discourage Emile from sexual activity; instead he actively utilizes Emile's imagination of a sexual object so as to discourage him from sexual activity. Thus he "repress[es Emile's] senses by his [sexual] imagination" (*Emile*, IV, p. 329).

The tutor describes to Emile a girl named Sophie, whom he has never met. The description attracts Emile, who, like Valère, the hero of Rousseau's play *Narcisse*, falls in love with a girl whom he can only imagine. Unlike the object of Valère's infatuation, however, the girl in question actually *is* a girl, and not Emile's male self dressed to resemble a girl. The asocial Valère at first loves only himself; Emile is relatively mature before he can love, but when he does he loves another. Because Emile has been properly educated, his sexuality socializes him.

Emile's love for Sophie makes his sexual desire moral. It does so at first by particularizing his desire. "Far from arising from nature, love is the rule and bridle of nature's inclinations. It is due to love that, except for the beloved object, one sex ceases to be anything for the other" (*Emile*, IV, p. 214). Love limits the number of women who are desired; more importantly, it also changes the manner in which men desire them. For love implies mutuality, which precludes a crudely instrumental view of the woman as object. "One wants to obtain the preference that one grants. Love must be reciprocal. To be loved, one has to make oneself . . . lovable" (*Emile*, IV, p. 214). The object of one's love must be a subject as well, for whom one is oneself in turn an object. For these reasons Rousseau contends that "a young man must either love or be debauched" (*Emile*, IV, p. 214; see also *Dialogues*, I, p. 688).

Thus the tutor's technique is to inspire Emile with romantic notions, to kindle his erotic imagination, so as to channel and repress his physical desire.

I shall depict ["the sweet sentiment for which he has such a thirst"] as the supreme happiness of life, because in fact it is. In depicting it to him, I want him to yield to it. In making him sense how much charm the union of hearts adds to the attraction of the senses, I shall disgust him with libertinism, and I shall make him moderate by making him fall in love (*Emile*, IV, p. 327).

Emile is made "moderate" because he is made to love an imaginary object.

I would have to be the clumsiest of men not to be able to make him passionate in advance of his knowing about whom. It is unimportant whether the object I depict for him is imaginary; it suffices that it will make him disgusted with those that could tempt him; it suffices that he everywhere find comparisons which make him prefer his chimera to the real objects that strike his eye (*Emile*, IV, p. 329).

Nor does it trouble the tutor that his charge is taught to act morally in the world because of his idealized image of someone who is not in the world. For Rousseau contends that in truth the object of one's love is never strictly speaking in the world, at least as he or she is perceived by the lover.

What is true love itself if it is not chimera, lie, and illusion? We love the image we make for ourselves far more than we love the object to which we apply it. If we saw what we love exactly as it is, there would be no more love on earth. When we stop loving, the person we loved remains the same as before, but we no longer see her in the same way. The magic veil drops, and love disappears (*Emile*, IV, p. 329).

Because Emile loves an imaginary woman, he does not exploit the women whom he encounters. (In addition, he exploits neither men nor women because of another being whom he imagines—his God.)[6] The necessary condition for the moral interaction of men and women within society seems to be an imagined and illusory influence—that is, the influence of someone not really to be found within society. The imagination is supposed to restrain the actual manifestation of desire by creating an illusory object of desire, one not easily to be encountered in actuality; as a result, one is supposed not to desire too much (or too many).

But the imagination is not simply the loyal and efficient servant of civil society, ministering to the moral needs of the individuals who compose it. For the imagination, or the world it produces, is also the great rival of and alternative to civil society. The imagination may be too effective at its task. If the illusory object is clearly preferable to its actual counterparts, actual desire might be not restricted and moralized (that which benefits society) but altogether transcended. If the effect of the imagination is to produce acute dissatisfaction with all existing individuals, it can hardly be said to accord with the interests of society—whose perpetuation requires the mutual desire of those individuals.

This ambiguity in the relationship between society and the imagination emerges in an interesting story in *Emile* (and also in a second story, to be discussed below, in the *Confessions*).[7] Rousseau discusses a girl like Sophie, the girl whom Emile is to marry. She is "so similar to Sophie that her story could be Sophie's without occasioning any surprise" (*Emile*, V, p. 402). Just as Emile is in love with the image he has of Sophie before he has met her, the girl like Sophie also has the image of a lover, according to whose standard she judges all her suitors. He is Telemachus, the son of Ulysses, and hero of Fénelon's epic novel. Not surprisingly, the young men whom she encounters fall short of this standard, and she is left with the desire to love, but with nothing approaching a lovable object. "She sought a man and she found monkeys; she sought a soul and found none" (*Emile*, V, p. 404). She pleads with her parents:

> Pity me; I am unhappy, not mad. . . . Is it my fault if I love what does not exist? . . . I do not seek Telemachus. I know that he is only a fiction. I seek someone who resembles him. And why cannot this someone exist, since I exist—I who feel within myself a heart so similar to his? No, let us not thus dishonor humanity. Let us not think that a lovable and virtuous man is only a chimera (*Emile*, V, p. 405).

Rousseau does not finish the story of the girl like Sophie; he does however suggest that her parents attempt to force her to marry a young man who fails sufficiently to resemble Telemachus, which brings on her death. Rousseau claims that he introduced this story in order to show that "enthusiasm for the decent and the fine is no more foreign to women than to men" (*Emile*, V, p. 405). Unfortunately, the girl like Sophie is doomed because of the "elevat[ion of] her soul," which has "disturbed her reason." The real Sophie, by contrast, has "only a good nature in a common soul." She has "a less lively imagination and [in consequence, presumably] a happier destiny" (*Emile*, V, pp. 405–06).

It is dangerous to have too great a soul, to have too vivid an imagination, to judge mankind by too lofty a standard. One risks isolation from and inability to deal with the actual human, all-too-human world. Effective integration into society requires limits on the activity of the imagination.[8] Rousseau says this of a woman, but the doctrine applies to men as well. Specifically, we shall see that it applies to Rousseau himself.

The story of the girl like Sophie teaches us that the exceptional individual will adjust to society and to sexuality with difficulty. The social integration of Emile, who has "only a common mind," poses fewer problems. Yet even Emile's social and sexual completion must be arranged for him by his tutor, who is omniscient and omnipotent. The tutor chooses a suitable mate for Emile. In order to be suitable she cannot be truly perfect. "I do not want to deceive a young man by depicting for him a model of perfection which cannot exist. But I shall choose such defects in his beloved as to suit him, so as to please him, and to serve to correct his own" (*Emile*, IV, p. 329). Moreover, the tutor is already acquainted with the suitable mate. At first "it was important that she not be found so quickly." Later, however, "the moment has come. It is time to seek her in earnest, lest he find someone on his own whom he takes for her and not learn his error until it is too late" (*Emile*, IV, pp. 354–55). The search for her "is only a pretext for making him learn about women, so that he will sense the value of the one who suits him. For a long time Sophie has been found" (*Emile*, V, p. 407).

The Interdependence of Men and Women

Sophie and Emile will make a good couple because neither is an exceptional individual. "Emile is no prodigy, and Sophie is not one either" (*Emile*, V, p. 393). Ordinary men like Emile and ordinary women like Sophie are necessarily social creatures who complement one another. Nevertheless, Rousseau believes that the sociability of women differs qualitatively from the sociability of men. Because women are weaker than men, he argues that they are more social than are men, and that they cause men to be as social as men are. Women are more dependent than are men; women's success in coping with this dependence leads Rousseau both to admire them and to fear them.

"Woman and man are made for one another, but their mutual dependence is not equal. Men depend on women because of their desires; women depend on men because of both their desires and their needs. We would survive more easily without them than they would without us" (*Emile*, V, p. 364). Thus men and women are mutually but not equally dependent. Men cannot be self-sufficient insofar as they desire women, but women could not be self-sufficient even if they did not desire men. Men do not need women; they are stronger than women, hence potentially better able to fend for and protect themselves. Thus men's greater physical strength, which Rousseau denies entitles them to rule women, nevertheless has an important consequence: were men not to desire women, they could conceivably be independent of women. Women, by contrast, do need men, because they are too weak in civilized society (as opposed to the state of nature) to fend for themselves. Although greater physical strength is not a title to rule, it does enable men potentially to be independent, or to escape rule. Men do not naturally rule women, but they are perhaps able to avoid being ruled by women. Because of women's weakness, they have no alternative but to rule men. They cannot be independent, and so their only recourse is to exploit men's desires, hence to make men as dependent on them as they are on men.

Rousseau's insistence on the necessity of female dependence on males is understandably offensive to feminists. For that very reason, it is worth pausing here to consider the disagreement between Rousseau and feminism. Surprisingly, on reflection it emerges that Rousseau is in considerable sympathy with the aim of feminism (equality between the sexes); his chief disagreement is with respect to the means to that end. We can see this by considering the objections of Mary Wollstonecraft, one of Rousseau's earliest and most thoughtful feminist critics, to his emphasis on the necessity of the interdependence of men and women. She criticizes Rousseau for failing to consider either men or women as independent moral beings; instead he is at fault for attempting to "make one moral being of a man and woman."[9] In opposition to Rousseau, Wollstonecraft argues that women are whole moral beings, who "ought to endeavor to acquire human virtues (or perfections) by the *same* means as men, instead of being educated like a fanciful kind of *half* being—one of Rousseau's wild chimeras."[10]

For Wollstonecraft, to exaggerate the weakness of women and their differentiation from men is also unjustly to exaggerate their dependence on men. Instead she wants women more to resemble men so that they will depend less on men. Rousseau, however, argues that it is necessary from women's own standpoint that they not resemble men. "The more women want to resemble [men], the less women will govern men, and then men will truly be the masters" (*Emile*, V, p. 363).[11] Here the basis of the dispute between Wollstonecraft and Rousseau emerges. She quotes this passage, and comments: "This is the very point I aim at. I do not wish them to have power over men; but over themselves."[12] "It is not empire,—but equality, that [women] should contend for."[13] But Rousseau contends that women can achieve equality only by virtue of asserting their empire. Because of their weakness, women cannot avoid depending on men, or being ruled by them. They are inevitably subject to men's empire. All they can do is ensure that men also depend on them. Since women are necessarily ruled by men, they can attain equality only by ruling men in turn. In other words, the disagreement between Wollstonecraft and Rousseau reduces itself in a sense to a question of tactics. For Wollstonecraft, women can be equal only if they make themselves as independent of men as men are of women; for Rousseau, women can be equal only if they make men as dependent on women as women are on men. For Rousseau, the bodily differences between men and women unalterably differentiate women from men. Men, perhaps, could be asexual anarchists; perhaps they could avoid both ruling and being ruled by the opposite sex. Women lack this option. For this reason women, not men, are in some respects the more political sex by nature; for those who are less self-sufficient have more need to rule others.[14] Strength is popularly (though wrongly) considered a title to rule; in fact, only weakness provides a motive for ruling.

Women seem to be less political than men, because they are more submissive. By nature men and not women revolt against injustice (*Emile*, V, p. 396). Once again, Rousseau's emphasis on female submissiveness must offend feminist sensibilities.

> [Women] never to cease to be subjected either to a man or to the judgments of men and they are never permitted to put themselves above these judgments. The first and most important quality of a woman is gentleness. As she is made to obey a being who is so imperfect, often so full of vices, and always so full of defects as man, she ought to learn early to endure even injustice and to bear a husband's wrongs without complaining (*Emile*, V, p. 370).[15]

Wollstonecraft responds to this passage by contending that Rousseau wishes to deprive women of their moral autonomy and wholly to subjugate them to men. "Women are . . . to be considered either as moral beings, or so weak that they must be entirely subjected to the superior faculties of men."[16] But in fact, Rousseau would argue, Wollstonecraft poses the alternatives unfairly. For in spite of first appearances, he denies that women are "entirely" subjected, he denies that men's faculties are simply "superior," and therefore he can indeed consider women as "moral beings." In reality, women's submissiveness is a political tool which they employ in order ultimately to exert control over men. For this reason women's submission indicates that they are in some sense more political than are men. "Unless a man is a monster, the gentleness of a woman brings him around and triumphs over him sooner or later" (*Emile*, V, p. 370).

Rousseau emphasizes that women are able to triumph over men in spite of their weakness. They can do so because in many respects their minds are superior to the minds of men. Rousseau speaks of the "peculiar cleverness given to the fair sex," describing it as "a very equitable compensation for their lesser share of strength" (*Emile*, V, p. 371). Nature has given women "agreeable and nimble minds" (*Emile*, V, p. 364).

One could of course object that there is something very condescending about this sort of praise: no one would ever speak of Newton's "peculiar cleverness," or comment on the "agreeable and nimble" character of Einstein's mind. There is some truth to this objection; in a way, however, the objection is also beside the point.

As the Newton and Einstein examples are designed to suggest, Rousseau believes that men are women's superiors in the realm of theoretical reason.[17] But he also believes that women are men's superiors in the realm of practical reason.[18] It is necessary that women be superior in practical and not theoretical reason, because the problem which confronts them is a practical and not a theoretical problem: women must be able to attain equality with men, notwithstanding male superiority in physical strength. In other words, women must be able to persuade men to put some of their greater physical strength at women's disposal. Rousseau begins with the premise that nature is beneficent, that it gives us what we truly need; it is therefore appropriate that he should speak of nature's bestowing superiority in practical and not in theoretical reason upon women. Desirable as it might be in many other respects, women's equal or greater capacity for theoretical reason would be of no particular use to women in solving the problem which Rousseau contends they face.[19]

Women's superiority to men in the realm of practical reason is indicated by their greater aptitude for the observation of others and the comprehension of their psychological proclivities.[20] Women resolve their practical problem by means of their superiority in practical reason, which enables them to rule men (even as they are also ruled by men). "It is by means of this superiority in talent that she keeps herself his equal and that she governs him while obeying him" (*Emile*, V, p. 371).

Because women are cleverer than men, men are directed to do things for women which women cannot do for themselves. "Nature wants [women] to think, to judge, to love, to know, to cultivate their minds as well as their looks. These are the weapons nature gives them to take the place of the strength they lack and to direct ours" (*Emile*, V, p. 364). "Wit alone is the true resource of the fair sex— . . . the wit which suits their position and consists in an art of exploiting man's position and putting our peculiar advantages to their use" (*Emile*, V, pp. 371–72).

> Woman, who is weak and who sees nothing outside the house, estimates and judges the forces she can put to work to make up for her weakness, and those forces are men's passions. Her science of mechanics is more powerful than ours; all her levers unsettle the human heart. She must have the art to make us want to do everything which her sex cannot do by itself and which is necessary or agreeable to it (*Emile*, V, p. 387).[21]

Not only can women rule men and get men to do things for them; because of women's greater cleverness and psychological acumen, men are largely oblivious to their rule. "Guile is a natural talent with the fair sex" (*Emile*, V, p. 370).[22] Women's rule, being guileful, is also hidden or indirect. What we have seen in chapter 3 to be true on a societal level is therefore equally true on an individual level.

In one sense, Rousseau clearly admires the ability of women, despite their own weakness, to rule men so as to supplement that weakness. And as we have already seen and shall see again, he also believes that their interest in ruling men could be directed toward the moral regeneration of society as a whole; in other words, the female will to power might be said to benefit all of society, not just the female sex. Nevertheless, he is also profoundly ambivalent about their will to power, because he is ambivalent about *any* will to power. Rousseau grounds his discussion of the innate goodness of human beings in their alleged lack of interest in domination; yet it is apparent from his analysis of women that that lack of interest characterizes at most only half the species. Rousseau's ambivalence toward women is thus unavoidable, given his emphasis on their need to dominate and his basic suspicion of all domination. His ambivalence comes out most clearly if one compares two different passages in *Emile*. In the first, he comments on the great moral dangers that follow from the physical weakness of children, who, because of their unavoidable dependence on adults, tend easily to want to dominate or manipulate adults. According to Rousseau, it is the weak person, not the strong, who is the potential tyrant.

> As soon as [children] can consider the people who surround them as instruments depending on them to be set in motion, they make use of those people to follow their inclination and to supplement their own weakness. That is how they become difficult, tyrannical, imperious, wicked, unmanageable—a development which does not come from a natural spirit of domination but which rather gives one to them, for it does not require long experience to sense how pleasant it is to act with the hands of others and to need only to stir one's tongue to make the universe move (*Emile*, I, pp. 67–68).

This passage can usefully be contrasted with one of Rousseau's descriptions of women which we have just discussed.

> Woman, who is weak . . . , estimates and judges the forces she can put to work to make up for her weakness, and those forces are men's passions. Her science of mechanics is more powerful than ours; all her levers unsettle the human heart. She must have the art to make us want to do everything which her sex cannot do by itself and which is necessary or agreeable to it (*Emile*, V, p. 387).[23]

(Male) children are potentially tyrants until they become strong enough to become self-sufficient, so that they no longer need to depend on others. Women's biology seems unfortunately to dictate that they necessarily always remain potential tyrants. Rousseau would enjoin male children from "acting with the hands of others," but he nevertheless urges adult women to do exactly that. Thus he is compelled to excuse in the adult female what he blames in the male child, but he cannot be completely comfortable in excusing it. In view of this similarity between weak children and weak women, it is not surprising that Rousseau remarks that "women . . . seem in many respects never to be anything else [but big children]" (*Emile*, IV, p. 211).[24] Women naturally manipulate others, and their manipulations may well produce great social benefits; but Rousseau's defense and praise of women cannot but be ambivalent, in view of his overall praise of autonomy and condemnation of manipulation.

Nevertheless, although female manipulation is in one sense suspect, it is still defensible inasmuch as it is in the service of equality and sociality. Woman "keeps herself [man's] equal" because she "governs him while obeying." For Rousseau, unlike Wollstonecraft, the dependence occasioned by the sexual distinction is fundamental, because it is in the interest of women and of humanity generally that it be fundamental. Neither men nor women are whole moral beings; men may come closer to human wholeness than do women, but to come close to being a whole is still to be only a part. Men in general (leaving aside exceptional individual men such as Rousseau) are no more whole human beings than are women. If men and women were "independent of one another, they would live in eternal discord, and their partnership could not exist. But in the harmony which reigns between them, everything tends to the common end; they do not know who contributes more. Each follows the prompting of the other; each obeys, and both are masters." Rousseau here makes the observation for which Wollstonecraft criticizes him: "The social relation of the sexes . . . produces a moral person of which the woman is the eye and the man the arm" (*Emile*, V, p. 377). In other words, for Rousseau neither man nor woman is a moral person by himself or herself, independent of the other. Men and women are not equal wholes; they are parts that are equal because each part alternately rules and is ruled. Only in the absence of rule would men's greater physical strength be a decisive inequality.

The Interdependence of Emile and Sophie

Rousseau's description of Sophie confirms the view that women are naturally more political than are men, in the sense that rule is more necessary to them than it is to men. Sophie is said to have her defects, but they "suit" Emile and "serve to correct his own." One defect of Sophie's of which Rousseau speaks specifically is her pride. She is proud even though "she is a pupil of nature just as Emile is, and she, more than any other, is made for him" (*Emile*, V, p. 410). Her pride is natural. It serves two functions: first, it preserves her modesty. "Possessing the temperament of an Italian woman and the sensitivity of an Englishwoman, Sophie combines with them—in order to control her heart and her senses—the pride of a Spanish woman, who, even when she is seeking a lover, does not easily find one she esteems worthy of her" (*Emile*, V, p. 402). In fact, "this pretended pride for which others reproach her is only a very wise precaution to protect her from herself. Since she has the misfortune to sense a combustible temperament within herself, she dreads the first spark and keeps it at a distance with all her power" (*Emile*, V, p. 428). To wish to rule others is to be proud, and pride is commonly considered a vice. Yet Sophie's pride is not really a vice, and Rousseau makes it clear that it would be incorrect to reproach her for it. Women's pride is "a very wise precaution," and it seems a necessary precaution. Nature seems to have left women no alternative but to be proud and to rule men.

For women must be proud not only to control themselves, but also to control men. This is the second function served by women's pride. "[Sophie] sees her triumph [over Emile]. She enjoys it" (*Emile*, V, p. 415). "The proud girl observes him stealthily and smiles secretly at her slave's pride" (*Emile*, V, p. 424).[25] Because women are weak, they cannot be independent, and must be ruled. But although they are weak, they rule in turn, and because they are weak, they enjoy doing so. The basis of Rousseau's psychology of women is that women, being the weaker sex, enjoy ruling the supposedly stronger sex. Women's love of rule provides the grounds for Rousseau's hope that sexual morality can be purified, that women can reform men. Thus he argues that women will not be chaste in this life because of the prospect of an afterlife. A religious motive will not guarantee feminine chastity, because women will always be proud of their desirability.

> A young and beautiful girl will never despise her body, she will never in good faith grieve for the great sins her beauty causes to be committed, she will never sincerely shed tears before God for being a coveted object, and she will never be able to believe within herself that the sweetest sentiment of the heart is an invention of Satan. Give her other reasons that she can believe within and for herself, for these will never get through to her (*Emile*, V, p. 392).[26]

Nevertheless, women can quite easily be encouraged to be chaste, for their pride supports their chastity; their desirability is heightened by their chastity.

> Chastity must be a delicious virtue for a beautiful woman who has an elevated soul. While she sees the whole earth at her feet, she triumphs over all and over herself. She raises in her own heart a throne to which all come to render homage. The tender or jealous but always respectful feelings of both sexes toward her, the universal esteem she enjoys, and her own self-esteem constantly reward her with a tribute of glory for a few momentary struggles. The privations are fleeting, but the reward for them is permanent. What a joy for a noble soul when the pride of virtue is joined to beauty! (*Emile*, V, p. 391).

Because women desire to rule men, they can be made to desire to be chaste. Women cannot be independent of men, and must not think that they can be; they must be convinced that "the good man . . . alone can make the women to whom he is attached—wives or beloveds—happy" (*Emile*, V, p. 392).

Men make women happy in two different ways.[27] Men make women happy (just as women make men happy) by completing them. This is Rousseau's understanding of love; we love that which we need in order to be complete. "I do not conceive how someone who needs nothing can love anything. I do not conceive how someone who loves nothing can be happy" (*Emile*, IV, p. 221).[28] Women, like men, when well educated are aware of their virtues but also of their shortcomings. They are aware that perfection is possible only in the context of heterosexual union. The perfected whole, the "moral person," is the product of that union alone; in its absence, the well-educated woman realizes that she is only an "eye" which does not know what to see (as the well-educated man realizes that he is only an "arm" which does not know what to do [*Emile*, V, p. 377]). Thus women and men are able to love one another, because they can recognize how much they need one another. As a result of the excellence of her education, Sophie is more aware than are most women of the necessity and the desirability of being completed by a virtuous man. For this reason, Rousseau can say of her what he would not say of most women—that "the need to love . . . devours her" (*Emile*, V, p. 397). Because of the intensity of her desire to love, Sophie is not fully representative of the average woman: nevertheless, one can say that as a lover Sophie successfully actualizes a potential inherent in women (and men) generally.

Men also make women happy in a second respect, however, in which similarity between the sexes is less evident. For women desire not only to be completed by men, but also to rule men. Only a good man cares enough about women to be dependent upon them and ruled by them.

> Make [women] feel that the empire of their sex and all its advantages depend not only on the good conduct and the morals of women but also on those of men, that they have little hold over vile and base souls, and that a man will serve his mistress no better than he serves virtue. . . . You will cause a nobler passion to be born in them—that of reigning over great and strong souls, the ambition of the women of Sparta, which was to command men. . . . The woman who is at once decent, lovable, and self-controlled, who forces those about her to respect her, who has reserve and modesty, who, in a word, sustains love by means of esteem, sends her lovers with a nod to the end of the world, to combat, to glory, to death, to anything she pleases. This seems to me to be a noble empire, and one well worth the price of its purchase (*Emile*, V, pp. 392–93).

Women's desire to rule men enables them to be the agents of a general moral reformation. This is because women cannot rule immoral men, and (when well educated) will not desire to rule slavish men. Only a man who is virtuous can be ruled, but rule over a virtuous man must be limited, for it must be consonant with his virtue. Women's pride therefore requires them to rule virtuous men. Sophie illustrates this in her relation to Emile.

> She has that noble pride based on merit which is conscious of itself, esteems itself, and wants to be honored as it honors itself. She would disdain a heart which did not find the full value of her heart, which did not love her for her virtues as much as, and more than, for her charms, and which did not prefer its own duty to her and to everything else. She did not want a lover who knew no law other than hers. She wants to reign over a man whom she has not disfigured (*Emile*, V, p. 339).[29]

She wishes to rule over a man who is capable in turn of ruling her. She therefore exemplifies the Aristotelian contention that political rule, in which ruling and being ruled are interchanged, is preferable to the absolute rule of a master over a slave.[30]

This defect of Sophie's, then, is natural to her sex: she is proud and desires to rule others. Emile does not share this defect. Thus their relationship mirrors the peaceful complementarity of the primeval relations between the sexes: men have the physical strength but not the desire to rule women, whereas women have the desire but not the physical strength to rule men.[31] Emile could be a "master" if he chose, but he does not condescend to make others his slaves. He does not wish to rule others; he "enter[s] society not in order to excel in it, but to know it and to find there a companion worthy of him" (*Emile*, IV, p. 335).[32] Emile needs to find a wife, just as Sophie needs to find a husband; but Rousseau does not suggest that Emile desires to rule his wife (as Sophie desires to rule her husband).[33]

By contrast, Rousseau does emphasize that because of his sexuality Emile is ruled. Upon first hearing Sophie's voice, "Emile surrenders [and bids] farewell [to] freedom" (*Emile*, V, p. 415).[34] "Softened by an idle life, he now lets himself be governed by women. Their amusements are his occupations, their wills are his laws; a young girl is the arbiter of his destiny, and he crawls and bends before her. The grave Emile is a child's plaything" (*Emile*, V, p. 431). Emile's dependence on Sophie is confirmed at the book's conclusion, when the tutor abdicates his authority over Emile, saying that Sophie, having married Emile, is henceforth to be regarded as Emile's "governor" (*Emile*, V, p. 479). Emile recognizes that his sexuality makes him dependent:

"If I were without passions, I would, in my condition as a man, be independent like God himself; for I would want only what is. . . . At least I have no more than one chain. It is the only one I shall ever bear, and I can glory in it. Come, then, give me Sophie, and I am free" (*Emile*, V, pp. 472–73).

The dependence of Emile upon Sophie (and of men upon women generally) is at once both moral and natural, which is why Rousseau advocates such dependence (notwithstanding his ambivalence). It is natural because men desire women (even if they do not need them). Even if women manipulate men in sexual relationships, women could not do so if male desire did not provide a more or less natural basis for their manipulation.

Of equal importance is the fact that the sexual relationship can be moral. Because "love must be reciprocal," the lover must "make [him]self lovable" (*Emile*, IV, p. 214). The lover does not desire to exploit the beloved, but instead to please her. For this reason, Rousseau believes that the love relationship is of unique moral significance in the modern bourgeois world. Citizenship is no longer an available option in this world, and all other social ties outside of the family are merely reflections of the calculated self-interest of individuals. In principle, the calculating and self-interested individual is an exploiter; only the fear of discovery and punishment restrains him. The general rule of bourgeois society, Rousseau contends, is that "someone's loss almost always creates another's prosperity" (*Second*, p. 194). This is not true of the legitimate society envisioned in the *Social Contract*, wherein "one cannot work for someone else without also working for oneself" (*Social*, II, 4, p. 62). But because the existence of legitimate societies depends on the denaturing of human beings (and because it presupposes a non-Christian religious foundation), this political solution is not of great practical relevance. By contrast, because Rousseau builds on a natural passion when he attempts to unite sexuality to morality through the medium of romantic love, he believes that this second solution to the problem of bourgeois self-interest, exemplified in *Emile*, is of far greater practical importance. "The attraction of domestic life is the best counterpoison for bad morals" (*Emile*, I, p. 46). Rousseau therefore presents the family, or the sexual interdependence of bourgeois men and women, as the only practical solution to the bourgeois phenomenon of narcissistic individualism.

Emile's sexual interest is important because it necessitates his more general socialization or politicization.

"In aspiring to the status of husband and father, have you meditated enough upon its duties? When you become the head of a family, you are going to become a member of the state, and do you know what it is to be a member of the state? Do you know what government, laws, and fatherland are?" (*Emile*, V, p. 348).[35]

Insofar as he is sexual, Emile must also be prepared to be political. Like the citizens of antiquity, Emile must be able to act in public, so as to defend his family, or those to whom he is most attached in private.[36] Rousseau remarks that in *Emile* he attempts to write "the history of my species," although it appears as a "romance" (*Emile*, V, p. 416). And the romance of Emile and Sophie does in fact recapitulate "the history of [the human] species" as we see it in the *Second Discourse*; for both primitive man and Emile, sex serves as the bridge to politics.[37]

Women make men political, but political men spend much of their time apart from women. This was certainly true of the political men of antiquity. In the classical republics, women were restricted to domestic life, and men deliberated publicly in their absence. In this respect too Emile resembles an ancient citizen. His political education takes place in the absence of women. Although he must learn about politics because of his engagement to Sophie, Emile leaves Sophie (at his tutor's command, and very much against his inclination) in order to learn about politics.

Yet the tutor has Emile leave Sophie for personal, not political, reasons. Although Emile depends on Sophie, he also must leave Sophie so as to lessen his dependence upon her. His dependence can and should be lessened because Sophie is not the cause of Emile's virtue.

> She was won by all the sentiments natural to her lover's heart: esteem of true goods, frugality, simplicity, generous disinterestedness, contempt for show and riches. Emile had these virtues before love imposed them on him. How, then, has Emile truly changed? He has new reasons to be himself. This is the single point where he differs from what he was (*Emile*, V, p. 433).

Emile is not virtuous because he loves; he loves because he is virtuous. For this reason he differs from the foolish theatergoers, infatuated with the image of a theatrical heroine, whom Rousseau criticizes in the *Letter to D'Alembert*: "If a young man has seen the world only on the stage, the first way to approach virtue which presents itself to him is to look for a mistress who will lead him there" (*Letter*, p. 48). Sophie merely confirms Emile's virtue; she does not cause him to approach it.

But Emile must come to know that she is not the cause of his virtue, that he can continue to be virtuous in her absence. Here Emile is both alike and unlike the ancient citizen. For the citizens of antiquity depended upon women, but were able to restrict their dependence, and to be chaste, in the name of their attachment to their city.[38] Like them, Emile depends upon a woman, and like them he is taught to restrict his dependence upon her. But unlike them, he is limited in his dependence by a vision of moral autonomy, not by one of political solidarity. The citizen is virtuous insofar as he submits to the general will; Emile is virtuous insofar as he is autonomous (able to do without Sophie). " 'Up to now you were only apparently free. You had only the precarious freedom of a slave to whom nothing has been commanded. Now be really free. Learn to become your own master. Command your heart, Emile, and you will be virtuous' " (*Emile*, V, p. 445).[39] Emile is a natural man. Because of his sexuality (the sexuality of a natural man "in the civil state"), Emile resembles a citizen far more than would a natural man "in the savage state," who more nearly approaches true self-sufficiency. Sexuality makes a natural man such as Emile resemble the citizen; what transcends the sexual (the city, or the morally autonomous self) causes the two to diverge again.

In learning to approach autonomy, Emile is now taught to distrust his illusions. Earlier Rousseau defended the pleasures of love, despite their illusory character, because of the moral consequences that they produce: "In love everything is only illusion. I admit it. But what is real are the sentiments for the truly beautiful with which love animates us. . . . So, what of it? Does the lover any the less sacrifice all of his low sentiments to this imaginary model?" (*Emile*, V, p. 391). It now seems that morality requires Emile to be liberated from any illusions he may harbor regarding Sophie. In order to be capable of independence, Emile must now imagine less actively. He is told that he must "attach [his] heart only to imperishable beauty" (*Emile*, V, p. 446). By doing so, the tutor concedes, he "will not . . . have the illusion of imaginary pleasures"; on the other hand, neither "will [he] have the pains which are their fruit" (*Emile*, V, p. 446). Yet despite his loss of illusions, Emile continues to depend upon women. He learns to be capable of independence—but his capacity is to be exercised only in case of emergency. As a matter of course, Emile is expected to remain social, and to remain dependent on women. In losing his illusions he merely shifts from a less to a more natural dependence upon women. "True love . . . is not as natural as is thought. . . . There is a great difference between the sweet habit which makes a man affectionate toward his companion and that unbridled ardor which intoxicates him with the chimerical attractions of an object which he no longer sees as it really is" (*Emile*, V, p. 430). Conjugal affection differs dramatically from romantic love, as we have seen in discussing the *Second Discourse*.[40] But even the man bound to his companion by "sweet habit" is far more dependent upon a woman than is the primordial natural man. At the conclusion of *Emile*, the tutor predicts that Emile's love for Sophie is necessarily impermanent. " 'Whatever precautions anyone may take, enjoyment wears out pleasures, and love is worn out before all others. But when love has lasted a long time, a sweet habit fills the void it leaves behind, and the attraction of mutual confidence succeeds the transports of passion' " (*Emile*, V, p. 479). But even when the illusions of love cease, Sophie can continue to govern Emile. " 'Become his other half to such an extent that he can no longer do without you, and that as soon as he leaves you, he feels he is far from himself' " (*Emile*, V, p. 479). Rousseau does not seem to expect Emile to be truly independent of women.

Émile et Sophie, the unfinished, unpublished sequel to *Emile*, may call the above statement into question. For in the fragment that we have of this work, Emile does abandon Sophie; Rousseau resumes the narrative with Emile and Sophie married and (after the death of their daughter) living in Paris. Sophie is unfaithful to Emile, and is impregnated by another man; Emile responds by leaving her.[41] Thus Rousseau vindicates Emile's education (at the price of conceding the failure of Sophie's education).[42] For the premise of Sophie's education is that in modern times a woman's reason must be cultivated. Otherwise, "in big cities and among immoral men, [an uncultivated] woman would be too easy to seduce. Often her virtue would depend only on the occasion; in this philosophic age she needs a virtue that can be put to the test. She needs to know beforehand what might be said to her and what she ought to think about it" (*Emile*, V, p. 383).

"She needs a virtue that can be put to the test," the test of big cities and immoral men. Sophie's education evidently fails here; she is seduced by an immoral man in the big city of Paris. But if her education fails, Emile's succeeds—he avoids the temptation to remain dependent upon Sophie.[43] In *Emile*, Emile must be forced by his tutor to leave Sophie temporarily; in *Émile et Sophie*, he decides of his own accord to abandon her forever.

Because of its extremely fragmentary nature, one hesitates to explicate *Émile et Sophie*. The work's subtitle, however, might seem to provide a clue: *Les Solitaires*. It seems to suggest that the book was to have told the story of Emile and Sophie achieving independence of one another; that Emile and Sophie were to have been portrayed as solitary beings, akin to Rousseau the solitary walker, and no longer united as one moral being.

Passages from the work support this interpretation, at least with respect to Emile. He realizes that Sophie's infidelity requires him to live alone, independent of women and of men alike (*Émile et Sophie*, pp. 905–06).

Yet this interpretation is by no means a necessary one. For we have three sources that inform us about the plot of the completed *Émile et Sophie*, as envisioned by Rousseau.[44] The first is a preface to the fragment written by Moultou and Du Peyrou, editors of an early collection of Rousseau's works; it explains that Sophie was not responsible for her infidelity (like the heroine of Samuel Richardson's novel *Clarissa Harlowe*, she was drugged into submission). This explanation, however, adds little to what is already implied in Rousseau's text (*Émile et Sophie*, p. 910).[45] The other two sources are reports by Pierre Prevost and Bernardin de Saint-Pierre, two of Rousseau's acquaintances, of his plans as confided to them for the completion of the novel. Their reports are more informative, but unfortunately they contradict one another. Both agree, however, that Emile and Sophie are eventually reunited. This again confirms an indication in the text (*Émile et Sophie*, p. 909). Prevost's account does not however mention Sophie's death following the reconciliation, which is clearly indicated in the text (*Émile et Sophie*, pp. 882 and 910).

The version of Bernardin de Saint-Pierre best corresponds to Rousseau's text. In addition, it is substantiated by three recently discovered preparatory notes written by Rousseau while planning *Émile et Sophie*.[46] According to Saint-Pierre, Emile travels to a desert island, where he marries a young Spanish woman. Sophie then arrives on the island; Emile takes her as a second wife. Sophie dies, having never been able to forgive herself for her infidelity. She leaves behind a letter for Emile, which explains the somewhat extenuating circumstances that led to her infidelity.

The denouement of *Émile et Sophie*, as we have it from Saint-Pierre, therefore renders it plausible that the sequel was not intended to demonstrate Emile's achievement of self-sufficiency. Emile leaves Sophie only to be reconciled to her, and to remarry—in fact both to marry another and also to remarry her. Emile does not then achieve independence from women in the sequel. If anything, by becoming a bigamist he doubles his dependence upon women. It is therefore conceivable that the work Rousseau subtitled *Les Solitaires* was intended as much to portray Emile's flight from solitude as his progress toward it. Emile is a natural man, but one who is capable of self-sufficiency only in extraordinary circumstances; for the most part he is a natural man who remains dependent upon women.

Thus even *Émile et Sophie*, if completed, might have confirmed the view that men and women are sexual dependents, beings whose different but complementary sexual capacities entail differing but complementary political orientations as well. Women embody the understanding of sexual politics expounded in *Emile*.[47] For women, to be sexual is to be political; as sexual beings, they are able to rule the stronger sex. Because they are weak, and must in part be ruled, they have no alternative but in part to rule the strong as well. By contrast, men confirm the *Second Discourse*'s explanation of sexual politics. Because men are sexual, they must as a consequence be political—so as to protect the lives and welfare of those dependent upon them.[48] But political men depend on those who depend on their protection.

"This little boy that you see there," said Themistocles to his friends, "is the master of Greece, for he governs his mother, his mother governs me, I govern the Athenians, and the Athenians govern Greece." O what little leaders would often be found in the greatest empires, if from the prince one descended by degrees to the first hand which secretly sets things in motion! (*Emile*, II, p. 84n).[49]

Although men are strong, insofar as they rule they inevitably are ruled as well. If men rule, they must also be ruled. Men are clearly not strong enough to rule absolutely; but the possibility remains that at least some men might be strong enough to avoid rule absolutely.

Rousseau as Natural Man

Rousseau's own life is of great interest and relevance because it illustrates this possibility. The experience of Emile shows us that women are not only social in themselves but the cause of men being social. And in *Emile* Rousseau presents us with a man who Rousseau thinks ought to be socialized; since women accomplish the task of socialization, Rousseau can view their influence favorably there. Rousseau himself resists socialization, however. Because he is an exceptional man, life in society and therefore life with women make him uncomfortable. He is unlike most men, for whom integration into society is the goal toward which they should be directed, the goal toward which women lead them. For there are a few men, such as Rousseau, who can be happy only by living apart from society. Because women socialize men, such men perceive the influence of women not as a benefit but as a threat. Thus Rousseau's experience gives us a very different perspective on the value of social life, and on the value of women, the agents who promote social life. This perspective suggests that social life and sexual life are beset with shortcomings, and are unable to accommodate all individuals successfully.

Rousseau differs from Emile because he is unsuited to civilized life. Like Emile he is a natural man. But he is a different sort of natural man than is Emile, because he is less social than Emile. He indicates this in his autobiographical work, *Rousseau Juge de Jean-Jacques*. There Rousseau contrasts natural man with man as we see him today. "All men are naturally lazy." But *amour-propre* transforms them. "It excites them, . . . because it is the only passion that always speaks to them: one sees them all thus in the world." It follows that a man without *amour-propre* would be natural man. "The man in whom *amour-propre* does not dominate and who does not seek his happiness far from himself is the only one who is carefree and has leisure; and Jean-Jacques is that man as far as I can judge myself" (*Dialogues*, II, pp. 846–47). Rousseau resembles the "savage man" of the *Second Discourse*, who unlike "civilized man . . . breathes only repose and freedom; he wishes only to live and remain idle" (*Second*, pp. 178–79). By contrast, Emile is taught a trade; he is not a solitary but a member of society, to which he owes the obligation to labor (*Emile*, III, p. 195). Emile is therefore unlike both the solitary savage and Rousseau. Emile "must work like a peasant and think like a philosopher so as not be as lazy as a savage" (*Emile*, III, p. 202). Jean-Jacques is to Emile as "what is natural in the savage state" is to "what is natural in the civil state."

Because he is like primeval natural man, Rousseau is not made to live in civil society. "I have never been truly suited for civil society where everything is annoyance, obligation, and duty. . . . My independent natural temperament always made me incapable of the subjection necessary to anyone who wants to live among men" (*Reveries*, VI, p. 83; cf. *Confessions*, I, p. 37). And just as Emile's "natural" sociability can be understood only in terms of his sexuality and his relationship with Sophie, so must Rousseau's "independent natural temperament," which separates him from civil society, be explained in terms of his sexuality and his relations with women. We have seen how Emile is made social and dependent by his need for a woman. He is like most men, who rule and are ruled by women. Like women, such men attain equality through empire. Again like women, they must engage in sexual politics because they cannot be asexual anarchists. Because most men cannot be independent, and must be ruled by women, they must rule them in turn.

Rousseau himself, by contrast, would like to be an asexual anarchist. He would like to be truly independent, to be able to avoid both ruling and being ruled. For men such as Rousseau, equality through empire, the interchange of ruling and being ruled, is unsatisfactory. It is unsatisfactory because empire is inherently unsatisfactory, involving as it does dependence on others. Rousseau's own goal therefore is not equality through empire but solitude through the avoidance of empire.

But women pose the greatest threat to Rousseau's quest for solitude. For like Emile he is inclined to depend upon women, and to enjoy depending upon them. Beginning with his formative sexual experience, Rousseau associates sexuality with feminine dominance. He first experiences sexual arousal at the age of eight, a consequence of the chastisement that he receives from one of his guardians, Mademoiselle Lambercier. The incident has vital consequences for him: "This childish punishment, inflicted upon me when only eight years old by a young woman of thirty, disposed of my tastes, my desires, my passions, and my own self for the remainder of my life" (*Confessions*, I, p. 14).[50] He "found in the pain, even in the disgrace, a mixture of sensuality which had left me less afraid than desirous of experiencing it again from the same hand" (*Confessions*, I, pp. 13–14). Rousseau's fundamental teaching about sexuality, that it involves a political relationship of command and obedience, emerges from his own sexual experience. In sexual relationships, women command. "To lie at the feet of an imperious mistress, to obey her commands, to ask her forgiveness—this was for me a sweet enjoyment" (*Confessions*, I, p. 16).[51] Much later in his life, Rousseau speaks of his wife and mother-in-law as his "*gouverneuses*" (*Confessions*, VIII, p. 393). In this second, much less erotic and exotic, context, women again appear as the rulers of men.

Sexual relationships are political because they normally entail the interchange of ruling and being ruled between the two partners. But Rousseau himself is not normal. He is a prodigy (*Confessions*, I, p. 6, II, p. 63). If Rousseau is a natural man, he is not for that reason an ordinary man. On the contrary: "I am not made like any of those who are in existence. If I am not better, at least I am different" (*Confessions*, I, p. 3). In an age of unnatural men, an authentically natural man, in many ways similar to a savage, is necessarily unique.

Among many other respects, Rousseau is abnormal in that he rejects the political character of sexual relationships, despite the evident attraction that he finds in submission to women. This rejection again indicates his similarity to savage man. For in the primordial state of nature, sex was not yet political; men and women united sexually at fleeting intervals, in brief encounters, but basically remained as self-sufficient integers. But what was true in the primordial state of nature obviously can no longer simply be true for Rousseau; for the man who enjoys lying "at the feet of an imperious mistress," sexual relations are no longer conceivable without sexual dominance. Sex was originally apolitical because savages enjoyed "the physical" without experiencing "the moral" "in the sentiment of love" (*Second*, p. 134). This is impossible for Rousseau; in this sense he cannot be considered a natural man.[52] If Rousseau is truly self-sufficient, his freedom from women must differ from savage man's; since "the physical" can no longer be separated from "the moral" in love, it appears that Rousseau must somehow manage to be free of even the physical in love. If Rousseau is to be independent and sex creates dependence, Rousseau must somehow transcend sexuality.

Rousseau's life illustrates a number of different strategies, some more successful than others, aimed at achieving such independence. Central to all of these strategies is his employment of a most unnatural faculty—his imagination. The imagination is Rousseau's unnatural means to the natural end of independence from society. Unlike Emile, Rousseau strives to be as independent as a savage; that he must strive to do so differentiates him from a savage.

Savage man is independent because he is altogether enclosed in his own existence, unaware of the existence of others. He is a whole because he cannot conceive of others; to be a part one must be aware that there are other parts who could make one into a whole. In short, savage man is too unimaginative to be anything but independent of others (*Second*, p. 117). But Rousseau is extraordinarily imaginative. Accordingly, Rousseau attempts to make use of his imagination so as to avoid being a part, dependent on other parts for his completion. In this first strategy, Rousseau constructs an imaginary world for himself, in which all the parts necessary for his completion are present, and in which he can be whole. The unimaginative savage is whole because he is unaware of the existence of other parts; the normal imaginative civilized man is not whole because he is aware of them; the extraordinarily imaginative Rousseau strives to be whole, despite his awareness of other parts, by virtue of the fact that he imaginatively creates and orders them. The imaginary world that Rousseau constructs is his preferred alternative to the real world of civil society, in which his state of dependence on others is only too obvious.

> The fictitious state in which I succeeded in putting myself made me forget my actual state with which I was so dissatisfied. This love of imaginary objects, and the readiness with which I occupied myself with them, ended by disgusting me with everything around me, and decided that liking for solitude which has never left me (*Confessions*, I, pp. 40–41; cf. *Reveries*, III, p. 28, VIII, p. 117, *Malesherbes*, I, p. 1131, III, p. 1140, and *Dialogues*, II, p. 814).

Society reflects our dependence upon others; the imagination seems to make possible our independence, or rather our dependence only upon those whom we create.

Because of his propensity to imagine ideal societies, Rousseau transcends his actual society. He is too imaginative to be a Genevan citizen. He says that "finding nothing around him that realized his ideas [of ancient valor and chivalric romance], he left his fatherland while still a young adolescent" (*Dialogues*, II, p. 815). The good citizen, as we saw earlier, must imagine that his city is devoid of ruling human wills. Rousseau leaves Geneva precisely because in this respect it is too good a city; he leaves it in search of the human wills that he imagines.

The exercise of Rousseau's imagination is intended to make him independent of society. But we have seen that Emile is made socially dependent as a result of his imagination of a woman; the liveliness of Rousseau's imagination could conceivably tie Rousseau to women, and through them to society. In fact, this is what happens. Rousseau's imagination of women can no more make him independent of society than can Emile's unless it also makes him independent of women. Rousseau's first strategy—of achieving self-sufficiency through the creation of his own imaginary world—ultimately fails, because it does not eliminate his dependence on women. So long as Rousseau continues to imagine women, he is unable to attain self-sufficiency; as is the case with Emile, Rousseau's sexuality is the key to his continued sociality, his continued experience of being ruled. In the end Rousseau does achieve independence through the imagination— but only after redirecting and limiting his imagination. The aging Rousseau becomes truly independent only when he himself follows the advice that governs the education of the prepubescent Emile. "The real world has its limits; the imaginary world is infinite. Unable to enlarge the one, let us restrict the other" (*Emile*, II, p. 81). Independence ultimately requires a restricted imaginary world.

Thus the vicissitudes of Rousseau's sexual imagination are decisive in explaining both his dependence and his ultimate independence. Rousseau's sexual imagination develops in the course of his encounters with the various women who were of importance in his life. In these encounters, one is repeatedly struck by the resemblances between Rousseau's self-descriptions and his characterizations of one or another of his literary creations. In particular, both at the beginning and the end of his sexual life he resembles Emile. But his development reverses that which he prescribes for Emile; for in the beginning he resembles the adolescent Emile and at the end the prepubescent Emile. In Rousseau's case, as opposed to Emile's, the man is father to the child, the child that the man ultimately becomes. Rousseau asserts that "None of us is philosophic enough to know how to put himself in a child's place" (*Emile*, II, p. 115). Rousseau achieves his independence only when he learns how to make himself once again into a child.

Rousseau's Relationships with Women

The first woman of importance in the life of the adolescent Rousseau is Madame de Warens, his preceptor in Catholicism. Rousseau is attracted to her (or rather to his image of her), and yet his attraction ensures his chastity.

> Her image, ever present to my heart, left room for no others; she was for me the only woman in the world; and the extreme sweetness of the feelings with which she inspired me did not allow my senses time to awake for others, and protected me against her and all her sex. In a word, I was chaste [*sage*], because I loved her (*Confessions*, III, p. 112).

The adolescent Rousseau resembles the adolescent Emile; he is chaste because of his image of his beloved. Rousseau's description of the impact of Madame de Warens's image upon him is in fact borrowed from the tutor's description of the impact of Sophie's image upon Emile. "I shall disgust him with libertinism, and I shall make him moderate [*sage*] by making him fall in love" (*Emile*, IV, p. 327). Madame de Warens, who is older than Rousseau, combines the functions of Sophie and the tutor in Rousseau's education.[53] The tutor sees to it that Emile possesses Sophie, and Madame de Warens arranges for Rousseau to possess her. Rousseau accedes: "I felt . . . that, in reality, there was only *one* woman who could protect me against other women and secure me against temptations" (*Confessions*, V, p. 202; the emphasis is the translator's). At first "her image . . . protected me against her and all her sex." Later, only her actual possession "could protect me against other women." Just as Emile's image of Sophie ultimately leads him to possess her, so does Rousseau ultimately possess Madame de Warens. Like the adolescent Emile, the adolescent

Rousseau proceeds from attachment to an image to dependence upon its real embodiment.[54]

But as Rousseau matures, the activity of his imagination complicates the relation between image and reality. No longer does his attraction to an image lead straightforwardly to the actual possession of its embodiment. We see this in Rousseau's account of his relations with the Venetian courtesan Zulietta. Rousseau strongly emphasizes the importance of the story of their encounter. "Whoever you may be, who desire to know the inmost heart of a man, have the courage to read the next two or three pages; you will become thoroughly acquainted with Jean Jacques Rousseau" (*Confessions*, VII, p. 329).

While in Venice, Rousseau encounters Zulietta, the loveliest young woman he ever met. She claims that he resembles a man whom she knew and with whom she was, and is, deeply in love; as a result, she offers herself to Rousseau. And yet Rousseau is unable to make love with her; although he idealizes her, he cannot accept that she really embodies the ideal. He soliloquizes:

> This object, which is at my disposal, is the masterpiece of nature and love; its mind and body, every part of it perfect. . . . And yet she is a miserable street-walker, on sale to everybody; . . . she comes and throws herself at my head, mine, although she knows that I am poor, while my real merits, being unknown to her, can have no value in her eyes.

He then sets out to resolve this seeming discrepancy between the real and the apparent—that is, to free himself of his illusion of her perfection.

> Either my heart deceives me, dazzles my senses, and makes me the dupe of a worthless slut, or some secret defect, with which I am unacquainted, must destroy the effect of her charms, and render her repulsive to those who would otherwise fight for the possession of her. I began to look for this defect with a singular intensity of mind.

In the end, he discovers that she is without a nipple on one breast.

> I immediately began to rack my brains for the reason of such a defect, and, feeling convinced that it was connected with some remarkable natural imperfection, by brooding so long over this idea, I saw, as clear as daylight, that, in the place of the most charming person that I could picture to myself, I only held in my arms a kind of monster, the outcast of nature, of mankind and of love.

Rousseau then questions her about her deformity. Not surprisingly, this rapidly cools her ardor (much to his subsequent regret). Her final remark, upon terminating their assignation, is that he should "Give up the ladies, and study mathematics" (*Confessions*, VII, pp. 329–31).

The moral which Rousseau draws from this story is that "Nature has not created me for enjoyment. She has put into my wretched head the poison of that ineffable happiness, the desire for which she has planted in my heart" (*Confessions*, VII, p. 329). In this story, Rousseau resembles not Emile but the girl like Sophie who possesses a "lively imagination" (*Emile*, V, p. 405). Like her, Rousseau's fixation upon an idealized image frustrates him in the real world. For by means of his imagination Rousseau first idealizes the world, but then, in Weber's phrase, proceeds to the "disenchantment of the world." Zulietta's concluding remark points toward Rousseau's imaginative destruction of the lover's happiness. Because Rousseau must question the enchantment of the world, he cannot be a lover, who thrives on enchantment. Instead he must stick to the dry, mundane, and more importantly, certain and certifiable reality of numbers.

One could, of course, invert the meaning of Zulietta's criticism with equal justification. As Platonists know, the mathematical world is not more mundane but precisely more ethereal, more "ideal" than the ephemeral world of men and women, no matter how lovely the latter may appear. Perhaps Rousseau should leave women and study mathematics not because he always subverts the seemingly ideal but because he would be at home only in the truly ideal. In the end, the two interpretations of Zulietta's remark arrive at the same conclusion from opposite beginnings: both suggest that Rousseau, the exceptional man, is uncomfortable in the world that is real, because he is aware that it is not ideal.

"Pity me. I am unhappy, not mad." This is the statement of the girl like Sophie, an exceptional individual overcome by the discrepancy between the real and the ideal. It could also be the statement of the Rousseau of the Venetian episode.

Rousseau is made miserable by the illusionary character of the ideal. He responds by attempting to live in the real world without idealizing it, or by accepting its unadorned reality. His most enduring sexual relationship, with the commonplace and illiterate Thérèse Levasseur, must be understood in these terms. Rousseau's relationship with Thérèse makes sense in chronological terms as a reaction against the failure of his experience with Zulietta; he meets Thérèse shortly after returning to Paris from Venice, and the story of their meeting occurs less than ten pages after the Zulietta episode in the *Confessions*. Rousseau lived with Thérèse for many years and married her in his old age. Rousseau in fact claims that his relationship with her alone made him a moral being, and hence a social being. "I have always considered the day which united me to my Thérèse as that which determined my moral being" (*Confessions*, IX, p. 426).

At first glance this claim would seem to make him decisively resemble Emile, whose moral being is equally determined by his relation with Sophie. One can therefore wonder whether Rousseau is truly any more independent of women than is Emile.

But in fact his relation with Thérèse differs decisively from Emile's with Sophie. Emile singles Sophie out from the entire female sex; he loves her because he imagines that she is unique among women. In the *Second Discourse*'s terms, his love for her is "moral"—"that which determines sexual desire and fixes it exclusively on a single object." Whereas Rousseau's attachment to Thérèse is "physical"—"that general desire which inclines one sex to unite with the other" (*Second*, p. 134). He makes this explicit: "I never felt the least spark of love for her; . . . the sensual needs, which I satisfied in her person, were only for me those of sexual impulse, without being in any way connected with the individual" (*Confessions*, IX, p. 427). Rousseau with Thérèse does not resemble Emile, but instead savage man, who knows only "physical love," for whom "any woman is good," to whose heart the "imagination . . . does not speak" (*Second*, p. 135).[55]

Rousseau is of course unlike savage man, in that he lives for a long time with one woman (whereas savage man unites for brief moments with a succession of many women). But the one woman with whom Rousseau lives for so long means very little to him—not much more than any of the women with whom savage man unites means to savage man.

Rousseau's dependence on Thérèse is minimal, since he does not imagine or particularize her. Starobinski puts this well; Thérèse is someone in response to whom Rousseau "never had to pose to himself the problem of the *other*. Thérèse is not a partner of a dialogue, but the auxiliary of physical existence. Beside other women, Rousseau seeks the miraculous moment when the presence of the body is no longer an obstacle; but in Thérèse, he finds a body which is not even an obstacle."[56]

Starobinski bases this judgment on a textual observation: he notes that Rousseau employs the same word, *supplément*, in describing both his relation to Thérèse and his practice of masturbation.[57] Here again the contrast with Emile is illuminating. The tutor insists that Emile be denied any opportunity to masturbate, because Emile must be a social being. "Emile enter[s] society . . . to find there a companion worthy of him" (*Emile*, IV, p. 335). Since this is so, Emile must need to seek a "companion"; hence he cannot masturbate, cannot attain sexual satisfaction by himself, because he must depend on another for his sexual satisfaction. "If a tyrant must subjugate you, I prefer to yield you to one from whom I can deliver you. Whatever happens, I shall tear you away more easily from women than from yourself" (*Emile*, IV, p. 334). It is better for Emile, a social being, to be tyrannized by women than by himself.

By contrast, Rousseau himself masturbates.

> This vice, which shame and timidity find so convenient, possesses, besides a great attraction for lively imaginations—that of being able to dispose of the whole sex as they desire, and to make the beauty which tempts them minister to their pleasures, without being obliged to obtain its consent (*Confessions*, III, p. 111).

The quotation helps to explain how Thérèse determined his "moral being"; for insofar as Rousseau restricted his sexual activity to his relations with her (to which she of course consented), he no longer "dispose[d] of the whole sex as [he] desire[d], . . . without being obliged to obtain its consent." Rousseau's love for Thérèse is not "moral" in the sense of being particular; he is not uniquely attracted to her. But it is moral in that she consents to his love, in that their love is reciprocal. In this sense, though, love is moral even in the primordial state of nature.[58]

But because Rousseau's love for Thérèse is not particular, does not involve the exercise of his imagination, it cannot satisfy him. This is the vital respect in which Rousseau differs from savage man; undifferentiated physical love cannot satisfy him. Because this is so, because he imagines and particularizes, sexuality threatens his independence more than it does savage man's.

Rousseau is given to masturbation because of his "lively imagination"— and as we have seen, Thérèse does not and cannot satisfy his imagination. He has no illusions about her, as he had with Zulietta. Because he never imagines that she "is the masterpiece of nature and love," he can never imagine her as "a kind of monster, the outcast of nature, of mankind and of love." But this is not enough to satisfy "lively imaginations," because lively imaginations are tempted by "beauty." Therefore it is not surprising that Thérèse does not cure Rousseau of the habit of masturbation; he prefers illusions without morality to morality without illusions. "Intercourse with women distinctly aggravated my ill health; the corresponding vice, of which I have never been able to cure myself completely, appeared to me to produce less injurious results" (*Confessions*, XII, p. 617). The tutor prefers that Emile, a social being without a lively imagination, be tyrannized by women rather than by himself. Because of Rousseau's lively imagination (and because intercourse with women is bad for his health), he masturbates. Masturbation is "less injurious" to Rousseau than would be the sexual life of a social being such as Emile. Because Rousseau does not imagine Thérèse, he depends less upon her than Emile depends upon Sophie. But also because he does not imagine her, the relationship with Thérèse leaves a void, requiring Rousseau to imagine someone. The inactivity of his imagination in dealing with Thérèse makes Rousseau comparatively independent in the real world, but also drives him back to the imagination, and to dependence in and upon an imaginary world.

Rousseau's masturbation, the sign of his continued recourse to the imaginary world, again suggests his kinship with the girl like Sophie. He seems to be condemned to frustration and unhappiness because of the nonexistence of the imaginary other on whom he depends. Nevertheless, it is possible to argue that the fertility of Rousseau's imagination enables him, unlike her, to achieve independence.

For the girl like Sophie is a young woman dependent upon an imaginary young man for her completion. By contrast, Rousseau claims that the precocious activity of his imagination has in a sense made him both man and woman. Influenced by his early readings (at ages six and seven) of romances and of Plutarch, he acquires "odd and romantic notions of human life, of which experience has never been able wholly to cure me," but also "the free and republican spirit, the proud and indomitable character unable to endure slavery or servitude, which has tormented me throughout my life" (*Confessions*, I, p. 7). The result of these varied readings is a peculiarly dualistic and bisexual character, "effeminate but yet indomitable" (*Confessions*, I, p. 10).[59] Prompted by his readings, Rousseau in some measure leaves the limiting character of his masculinity behind him. He claims to be effeminate; in his own estimation he is thus both female and male, which is to say that he transcends the differentiation between the sexes, and is a human whole, not merely a sexual part.[60] In Whitman's words one could say that Rousseau contradicts himself because he is large, he contains multitudes. Rousseau's imagination, which accounts for his doubleness, is nourished on the seemingly incompatible fare of (his mother's) romances and (his grandfather's) Plutarch; in Albert Schinz's useful formula, there is thus both a "Rousseau *romantique*" and a "Rousseau *romain*."[61] Rousseau's wholeness or independence is therefore linked intimately to the activity of his imagination. Because of his imaginative doubleness, his capacity for independence and his sexual self-sufficiency transcend the practice of masturbation. Rousseau's masturbation makes possible only his physical independence of women; but his effeminacy is far more important to the extent that it ensures his psychological transcendence of sexual differentiation and limitation.

In chapter 3 we considered Rousseau's discussion of spurious sexual independence in his comic play *Narcisse*. At the play's conclusion, the reformed hero declares to the heroine: "Come, beautiful Angelique; you have healed me of a ridicule which was the shame of my youth, and henceforth I am going to demonstrate with you that when one loves well, one no longer muses about oneself" (*Narcisse*, p. 1018). As we observed, in *Narcisse* the love of women is related to sociability, the positive standard according to which self-absorption is criticized. Before his reformation,

Valère imagines that he is in love with another (the girl whose portrait he is given), though in reality he is enslaved to himself (for he of course is the girl). Valère is not yet involved with a real woman, because in truth he is involved only with himself. Valère, or Narcisse, is taught in the play to depend upon women, and not upon himself alone. Because of the fertility of his imagination, Rousseau himself can be considered a more justifiable Narcisse. He can depend upon himself alone, because his self incorporates both masculinity and femininity. Rousseau is Narcisse, but insofar as he is truly whole, he stands in no need of a cure.[62]

Yet this assertion of Rousseau's wholeness and bisexuality is not wholly defensible. For at times Rousseau presents bisexuality and the consequent elimination of sexual dependence not as a characteristic that he possesses but only as a goal toward which he aims. Rousseau may be effeminate in the world created by his imagination; but he still recognizes that the imaginary world is not the only world in which he lives. In the world of reality, Rousseau continues to search for a completion which true bisexuality alone could afford him:

> The first, the greatest, the most powerful, the most irrepressible of all my needs was entirely in my heart; it was the need of a companionship as intimate as was possible; it was for that purpose especially that I needed a woman rather than a man, a female rather than a male friend. This singular want was such, that the most intimate corporal union had been unable to satisfy it; I should have wanted two souls in the same body (*Confessions*, IX, p. 428).

For Rousseau to say that he would like to have both a male and a female soul in his body is of course to say that he does not really have them both. But even if the effeminacy or bisexuality of the imagination is not wholly satisfactory, it nevertheless offers Rousseau considerable compensation. The compensation results from the fact that the liveliness of Rousseau's imagination still differentiates him from the girl like Sophie, condemned to search in vain for a nonexistent Telemachus. Rousseau's imagination is more active or creative than is the girl's. "The impossibility of grasping realities threw me into the land of chimeras, and, seeing nothing in existence which was worthy of my enthusiasm, I sought nourishment for it in an ideal world, which my fertile imagination soon peopled with beings after my own heart" (*Confessions*, IX, p. 441). When the girl like Sophie sees nothing in existence worthy of her enthusiasm, she becomes distraught. But this is because she can only read *Télémaque*; in effect the more imaginative Rousseau can write his *Télémaque*. Because of the active power of his imagination, Rousseau more closely resembles yet another of his literary creations—Pygmalion.

Pygmalion is a dramatic work of Rousseau's dating from 1762. In the piece, we see the sculptor Pygmalion dissatisfied with his master work, the statue of the female Galatea. The statue is inanimate, and Pygmalion wishes both to animate her with his soul (to unite with her) but also to be able to see and love her (to remain apart from her [*Pygmalion*, p. 1228]). His two contradictory desires are realized. Galatea comes to life. She speaks, touching herself while saying, "It is me." The sculptor asks that this "ravishing illusion . . . never abandon [his] senses." She then touches a piece of marble, realizing that "It is no longer me." And then at last she touches and kisses Pygmalion: "Ah! Me again" (*Pygmalion*, pp. 1230–31). As he wished, Pygmalion is both apart from his creation (hence able to love her) and a part of her (hence able to identify with her). He concludes: "It is you, it is you alone. I have given you all my being; I will no longer live except through you" (*Pygmalion*, p. 1231).

The conclusion of *Pygmalion* invites comparison with that of *Narcisse*. Because Valère loves Angelique, he "no longer muses about himself." But that is because Angelique is wholly apart from himself; he has not created her. Pygmalion has created Galatea. He can love her and in so doing love himself as her creator. Thus the highly imaginative man, the artistic creator (Rousseau as well as Pygmalion) appears as the justifiable narcissist.[63]

For Rousseau like Pygmalion creates ideal women and an ideal society, to compensate himself for his dissatisfaction with the real world. These creations ultimately become the characters of his romantic novel, *Julie*.

> I represented to myself love and friendship, the two idols of my heart, under the most enchanting forms. I took delight in adorning them with all the charms of the sex which I had always adored. I imagined two female friends, rather than two of my own sex, because if an instance of such friendship is rarer, it is at the same time more amiable (*Confessions*, IX, p. 444).

Rousseau compares himself to Pygmalion; he notes that he took such great pleasure in writing *Julie* because "nothing was sufficiently elegant or refined for the charming girls, with whom, like another Pygmalion, I was infatuated" (*Confessions*, IX, p. 451).

But Rousseau's attempt to content himself with the creatures of his imagination, and thereby to achieve self-sufficiency, is unsuccessful. Just as his experience with Thérèse drives him back to the world of imaginary women, so does his experience in writing *Julie* drive him back to the world of real women. For ultimately he shares the delusions of the infatuated theatergoers described in the *Letter to D'Alembert*: he ends by projecting the virtues of his imagined ideal onto a real woman (*Letter*, p. 48).[64] The composition of *Julie* occasions his one experience of true love, that for Madame d'Houdetot. "I was intoxicated with love without an object. This intoxication enchanted my eyes; this object became centered in her. I saw my Julie in Madame d'Houdetot, but invested with all the perfections with which I had just adorned the idol of my heart" (*Confessions*, IX, p. 455).

Madame d'Houdetot is the one woman whom Rousseau claims truly to have loved. In one respect, she is the perfect object of Rousseau's love; for she is in love with another (not to speak of being married to a third), hence Rousseau cannot hope to possess her. Since Rousseau contends that love is only a figment of the imagination, that love is in the eye of the beholder, not in the form of the beloved, he also contends that love is necessarily impermanent; the imagination's infatuation cannot long survive contact with the reality of the imagined object. "Imagination adorns what one desires but abandons it when it is in one's possession" (*Emile*, V, p. 447). Madame d'Houdetot is thus the perfect complement to Thérèse in Rousseau's love life; he possesses Thérèse without imagining her, and imagines Madame d'Houdetot without possessing her. Rousseau says of her that "I loved her too dearly to possess her" (*Confessions*, IX, p. 459).[65] It is also evident that he loved her so dearly because he could not possess her.

Thus, although Rousseau's imaginative creations drive him back toward dependence on a real woman, the woman who becomes the object of his love is still known to him only through his imagination, not through possession. Nevertheless, Rousseau's acquaintance with Madame d'Houdetot ultimately proves harmful to him. He is unable simply to rejoice in his imagination of Madame d'Houdetot. Imagining a perfect woman, not possessing her, still ties him to the real world and causes him misery in it. For this reason he can say that her first visit to him "unfortunately, was not the last" (*Confessions*, IX, p. 446). "The only amorous enjoyment of [Rousseau], the man of the most inflammable temperament, but, at the same time, of the most retiring disposition that Nature has perhaps ever produced," came to him as a result of his acquaintance with her. Yet his enjoyment does not sound particularly enjoyable:

> This time it was love—love in all its force and in all its frenzy. I will not describe the agitation, the shivering, the palpitation, the convulsive movements, or the faintness of the heart, which I felt continually. . . . This state, and, above all, its continuance during three months of excitement and self-restraint, so exhausted me that I did not recover for several years, and, finally, brought on a rupture, which I shall carry with me, or which will carry me with it, into the grave (*Confessions*, IX, pp. 460–61).

But Rousseau's infatuation with Madame d'Houdetot is not only painful in itself; it has painful consequences as well. His love excites the jealousy of Madame d'Épinay, furthering the conspiracy that he sees directed against him (*Confessions*, IX, p. 462). Rousseau is confirmed in his opinion that his supposed friends have been deceiving him. Accordingly, he feels "the sadness of a too loving and tender heart, which, deceived by those whom it believed to be of its own stamp, had been forced to retire into itself" (*Confessions*, X, p. 512). As a result of his experience with Madame d'Houdetot he resolves to bid "adieu to love for the remainder of [his] life" (*Confessions*, X, p. 562). The disproportion between the real and the ideal in love, the cause of Rousseau's unhappiness with Zulietta, is a problem that Rousseau never successfully resolves. He cannot idealize a woman without experiencing frustration and unsatisfying dependence in the real social world. Thérèse drives him back to the imaginary world in search of fulfillment, but Madame d'Houdetot teaches him that the imaginary world can never wholly be separated from the miseries of reality. As long as love is a concern of Rousseau's, he can never be happy whether in or out of love. "I was born to be the victim of my weaknesses, since victorious love was so fatal to me, and vanquished love even more fatal still" (*Confessions*, X, p. 562).

Rousseau bids adieu to love. In doing so, he redirects his attention from the human to the botanical world. "I have become solitary, or, as they say, unsociable and misanthropic, because to me the most desolate solitude seems preferable to the society of wicked men which is nourished only by betrayals and hatred." Yet "I am nevertheless unable to become entirely wrapped up in my own self, because in spite of my efforts, my expansive soul seeks to extend its feelings and existence over other beings" (*Reveries*, VII, p. 95). "The more profound the solitude in which I then live, the more necessary it is that some object fill the void; and those my imagination denies me or my memory pushes away are replaced [*supplées*] by the spontaneous products that the earth, not violated by men, offers my eyes on all sides" (*Reveries*, VII, p. 99).

Rousseau's shift in focus from the human to the botanical world can be explained in terms of his concern with sexuality. We have seen him regret the fact that the human world cannot provide him with "two souls in the same body." Humans are frustrated and incomplete because they are not bisexual. The bisexuality which Rousseau seeks in vain in the human world is, however, the basis of the botanical world:

> The constitution common to the greatest number of Flowers is to be hermaphrodites; and this constitution in effect appears to be the most convenient to the realm of plants, where individuals deprived of all progressive and spontaneous movement cannot go to seek one another when the sexes are separated. In the case where trees and plants are separated, nature, which knows how to vary its means, has provided for this obstacle; but it is not less true generally that immobile beings must, in order to perpetuate their species, have in themselves all the instruments appropriate to this end (*Botanique*, p. 1229).[66]

Only in the botanical world can Rousseau discover beings which are self-sufficient in spite of being sexual; he therefore comes ultimately to regard it as the most satisfactory world for him to contemplate.

In bidding adieu to love, and in focusing upon the botanical world, Rousseau does not, however, forsake the imaginary for the real world; his experience with Thérèse indicates that this would be an impossibility for him. Instead he continues to exercise his imagination while studying botany.

> I am attached to botany by the chain of accessory ideas. Botany gathers together and recalls to my imagination all the ideas which gratify it more. The meadows, the waters, the woods, the solitude, above all, the peace and rest to be found in the midst of all that are incessantly retraced in my memory by my imagination. Botany makes me forget men's persecutions (*Reveries*, VII, p. 103).

Yet his imagination now abstracts from the human world. Now what he lacks is "replaced" or supplemented, not by the body of a real woman, or by the image of an ideal woman, but by the plants that he observes. His stay on the island of Saint-Pierre, where his botanical interest was first aroused, again indicates his rejection of the human for the botanical world. "I should have liked to be shut up in this island so completely as to have no further intercourse with any living man" (*Confessions*, XII, p. 664). In his isolation on the island Rousseau fancies himself "a second Robinson" (*Confessions*, XII, p. 670). He is a second Robinson despite the presence of Thérèse; we see again that his relationship with her poses no obstacle to his solitude. The aging Rousseau is like Robinson Crusoe; in this respect he resembles the young Emile. For Robinson Crusoe is Emile's only model before puberty, at a time when it is still reasonable for him "to put [him]self in the place of an isolated man" (*Emile*, III, p. 185). But upon maturing, Emile can no longer be a solitary. As we have seen, if Emile was to have lived on a desert island in the unwritten portion of *Émile et Sophie*, he was to have done so not as a solitary but as a bigamist. Only before puberty does Emile imagine a world devoid of human wills. Thereafter, he must imagine instead a world that includes a female who must will to rule him in part. He imagines first a nonhuman world, and only later a human world.

Rousseau's course, it should now be clear, is precisely the opposite. He becomes an aging solitary as he orients his imagination, which peopled the world in his youth, away from the human world. His imagination turns from human wills to plants without wills. One specific purpose to which the aging Rousseau sets his imagination after his expulsion from the island of Saint-Pierre is to recreate his life upon it. He "transport[s himself] there each day on the wings of [the] imagination" (*Reveries*, V, p.

71). Rousseau can be a solitary because of his imagination of his life upon an island. By contrast, he admits that his educational program is in large measure impractical because the young Emile cannot live apart from humans "on a desert island" (*Emile*, II, p. 94). Humans are social beings because they are sexual; and they are sexual, in turn, because they are not solitaries, "raised in a desert." Anyone who was raised in a desert, "without books, without instruction, and without women, would die there a virgin at whatever age he had reached" (*Emile*, IV, p. 333).

If we lived in deserts and on islands, we could be asocial, asexual solitaries. In the end, Rousseau becomes such a solitary, to the extent that he is able to occupy himself with the image of his own life upon an island—although his was not a desert island, but one replete with vegetation. On that island of his imagination, Rousseau imagines that he can dispense with society and sexuality. No man is an island—unless he can imagine himself alone upon an island.

We have seen that societies are composed of and ruled by men who depend upon women. In Emile we see a child with "only a common mind" whose independence is qualified and ultimately terminated by his dependence upon a woman. Because of Sophie, Emile must learn to be social. In Rousseau himself we see an extraordinary individual, whose formative experience is subjection to a woman. He approaches self-sufficiency only insofar as he can free himself from the images of women, even the images of the women that he himself creates.

Women desire to rule men, and are uniquely successful at ruling men. They make men social, and prevent men from being self-sufficient. This is what Rousseau praises women for—and also why he blames them. Both the praise and the blame recur in Rousseau's lengthiest work devoted to the problem of sexual dependence—his romantic novel *Julie*, or the *Nouvelle Héloïse*.

❦ 5 ❧

Julie
Of Romance and Reality

Throughout our examination of Rousseau's theoretical works, we have seen his ambivalence about human sexuality—an ambivalence that can be understood only in terms of the political implications of human sexuality. For the sexual relations of civilized human beings necessitate the government of men by women. Insofar as Rousseau recognizes that men need to be governed, he portrays their female governors favorably. But insofar as he contends that at least some men could and should achieve independence of others, he criticizes women because they are the most powerful obstacles to men's independence.

Julie, Rousseau's novel of romantic love and unromantic marriage, consists of over seven hundred pages of variations upon the theme of the uses and abuses of women's political power over men, the theme that has been the focus of this study. Although *Julie* does not add an additional perspective on sexuality to those that we have already encountered in Rousseau, it synthesizes his various perspectives more successfully than any of his other works. For this reason *Julie* can be said to provide a synopsis of Rousseau's sexual politics. For the novel worships women and especially their tremendous power, and indicates that their power is often put to beneficial uses; and yet it also suggests that women are terrible as well as wonderful by virtue of their power.

Julie is Rousseau's principle meditation about the power of women. The novel stresses women's capacity to shape men, to make of men what they will. Thus Saint-Preux, a character in the novel who loves Julie passionately, takes note of the influence of his beloved upon all men: "What men we would all be, if the world were full of Julies" (*Julie*, II, 13, p. 229). In an editorial note toward the end of the epistolary novel, Rousseau speaks in his own name and concurs: "Only find Julie, and all the rest is found" (*Julie*, VI, 11, p. 731). Women such as Julie have a profound impact upon men. Julie's particular mastery is made manifest while she guides Saint-Preux through a garden on her estate. He believes that her garden is entirely the work of nature, not of man or woman. She corrects him: "It is true . . . that nature has done all, but under my direction, and there is nothing here that I have not commanded" (*Julie*, IV, 11, p. 472). The power of women such as Julie may not be fully apparent to Saint-Preux, but it commands all of nature. Primarily, of course, we see the power of Julie as she exercises it in the human world. Julie exemplifies the power which we have seen Rousseau ascribe to women—the informal power to control the *moeurs*, opinions, and ultimately the behavior of the men whom they know.[1] In the *Letter to D'Alembert*, Rousseau provides a specific case where he believes that women could and should use their power: he argues that duelling can be abolished only by means of "the intervention of women, on whom men's way of thinking in large measure depends" (*Letter*, p. 72). In the novel, Julie employs her power in the manner recommended by Rousseau: she uses her influence to prevent a duel between her lover Saint-Preux and another man (*Julie*, I, 57–58, pp. 152–62). She says that in so doing she "employs . . . an authority that a wise man has never resisted" (*Julie*, I, 57, p. 160). Thus *Julie* tells the story of a woman's employment of authority. Women such as Julie use their authority to fashion men according to their feminine desires. We shall see that Rousseau's novelistic portrait of Julie, like his theoretical presentation of human female nature, is ambivalent: although Rousseau respects Julie's political power, he is not sure that her exercise of it fully benefits either others or herself.

Julie is a romantic novel, but also a didactic work. Rousseau states this explicitly. He is led to write *Julie* because of "the desire of loving, which I had never been able to satisfy, and by which I felt myself devoured" (*Confessions*, IX, p. 445). The novel is a product of his "erotic transports" (*Confessions*, IX, p. 453). But he is embarrassed to find himself writing a romantic novel, because of "the biting invectives which [he] had launched against . . . effeminate books which breathed nothing but love and tenderness" (*Confessions*, IX, p. 449). He is reconciled to his romantic reveries, however, because "the love of the good, which has never left my heart, turned them naturally towards useful objects, which might have been productive of moral advantage." Thus *Julie* is not only an evocation of romantic love; it is also a defense of "morality and conjugal fidelity, which are radically connected with all social order," and a plea for "harmony and public peace" between "Christians and philosophers" (*Confessions*, IX, pp. 449–50). For this reason *Julie* is not an ordinary collection of love letters; as Saint-Preux remarks, Julie's letters to him "will be in my opinion the first love letters from which [moral edification and instruction] can be drawn" (*Julie*, II, 13, p. 229).

In the second preface to *Julie*, Rousseau remarks that he has "changed the means, but not the object." Earlier, in more philosophical works, he was not understood; he hopes that the novel, consisting of "badly disguised remedies," will be swallowed more readily than was "naked reason" (*Julie*, Second Preface, p. 17). *Julie* can therefore be considered the work of a citizen. "The citizen who is worried about the success [of his discourse] must not stupidly cry out to us: 'Be good'; but he must make us love the state which leads us to be good" (*Julie*, Second Preface, p. 20).[2] Rousseau wishes his novel to be judged by the standard employed by Julie herself in evaluating literature: "I can hardly imagine what sort of goodness a book that does not lead its readers to the good can have" (*Julie*, Second Preface, p. 23, and II, 18, p. 261). Finally, the *Letter to D'Alembert* itself, the locus of Rousseau's "biting invectives . . . against . . . effeminate books which breathed nothing but love," serves as an advance prospectus for the novel: Rousseau declares that in his forthcoming manuscript he will develop the "principle on which all good *moeurs* depend"—that "the plan of nature . . . gives different tasks to the two sexes, so that they live apart and each in [its] own way" (*Letter*, p. 107). It is very clear that *Julie* is intended to be as morally advantageous for us to read as it was erotically pleasurable for Rousseau to imagine and write.

Julie's story runs as follows. She is the only living child of Baron d'Étange, a nobleman of the Swiss town of Vevey. She and her tutor, Saint-Preux, who is a commoner, fall passionately in love. However, it seems impossible for them to marry because of Baron d'Étange's strict prejudices about social position. Because of the baron's opposition, Julie is torn between her passion for her lover and her devotion to her father, and is made miserable. Noting Julie's misery, Claire (who is Julie's cousin) prevails upon Saint-Preux to exile himself from the household. Julie and Saint-Preux continue to correspond until their letters are discovered by Madame d'Étange, who had been far more receptive than her husband to their union. Madame d'Étange dies shortly after her discovery, and Julie blames herself because she feels that the grief experienced by Madame d'Étange upon her discovery led to her demise.

The baron, we learn, opposes the wedding not only because of his social prejudices, but also because he has promised to marry Julie to Wolmar, an old friend who once saved his life. Julie asks and receives Saint-Preux's permission to marry Wolmar. Subsequently she writes Saint-Preux describing her wedding and her marriage. Always religious, she reports that she has become far more devout as a result of her experience of the wedding ceremony. She praises Wolmar highly as a husband. Although she admits that she does not love him (and did love Saint-Preux), she declares that she is happier as Wolmar's wife than she could ever have been as Saint-Preux's. Saint-Preux's despair leads him to contemplate suicide. Édouard Bomston, an English nobleman who is a close friend of his and also of the d'Étange family, dissuades him. Bomston arranges a berth for Saint-Preux on board a ship leaving for a voyage around the world.

Several years pass. Julie is now a mother; her life at Clarens is almost ideal, but it is marred for her because Wolmar is an atheist. Saint-Preux returns from his expedition. Wolmar invites Saint-Preux to visit Julie at the estate of Clarens at which he and she now live, knowing full well that Saint-Preux had been her lover. Wolmar likes and is impressed by Saint-Preux, and asks him to reside at Clarens and eventually to tutor his children. He announces to Julie and Saint-Preux that he intends to cure them of their love, which has made Saint-Preux miserable because of his failure to repress it, and has limited Julie's happiness in spite of her apparent success at repressing the love. As part of their cure, he leaves them alone together at one point. During his absence Julie and Saint-Preux are tempted to commit adultery, but manage virtuously to resist the temptation.

Saint-Preux leaves Clarens for Rome, to give Bomston advice about his romantic entanglements. At Rome Saint-Preux dissuades Bomston from marrying a former prostitute who has reformed, despite his understanding that encouraging the marriage would serve his own interests; for Saint-Preux believes that if Bomston marries he will be free to return to Julie at Clarens, whereas if Bomston remains single, he will insist that Saint-Preux accompany him on his return to England. Saint-Preux's disinterested advice indicates to Bomston that Saint-Preux is truly cured of his love for Julie; Saint-Preux has shown him that he prefers the virtuous to the pleasurable course of action. Bomston thereupon informs Saint-Preux that he is quite content not to go back to England, but instead that the two of them (along with Claire, who was married but who is now a widow) should return to complete the happy community at Clarens. Before they can do so, however, Julie falls ill as a result of rescuing her drowning child. She dies, but before doing so writes a letter to Saint-Preux, in which she declares that her death was well-timed, because she now realizes that she has never overcome her love for him. The novel concludes with Claire bidding Saint-Preux to return to Clarens, and admitting that she too may love him. However, she declares that in memory of his love for Julie they must never marry, despite the fact that Julie had previously encouraged their union.

As Rousseau admits, *Julie* is two different novels—a novel of love and a novel of marriage. "I think . . . that the [moral] end of this collection [of letters, the part that describes the Wolmars' married life] would be redundant for readers repelled by the beginning [the part that describes the illicit love of Julie and Saint-Preux], and that this same beginning must be pleasing to those for whom the end can be of use" (*Julie*, Second Preface, p. 17). I shall begin my discussion of the novel with its moral end, with the theme of *Julie* as it is previewed in the *Letter to D'Alembert*—Rousseau's portrait of the mutual dependence and differentiation of the sexes in marriage as the basis of social morality. This portrait is already largely familiar from our consideration in previous chapters of Rousseau's more theoretical works. Then I shall turn to the beginning (as well as to what is really the end of the novel, Julie's death and not her married life), in order to discuss the somewhat fragile and unsatisfactory character of the moral order established through the sociability and mutual rule of men and women. What is least familiar in *Julie* is not the morality that it presents—we have already seen Rousseau declare that he has not changed his "object" in writing the novel—but its fictional presentation of the shortcomings that individuals perceive in practicing it. Rousseau's moral romance would be far less believable did not the romance call the morality into question.

The Interdependence of Julie and Wolmar

The wedding between Julie and Wolmar marks the break between the two novels.[3] After the ceremony, Julie writes to Saint-Preux, explaining to him that she is happy in spite of the fact that she did not marry the man she loves, and did marry one she does not love. Her argument rests on a distinction between marriage and love. It is an error, she writes, to believe that "love is necessary to have a happy marriage." Marriage must instead be based on a "very tender attachment which, for all that it is not precisely love, is not less sweet and is more durable than love" (*Julie*, III, 20, p. 372). Julie repeats the argument made by Rousseau in both *Emile* and the *Second Discourse*, in which he distinguishes between conjugal love and romantic love.[4]

What, according to Julie, are the shortcomings of romantic love? "Love is accompanied by a continual anxiety of jealousy or of privation, hardly suitable to marriage, which is a state of enjoyment and of peace." Again this is the argument of the *Second Discourse*; romantic love unites individuals but separates them as well (*Second*, pp. 148–49).[5] Romantic love is an insufficiently social sentiment on which to build as social an institution as marriage.

> One does not marry in order to think uniquely of one another, but in order jointly to fulfill the duties of civil life, to govern the household prudently, to raise children well. Lovers never see anyone but themselves, are occupied incessantly only with themselves, and the only thing they know how to do is to love one another. This is not enough for Spouses who have so many cares to look after (*Julie*, III, 20, p. 372).[6]

As Rousseau observes in the *Letter to D'Alembert*, "It is much better to love a mistress than to love oneself alone in the world. But whoever tenderly loves his parents, his friends, his country and humankind, degrades himself by a dissolute attachment which soon does damage to all the others and is without fail preferred to them" (*Letter*, p. 117).

"Lovers never see anyone but themselves." In fact, Julie goes on to argue, they do not even see one another properly. "There is no passion that brings forth for us so strong an illusion as love." Love is a violent passion, but not one of long duration. "Sooner or later [lovers] will cease to adore one another" (*Julie*, III, 20, pp. 372–73). The imagination, which once falsely adorned the beloved, will end by falsely disfiguring the beloved. The illusions of love cannot last, and for this reason cannot sustain an enduring relationship between man and woman. Such illusions can only engender and be succeeded by illusions of hate.

The relation between Julie and Wolmar, by contrast, is not at all illusory. "No illusion prejudices the one toward the other; we see one another such as we are" (*Julie*, III, 20, p. 373). They are two individuals, she contends, who complement one another perfectly. "It seems that if one had formed us expressly so as to unite us one could not have succeeded better." Julie and Wolmar are a woman and a man who are perfectly suited to live with one another. Because they differ from one another, they complement one another. They illustrate the sexual principle described in the *Letter to D'Alembert*; men and women "live apart and each in [their] own way." For Julie and Wolmar embody the differing and complementary orientations of the two sexes to the principle of rule associated with sexuality. In this respect (though not in others) Julie can be said to be a typical woman, and Wolmar a typical man.

Wolmar is asocial, but is socialized by Julie, because of his need for her. He loves to observe; if he could, he would like to become "a living eye." In principle, he would like to remain inactive. His *amour-propre* is satisfied only through his "continual studies." He "does not like to play a role, but only to see others play them" (*Julie*, IV, 12, p. 491). At one time Wolmar says that he is without passions (*Julie*, IV, 7, p. 429). Elsewhere, however, he denies this. "If I have some dominant passion, it is that of observation" (*Julie*, IV, 12, p. 491).[7] At first he becomes active only in order to observe better. "I sensed . . . that one sees nothing when one is content to look on, that one must act oneself in order to see men act, and I made myself an actor in order to be a spectator" (*Julie*, IV, 12, p. 492).

At this point, one could say that Wolmar is only instrumentally social; other humans provide him with material for observation, but otherwise they do not interest him. "My indifference to men does not make me independent of them; without being dear to me they are necessary to me" (*Julie*, IV, 12, p. 491). But ultimately Wolmar cannot be sociable only in order to observe. He becomes "less contemplative," having "perceived that I was alone. . . . Without having lost my coldness I needed an attachment" (*Julie*, IV, 12, p. 492). Rousseau uses exactly the same words in describing his relationship to Thérèse—"I needed an attachment" (*Confessions*, IX, p. 426). Like Rousseau, Wolmar is progressively attached to action in the real world (though Rousseau was previously detached by his imagination, and Wolmar by his love of observation). In both cases, a woman confirms and completes the attachment.

But Wolmar's attachment to Julie is far stronger than Rousseau's to Thérèse. Julie speaks not of Wolmar's passion to observe, but of his passion for her. "I have not been able to find any sort of passion in him except that which he has for me" (*Julie*, III, 20, p. 370). Wolmar confirms her statement. "I loved you, and loved only you. All the rest was indifferent to me. How can one repress even the most feeble passion, when it is without a counterweight?" (*Julie*, III, 20, p. 373). Wolmar's passion for Julie may be feeble, but it is real. Only because of this are they so well matched, Julie contends. "If he didn't love me, we would live badly together; if he loved me too much, he would be troublesome to me" (*Julie*, III, 20, p. 373). As it is, they complement each other perfectly. "Each of the two is precisely what the other needs; he enlightens me and I animate him" (*Julie*, III, 20, pp. 373–74).

Julie animates Wolmar; she activates or socializes him. Julie and Wolmar thus illustrate several of Rousseau's contentions about men and women in *Emile*. Women are more social than men (who are more intellectual than women). Men conduct the "quest for abstract and speculative truths," whereas women's "studies ought to be related to practice" (*Emile*, V, p. 386). Women's morality is "experimental," men "reduce it to a system" (*Emile*, V, p. 387). "The woman learns from the man what must be seen and the man learns from the woman what must be done" (*Emile*, V, p. 377). Rousseau contends that there are limits to the female intellect (though it should not be forgotten that he ascribes complementary limits to the male intellect as well, stating that "woman has more wit, man more genius" [*Emile*, V, p. 387]);[8] but he also declares that there are limits to male sociability. Women are not only more social than men are, they are the cause of men's being as social as men are. This is true of Emile's relation to Sophie, and of Wolmar's relation to Julie as well. Indeed, in some respects Wolmar calls Emile to mind. Before his involvement with a woman, Wolmar lives in society chiefly to observe; so does Emile (*Emile*, IV, pp. 236-37). Wolmar's first, perhaps his only, passion is for Julie; his first sight of her gives him "the first or rather the only emotion that [he] felt in [his] life" (*Julie*, IV, 12, p. 492). Emile's love for Sophie is his "first passion," "perhaps the only [one] worthy of [him]"; if controlled properly, "it will be the last" (*Emile*, V, p. 445).

The two most insightful commentaries on *Julie* that I have read contend that Wolmar is an analog of God on earth.[9] Rousseau's text supports this contention in some measure.[10] Here again, however, the example of Emile should be kept in mind: "'If I were without passions, I would in my condition as a man, be independent like God himself. . . . Give me Sophie, and I am free'" (*Emile*, V, pp. 472–73). No man who depends on a woman can be wholly a God.

Julie makes Wolmar social. Only with her help does he, the contemplative man, become a superlative manager of an estate; his success at directing others (no longer just at observing them) depends on a division of labor between the two of them (*Julie*, V, 2, p. 530). Through her death, she completes his socialization by converting him into a believer.[11] Earlier, Wolmar was an atheist, his lack of belief explained by his dispassionate character (*Julie*, V, 5, p. 594). His lack of passion, which made him an atheist, also, as we have seen, made him asocial. As one commentator remarks, Wolmar's atheism follows from the fact that earlier he was "a solitary, a man who does not truly participate either in society or in the life of another."[12] But as we have also seen, Julie causes Wolmar to feel passion. She does so most dramatically before dying, when her farewell to Wolmar reduces him to tears for the first time since his birth (*Julie*, VI, 11, p. 721). Wolmar's sexual involvement socializes him; for Wolmar, as for men generally, sex is the bridge to politics.

Julie as Ruler

Julie socializes Wolmar by ruling him. Nor does she rule him alone; the empire that Julie exercises over all who surround her is frequently emphasized in the novel. It is not surprising, perhaps, to see Julie rule her lover Saint-Preux. In freeing him from his vow never again to drink wine, she compares herself to Henri IV of France: "Your Sovereign wishes to imitate the clemency of the best of Kings" (*Julie*, I, 52, p. 142). She is not always so accommodating a sovereign, however. After an expedition of Saint-Preux's to a Parisian bordello, she warns him that "there must remain no trace of a crime that I have pardoned" (*Julie*, II, 27, p. 305). Saint-Preux submits to Julie, of whose "inconceivable empire" he speaks (*Julie*, III, 16, p. 336).

Julie does not rule her lover alone, however, as Claire observes: "My Julie, you are made to reign. Your empire is the most absolute that I know. It extends over the will, and I feel it more than anyone" (*Julie*, IV, 2, p. 409). Saint-Preux speaks of her "adorable and powerful empire" over the servants at Clarens, later adding that they fear her more than they do Wolmar (*Julie*, IV, 10, pp. 444, 465). The sage, cold Wolmar completes the list of tributes. Upon hearing that Louis XV is ill, and of the extent of the French people's love for him, Julie observes that she envies the ruling class only the pleasure that they attain in making themselves loved. To which Wolmar responds: "Envy nothing . . . ; for a long time we have all been your subjects" (*Julie*, V, 3, p. 559).

Julie compares herself to one French king and is compared to another. To be sure, she exercises her empire in private life. In this sense, like the women of antiquity, she is a secret cause of events.[13] "Politics," she admits, "is hardly the jurisdiction of women." She is not very interested in affairs of state.

> [The] utility [of politics] is too far from me to affect me much. . . . What good would it do me to know [that there are better governments than the one under which I was born], with so little power to establish them? Why should I sadden my soul by considering such great evils about which I can do nothing, when I see others around me that I am permitted to relieve? (*Julie*, II, 27, p. 305).[14]

Julie seems to exemplify the nonpolitical virtues, the superiority of the private to the political life.

> Heaven seems to have put her on earth in order to show at once the excellence of which a human soul is capable, and the happiness which it can enjoy in the obscurity of private life, without the assistance of the brilliant virtues which can raise it above itself, or of the glory which can honor them (*Julie*, V, 2, p. 532).

Yet in fact Julie illustrates not the divorce but the harmony of the political and nonpolitical spheres. She shows that women can best satisfy their political passions, their desire to rule men, in private life. She shows that, for women, sex is politics; women rule men through their sexual involvement with them. Saint-Preux compares Julie to Agrippina, the wife of the Roman commander Germanicus: "Julie! Incomparable woman! You exercise in the simplicity of private life the despotic empire of wisdom and beneficence. . . . You live more securely, more honorably in the middle of an entire people that loves you, than Kings surrounded by all their soldiers" (*Julie*, V, 7, p. 607).

Thus a woman such as Julie can combine despotic empire with private life. As she explains to Saint-Preux, she can and must rule, precisely because she is a woman. Women's reason is weaker than men's, but it also matures at an earlier age. "We find ourselves, from an early age, responsible for such a dangerous deposit, that the care of conserving it soon awakens our judgment; an excellent means of seeing the consequences of things well is to sense alertly all the risks that they make us run" (*Julie*, I, 11, p. 55).[15] Because women are weaker, and because of the premium placed on female chastity, women are cleverer and more prudent than are men. Julie immediately proceeds to illustrate this cleverness to Saint-Preux; having conceded that "reason is ordinarily weaker . . . among women," she then informs him that "the more I consider our situation, the more I find that reason asks of you what I ask of you in the name of love. Therefore be submissive to its sweet voice" (*Julie*, I, 11, pp. 55–56). Reason is weaker in women, but it is not so weak that they cannot know that their preferred course of action is the reasonable one.

The basis of Julie's claim to rule is the distinction between male and female sexual behavior; women must rule because their modesty demands it of them. Like Rousseau himself, Julie rejects Plato's *Republic* because it denies that sexual modesty is preeminently a female virtue. "Attack and defense, the boldness of men, the modesty of women, are not conventions, as your philosophers think, but natural institutions" (*Julie*, I, 47, p. 128). And indeed it is easy to see why a woman would want to assert that modesty is natural, since their modesty gives women power over men. Saint-Preux exclaims: "Sweet modesty! . . . How many women would take pains to conserve you, if they knew your empire" (*Julie*, II, 27, p. 296). Claire agrees: "The most decent women conserve in general the greatest ascendancy over their husbands; because with the aid of this wise and discreet reserve, without caprice and refusal, they know how to maintain a certain distance in the midst of the most tender union, and they prevent their husbands from ever becoming satiated" (*Julie*, V, 13, p. 501).[16] Rousseau assumes that women want to govern men; he then shows women how well their modesty serves them as a means to this end.

The Beneficence of Women's Rule

Julie is Rousseau's book about and generally in defense of feminine power. Claire contends that her and Julie's marriages (as opposed to that of Madame d'Étange) demonstrate that "when the woman governs, the household is not worse off" (*Julie*, IV, 9, p. 440). Saint-Preux too observes that "the sweetest empire on earth" is that of women and specifically mothers; if they are virtuous their empire can also be "the most respected" (*Julie*, V, 3, p. 585). The power of women benefits society. In *Julie*, even the harm that women do is viewed indulgently. Parisian women are said to be the true source of all activity in their society. No doubt because this is the case, Parisian society is corrupt; in the "gynecocracy," or government by women, there is no division of labor between the sexes (*Julie*, II, 21, p. 269). Because it is a bad society, the women do more harm than good. Nevertheless, they are excused because "they do the harm impelled by men, and the good from their own impulse" (*Julie*, II, 21, p. 275). Saint-Preux reports that the women alone in Paris "conserve . . . the bit of humanity that still reigns there. Without them one would see the men, avid and insatiable, devour one another like wolves" (*Julie*, II, 21, p. 277). Especially in Paris, women are sovereign over men; it is therefore fitting that they perform there the primary task that Thomas Hobbes assigns to sovereigns—maintenance of the peace. Without women, the Parisian men would be like wolves; and Hobbes in fact asserts with respect to men from different cities, who lack a common sovereign, that "Man to man is an arrant wolf."[17] Within the same city, however, men do not behave like wolves, because they are subjected to the same power ruling over them all. By ruling and keeping the peace, the women of Paris, like the Hobbesian sovereign, enable men to be humane rather than lupine with one another.

Julie accepts the truth of Saint-Preux's report on the Parisian women, but denies that they are unique in making society humane. Women fulfill this function everywhere. "In what country of the world are gentleness and commiseration not the amiable allotment of women?" (*Julie*, II, 27, p. 299). Like the Hobbesian sovereign, women keep the social peace by enjoying an empire; unlike his, theirs is "the sweetest empire on earth." Sweetness is the basis of their empire, not the limitation upon it; men obey women because women are the only rulers whom men enjoy obeying.[18]

Women socialize men, and *Julie* is mostly written in defense of women because it is intended to influence behavior in corrupt societies, wherein self-centered men stand most in need of socialization. The fact that the book defends women is stated explicitly in the book's Second Preface, which is written in dialogue form. Rousseau's interlocutor, a reader of the novel, remarks to him: "I am charmed to see you reconciled with the women; I was angry that you prohibited them from making sermons to us" (*Julie*, Second Preface, p. 25). The interlocutor presumably refers to the *Letter to D'Alembert*, in which Rousseau denies that men "ought to take counsel" from women (*Letter*, p. 47). In *Julie*, however, the interlocutor remarks, Rousseau presents his readers with a female "preacher" (*Julie*, Second Preface, p. 25),[19] as Julie is frequently described.

As he does in the *Letter*, Rousseau continues to criticize the immorality of women. But in *Julie* he extenuates their immorality. He speaks in his own name in the Second Preface: "Let us be just toward women; the cause of their disorder is less in them than in our bad institutions." Rousseau's defense of women here is representative of his defenses of human nature throughout his philosophy: human beings are naturally good, but they are corrupted because their natural benevolence is destroyed by the social institutions under which they live. Rousseau then discusses in detail the institutions that cause the corruption of women:

> Since all the sentiments of nature are smothered by extreme inequality, it is from the inequitable despotism of fathers that the vices and unhappiness of children come; it is in forced or badly matched unions that young women, victims of the avarice or the vanity of parents, efface the scandal of their earlier decency through a disorder that they glorify (*Julie*, Second Preface, p. 24).

One of Julie's most affecting and effective sermons is also about the plight of the unmarried young woman: "Always to speak differently than is thought; to disguise all that is felt; to be false out of duty; and to lie out of modesty: here is the habitual state of every girl of my age" (*Julie*, II, 7,

p. 212).[20] The infidelity of married women follows from the prohibition earlier imposed upon them by paternal power against marrying whom they please.[21]

Commenting in a private letter on a reader's reaction to the *Letter to D'Alembert*, Rousseau expresses a very different opinion: "I am not of your opinion when you say that if we are corrupted it is not the fault of women, it is our own; my whole book is undertaken to show how it is their fault" (letter to Lenieps of November 8, 1758, in *Correspondance*, 5:212–13). Rousseau criticizes women in the book intended to sustain a republic, but praises them in *Julie*, a novel, hence a work intended for a different audience. "Novels are perhaps the last form of instruction that remains to give to a people who are so corrupted that every other form would be useless to it" (*Julie*, II, 21, p. 277). Modern women may be the cause of the corruption of virtuous republics, but they also seem to be the main hope for the salvation of already corrupted monarchies. As Rousseau concedes in the *Letter*, "There are countries in the world where the *moeurs* are so bad that they would be only too happy to be able to raise themselves back up to the level of love" (*Letter*, p. 118). It is for such countries primarily, wherein women are no longer a secret but an open cause of social activity, that Rousseau writes his book in praise of women.

Julie demonstrates the capacity of women to improve corrupt regimes. This is indicated by the discussion of the political economy of Clarens, the Wolmars' estate. As many commentators have noted, Clarens is a highly inegalitarian society, sharply divided between the Wolmars, who are the masters, and their servants.[22] Clarens is in fact a despotism, as Rousseau makes perfectly evident. "I do not believe that there are Sovereigns in Asia who are served in their Palaces with more respect than are these good masters [the Wolmars] in their household" (*Julie*, IV, 10, p. 459). "In a Republic, citizens are restrained by *moeurs*, by principles, by virtue; but how can domestics or mercenaries be controlled, other than through constraint and hindrance?" (*Julie*, IV, 10, p. 453).[23] But Clarens is at least an enlightened despotism, or a despotism of the *éclaircissement*, as its name suggests.[24] Through the example of Clarens Rousseau suggests to the rulers of inegalitarian societies how to be better served by their subjects, so as to benefit both rulers and subjects.

The Social Utility of Sexual Propriety

A renewed emphasis upon sexual propriety (which would stem from the differentiation and division of labor of the sexes) can best accomplish this purpose. We have previously seen Rousseau assert that the habits of debauchery make young men "inhuman and cruel" (*Emile*, IV, p. 220).[25] But this is not the only reason for Rousseau's indictment of sexual incontinence. Those who are promiscuous deceive their acquaintances, and subordinate everything else in life to the search for personal pleasure. They therefore tend to be untrustworthy in person, unconscientious in their work.

The subjects of a despotism are not citizens; by definition, the morality of public action is no concern of theirs (or of their rulers). The morality of private life is, however, (or should be) a concern of both the rulers and the subjects of despotisms. And it is in the interest of both the rulers and subjects of despotisms, Rousseau contends, to preserve the morality of private life, if possible to elevate it: people must learn to keep their word, to perform their tasks conscientiously. Hence Rousseau emphasizes the importance of sexual behavior in a despotic society such as Clarens: the root of private morality generally is to be found in sexual morality specifically. Only if people are trustworthy with regard to what is most pleasurable can they be expected to be trustworthy with regard to anything and everything else.

At Clarens, "there is little communication between the sexes," because "excessively intimate liaisons between the sexes never produce anything but harm." The interest of the masters explain this policy. "It is always between men and women that the secret monopolies are established that finally ruin the most opulent families. . . . No one does his duty well if he does not love it, and only honorable people know how to love their duty" (*Julie*, IV, 10, p. 449).

Because the sexes are kept apart, the servants at Clarens do not corrupt one another, do not learn to value their pleasure above everything else. As we have already seen, this is Julie's policy. "According to her, husband and wife are destined to live together, but not in the same manner; they must act in concert without doing the same things" (*Julie*, IV, 10, p. 450). In France, where the men and women lead identical lives, the men's existence is one of "effeminate indolence." The Italians too are "effeminate," as is indicated by the fact that there is too close a correspondence between the male and female diet (*Julie*, IV, 10, pp. 451, 453).

At Clarens, however, the sexes live separately. Both men and women work very hard, which leads them to live different lives. "For their tasks are so different that only idleness brings them together" (*Julie*, IV, 10, p. 451). Again we see the sexual division of labor benefiting the masters; if the men and women saw more of one another, the servants would be lazier. Their search for pleasure would undermine their labor.

Why are the servants willing to work hard, and be separated by sex? The women take pride in excluding men from their company; as before, we see that female pride is the psychological factor making sexual modesty possible. During their leisure hours, the female servants, together with Julie, assemble together to amuse themselves. If they are proud to be on a seemingly equal level with Julie, they are still prouder to be seemingly

superior to Wolmar. For Wolmar is refused admittance to these gather-
ings; "imagine if this flatters petty female vanity" (*Julie*, IV, 10, p. 452).

Why do the men submit? This is the question that leads Saint-Preux to
differentiate Clarens from a republic. Because it is not a republic, this
submission cannot be because of the male servants' "*moeurs*, . . . principles, [or] virtue." Yet since men are bolder than women, or naturally less
modest, it is all the more necessary to restrain them if promiscuity is to be
avoided. Only "constraint and hindrance" remain as means to be employed. Because the male servants at Clarens are governed by these
means, and do not govern themselves, Clarens is not a republic. Nevertheless, despots can rule their subjects more or less cleverly, and the
despots of Clarens are exceptionally clever. "The whole art of the master
is to hide this hindrance under a veil of pleasure or of interest, in such a
way that [the servants] think that they will all that they are obliged to do"
(*Julie*, IV, 10, p. 453). The servants are allowed to drink and compete in
games at the estate, in the presence of their masters, lest they drink and
gamble elsewhere, in the company of "debauched women" (*Julie*, IV, 10,
p. 452).

Thus, despite their submission, the servants at Clarens live moral and
productive lives. Since they cannot achieve equality, at least they manage
to serve with dignity. The only alternative that seems to be available is the
debauched inequality that characterizes French monarchic society, in
which neither masters nor servants are better off. Rousseau knows this
from his personal experience in that society as a servant. He writes of
Madame de Vercellis, who was the first to employ him as a servant: "She
. . . never spoke to me except to give me an order. She judged me less
according to what I was than according to what she had made me; and, as
she never saw anything in me but a lackey, she prevented me from
appearing anything else" (*Confessions*, II, p. 83).[26] Just as women shape
men, masters shape servants; when they do so badly, like Madame de
Vercellis, they benefit neither their servants nor themselves.

At Clarens, by contrast, the masters take a personal interest in the lives
of their servants. For this reason the servants willingly accept the regimen
of sexual restraint that is imposed upon them. But it would be wrong to
overstate the extent of the restraint; if the servants are not libertines,
neither are they ascetics. Rousseau suggests that libertinism and asceti-
cism feed on one another. This explains the immorality of monks, who,
being "subject to a thousand useless rules, do not know what honor and
virtue are" (*Julie*, IV, 10, p. 456). "Men and women are destined for one
another, the end of nature is that they be united by marriage" (*Julie*, IV,
10, p. 456). For this reason there are public dances at Clarens, so as to
facilitate meetings, courtships, and ultimately marriages between young
men and women.[27]

Chapter Five

The sexual morality of Clarens is the key to the relative success of its highly inegalitarian social structure.[28] One can take this to be Rousseau's advice to the rulers of highly inegalitarian European societies. "Nowhere but here have I seen masters form at once in the same men good domestics for the service of their persons, good peasants to cultivate their lands, good soldiers for the defense of the fatherland, and good people for all the estates to which fortune can call them" (*Julie*, IV, 10, p. 455). The division of labor between the sexes, a seemingly insignificant principle, is the basis of all these accomplishments.[29] And yet, as Saint-Preux remarks of Wolmar, "It is the attribute of true genius to produce great effects through small means" (*Julie*, IV, 10, p. 455). One can see in Saint-Preux's remark Rousseau's assessment of his own intended accomplishment. For as he says of himself in the Second Preface, "I have changed the means, but not the object" (*Julie*, Second Preface, p. 17). *Julie* is hardly "small" in size, but as a love novel addressed to women it seems to be far less significant than Rousseau's political and philosophical works. But in fact Rousseau presents the reformation of sexual relations that the novel depicts as the basis for all conceivable political reform. "If some reform of public *moeurs* is to be attempted, it must begin with domestic *moeurs*, and that depends absolutely on fathers and mothers" (*Julie*, Second Preface, p. 24). At least in the context of the corrupted Europe for which *Julie* is written, such political reform as is conceivable must be based on the role of women.

Julie as Lover

Thus far I have interpreted *Julie* as a book in praise of women and of their sexual rule as a socializing force. But this is not all that there is to the novel, in which Rousseau's ambivalence toward the political implications of sexuality is very evident. For *Julie* is not only about marriage; it is about love as well. *Julie* teaches that love can be as subversive of the social order as marriage is necessary to it. To see this we must consider Julie's nature and her effect upon the other characters in the work.

Despite her remarkable success at ruling others, Julie is presented to us in one respect as an ordinary woman. Rousseau insists upon this; it is the basis of his claim to have written a moral novel. "Perfect beings do not exist; the lessons which they give are too . . . remote from us" (*Confessions*, IX, p. 450). Or as his interlocutor remarks in the Second Preface: "If your Héloïse had been always wise, she would instruct much less; for to whom would she serve as a model?" (*Julie*, Second Preface, p. 26). Thus Saint-Preux speaks for Rousseau when he observes that novels can instruct corrupt peoples only if they are written by authors who are not "above the weaknesses of humanity, who do not all of a sudden show virtue in Heaven out of the reach of men" (*Julie*, III, 21, p. 277). Because she falls,

Rousseau's Julie, and not Richardson's Clarissa Harlowe (nor, for that matter, Rousseau's Lucretia) is a plausible heroine who can provide moral instruction in an immoral age.[30]

But in truth Julie is very far from being an ordinary woman, despite her fall from unsullied virtue. "There will never be more than one Julie in the world" (*Julie*, V, 2, p. 532). Julie is unique because of her exceptional capacity for loving. "My heart was made for love" (*Julie*, VI, 11, p. 724). In this respect, she is to some extent comparable to Sophie. For the same claim is made about Julie that Rousseau makes about Sophie: she "is consumed [*devorée*]," Saint-Preux remarks, by the "need [*besoin*] to love" (*Julie*, V, 5, pp. 589–90).[31] In fact, however, the intensity of Julie's desire to love (and her resultant inability to satisfy that desire in the world of reality) make her more reminiscent of the girl like Sophie, who "loved [Telemachus] with a passion of which nothing could cure her," and who is not "an ordinary woman" because of her "elevat[ed] . . . soul." The parallel between the two girls could in fact be greatly extended; as in the case of the girl like Sophie, Julie's parents, in "leading her to the altar," eventually cause her to "descend into the grave" (*Emile*, V, pp. 404–05).

Julie is unique among women because she needs and wants to love so badly. This claim makes sense in terms of the genesis of the novel as Rousseau describes it to us. Rousseau invents Julie because he too is "consumed [*devoré*] by the desire [*besoin*] to love" (*Confessions*, IX, p. 440).[32] Because he does not find a woman like Julie in the world, his imagination creates her. "The impossibility of grasping realities threw me into the land of chimeras, and seeing nothing in existence which was worthy of my enthusiasm, I sought nourishment for it in an ideal world, which my fertile imagination soon peopled with beings after my own heart" (*Confessions*, IX, p. 441). Julie is the woman whom Rousseau imagines but (at least until he encounters Madame d'Houdetot) never meets; she is also the female counterpart of Rousseau, since the need to love devours them both. Julie is truly a woman after Rousseau's own heart.

Although he cannot be happy in the world of reality, Rousseau lives in it and through his writings, in fact, attempts to improve it. Rousseau's relation to reality is thus ambivalent, both reformist and escapist. *Julie* the novel and Julie the character mirror this ambivalence. Rousseau contends that his novel serves a moral purpose because it is not escapist, or because it does not lead its readers to choose to escape their actual condition.

People complain that Novels disturb judgment: I believe it. In incessantly showing to those who read them, the purported charms of an estate that is not theirs, they seduce the readers, they cause them to hold their estate in disdain, and to make an imaginary exchange for the estate that they are led to love. Wanting to be what they are not, they manage to believe themselves other than they are, and thus they become fools. If Novels offered their Readers only portraits of objects that surround them, only duties that they can perform, only the pleasures of their condition, Novels would make them not foolish but wise (*Julie*, Second Preface, pp. 21–22).

So unlike other novels, *Julie* is praiseworthy because it is the romance of reality. But is it? Elsewhere in the Second Preface Rousseau calls this claim into question. For *Julie* is a collection of love letters, and "love is only an illusion; it makes for itself, so to speak, another Universe; it surrounds itself with nonexistent objects, or objects to which it alone has given being" (*Julie*, Second Preface, p. 15). The "simple people" depicted in *Julie*, who "know how to love, . . . finding nowhere what they feel, fall back on themselves; they detach themselves from the rest of the Universe; and creating among themselves a little world different from ours, they form therein a truly new spectacle" (*Julie*, Second Preface, pp. 16–17). Novels should not lead people to want to be "what they are not," yet *Julie* depicts the "nonexistent"; people should not "believe themselves other than they are," yet *Julie* celebrates "a little world different from ours," "detach[ed] . . . from the rest of the Universe." *Julie* purports to celebrate reality, yet the love that it portrays entails the creation of "another Universe." Love and reality seem to be in tension.

Thus far we have seen *Julie* celebrate society in the harmonious marriage of Julie and Wolmar. *Julie* also portrays the love between Julie and Saint-Preux, and its impact on society. It is part of Wolmar's project to make their love safe both for themselves and for society. Wolmar invites Saint-Preux to live with him and Julie, although he knows of their love. "I understood that there held sway over you ties that it was necessary not to break; that your mutual attachment related to so many praiseworthy things, that it was necessary rather to regulate it than to annihilate it; and that in forgetting one another you would both lose much of your value" (*Julie*, IV, 12, p. 495).[33]

It seems paradoxical that the impassive Wolmar emerges as a greater advocate of passion than the volatile Julie. In fact he admires passion because he has so little of it. He marries Julie because of his passion for her, despite her far greater passion for another man. He confesses: "This conduct was inexcusable. . . . I offended against delicacy; I sinned against prudence; I exposed your [Julie's] honor and mine; I should have feared to hurl us both into misfortune without resort: but I loved you, and loved only you. All the rest was indifferent to me" (*Julie*, IV, 12, p. 493). Wolmar contends that he sinned because he lacked passion.

How can one repress even the most feeble passion, when it is without a counterweight? Here is the disadvantage of cold and tranquil characters. . . . I have been tempted only once, and I succumbed. If the intoxication of another passion had made me waver again, I would have fallen as often as I slipped: only fiery souls know how to combat and win. All great efforts, all sublime actions are their work; cold reason has never done anything illustrious, and one triumphs over the passions only by opposing one to another. . . . The true sage . . . is no more sheltered from the passions than any other, but [he] alone knows how to vanquish them by themselves (*Julie*, IV, 12, p. 493).[34]

Only the passionate man can be virtuous, Wolmar claims. Earlier Julie asserted that the passion of love was incompatible with socially responsible behavior; Wolmar argues that socially responsible behavior is inconceivable without a basis in passion. Wolmar can speak of the passion for virtue (*Julie*, IV, 12, p. 493); yet it is clear that not all passions are virtuous. Wolmar can be confident not only because the love of Julie for Saint-Preux is a passion; he must also trust that her love can be transformed to be compatible with her continued virtue as the wife of another.

Wolmar believes that Julie's passion alone makes possible her virtue; if she could not love she could not be as virtuous a woman. And since she cannot learn to love Wolmar, she must continue to love Saint-Preux. The "disproportion of ages" takes from Wolmar "the right to aspire to a sentiment which its object was unable to enjoy, a sentiment that no other can obtain" (*Julie*, IV, 12, p. 494). Thus he and she can properly socialize one another, or make one another moral beings, despite the fact that she loves a third. Wolmar's ground for this remarkable assertion is his "discovery" about love. He explains to Claire:

To tell you that [Julie and Saint-Preux] are more in love than ever no doubt is not to teach you anything marvelous. To assure you on the contrary that they are perfectly healed is not a miracle either, for you know what reason and virtue can do: but that these two opposites are true at the same time; that they burn more ardently than ever for one another, and that between them there is now only an honorable attachment; that they are lovers forever but are now only friends; that, I think, is what you expect less, what will be harder for you to understand. Yet this is the exact truth (*Julie*, IV, 14, p. 508).

Wolmar is more certain of this explanation of Saint-Preux's behavior than of his wife's. His wife's heart is covered by "a veil of wisdom and of decency," so that "it is no longer possible for the human eye to penetrate it" (*Julie*, IV, 14, p. 509). Of Saint-Preux, however, he is certain: "He does not love Julie de Wolmar, but Julie d'Étange. . . . He loves in the past tense; love is the true explanation of the enigma. Take from him his memory, and he will no longer love" (*Julie*, IV, 14, p. 509).

For Wolmar, like Julie, holds that love is only temporary. Julie and

Saint-Preux were separated "when their passion was at its height of vehemence. Perhaps if they had remained together for longer they would again have become cooler little by little; but their vividly moved imagination incessantly offers one to the other such as they were at the instant of their separation." Hence Wolmar is confident. Eventually reality will triumph over illusion:

> She has become more beautiful, but she has changed; in this sense what she has gained is to her detriment; for he loves the old Julie and not another. . . . In place of his mistress I force him always to see the wife of an honest man and the mother of my children: I erase one picture with another, and cover the past with the present (*Julie*, IV, 14, pp. 509–11).

Wolmar, who is not passionate, lives in the present. His task is to compel Julie and Saint-Preux to live there as well. He realizes that love signifies the triumph of the remembered past (or the imagined future) over the present because he is a man; he says that "No woman in the world, with all the subtlety that is ascribed to your sex, would ever have made [his discovery]" (*Julie*, IV, 14, p. 508). Like Julie, Wolmar is an extraordinary individual who in some respects is also representative of his sex. His powers of observation and his remarkable capacity to penetrate the motives of others obviously set him apart from the run of men. But Wolmar's discovery differentiates him more from women than from men. Wolmar is like other men because his interest in governing women is not great, and because he recognizes the impermanence of passionate desire. He differs from other men (and admittedly it is a vast difference) only because he understands so acutely what they understand so imperfectly.

Rousseau advises women to recognize the inconstancy of love, the fact that present eventually triumphs over past, or reality over memory and imagination. He speaks for himself in a note appended to Wolmar's discovery:

> All changes in nature, all is in a continual flux, and you want to inspire constant order? And with what right do you aspire to be loved today because you were loved yesterday? . . . Always be the same and you will always be loved, if you can be. But to change without cease and to want always to be loved, is to want at each instant that one no longer be loved; it is not to seek constant hearts, but hearts as subject to change as you are (*Julie*, IV, 14, pp. 509–10).

Love cannot be permanent because nothing human is permanent. In *Emile* Rousseau asserts that in particular the love of males for females is impermanent (because men's desire is weaker than is women's); hence women must be modest even in marriage. Women must augment men's desire for them by seldom allowing men to satisfy men's desire. Only then will men depend upon women, and women govern men (*Emile*, V, pp. 476–79). Insofar as women's government of men is based on men's passion alone, it is necessarily impermanent.[35]

Thus Wolmar's project to rehabilitate Saint-Preux and Julie, to make their passion safe for themselves and for society, depends on the impermanence of their passion. Because Wolmar himself is so cold, so comparatively dispassionate, passion must seem particularly evanescent to him; in this respect he is the embodiment of masculinity as it is conceived by Rousseau. By nature he is solitary because his desire for others is weak. For the same reason he is an "atheist" (*Julie*, V, 5, p. 589). He is too "cold," Saint-Preux fears, to become a believer. "He lacks sentiment, or the interior proof, and that proof alone can render all the others invincible" (*Julie*, V, 5, p. 594).[36] A man of weak passions, Wolmar seems to need neither man nor God. He does not need God because he affirms the evanescence that he thinks characteristic of the world. "The spectacle of nature . . . is dead in the eyes of the unfortunate Wolmar." Wolmar is not concerned with permanence; the only eternity that he admits is the "eternal silence" (*Julie*, V, 5, pp. 593–94) of a world in which humanity does not hear God because God never speaks.

If Wolmar embodies the masculine principle of self-sufficiency, Julie equally embodies the feminine principle of sociability. Like all women, she engages in sexual politics; she desires to rule men, and exploits the sexual difference in order to do so. But Julie is exceptional among women because of her extraordinary capacity to love. Only in terms of this capacity can her intense religiosity be understood.[37] For Julie religion is the ultimate expression of her love for others. "One would say that nothing terrestrial being able to satisfy the need to love with which she is consumed, this excess of sensibility is forced to ascend back to its source." Julie has

a truly inexhaustible heart that love and friendship have not been able to drain, and which carries its superabundant affections to the only Being worthy of absorbing them. The love of God does not detach her from His creatures; it gives her neither harshness nor bitterness. All these attachments [are] produced by the same cause; in being animated by one another they become sweeter and more charming (*Julie*, V, 5, pp. 589–90).

Julie expresses her love in her devotion to her fellows, and supplements this expression with her love of God. She is socially active in the temporal world, but seeks spriritual solace in her love for an eternal being. *Julie*, we have said, is the romance of reality that celebrates a world different from ours; both social activist and devotée, Julie well illustrates the tensions of the novel that bears her name.

But Julie and her world are ultimately overcome by the tension between social reality and love, the illusionary product of the imagination; it proves to be impossible to be altogether faithful both to the world of social reality and to the ideal of love. Rousseau's novel can reasonably be understood as a qualified defense of romantic love, of the world of illusions that it harbors; but his defense is made not because romantic love can be harnessed to serve society's interests but in spite of (and even because of) the fact that it cannot.[38]

Arguments against Marriage in the Nouvelle Héloïse

We have already seen Rousseau depict *Julie* as a defense of conjugal fidelity and married life. "I love to represent to myself two spouses reading this collection [of letters], extracting from it new courage in order to support their common labors, and perhaps new views in order to make them useful. How could they contemplate the [novel's] portrait of a happy household without wishing to imitate such a sweet model?" (*Julie*, Second Preface, p. 23). Julie speaks repeatedly in the course of the novel in defense of marriage. "Men and women are destined for one another, the end of nature is that they be united by marriage" (*Julie*, IV, 10, p. 456). "Is there shame in marrying the man you love, or loving him without marrying him? . . . The wife of a Coal Dealer is more reputable than the mistress of a Prince" (*Julie*, V, 13, p. 633). "Man is not made for celibacy, and it is hard for a state so contrary to nature not to lead to some public or hidden disorder" (*Julie*, VI, 6, p. 668).

This is the official position of the novel, so to speak; men and women are social beings who must complete and rule one another. But Rousseau's ambivalence about human sexuality and the social and political relations that it creates is very much evident in the novel. For Julie may preach as much as she wants in favor of marriage; the fact is, none of the major characters in the book listens to her.[39] Of the major characters alive at the book's end, Baron d'Étange and Wolmar are widowers with no prospect of remarrying, Claire is a widow with no prospect of remarrying, and Saint-Preux and Bomston are bachelors with no prospect of marrying. In some measure the actions of the book's characters rebut its explicit support of married life.[40]

Bomston, Saint-Preux, and Claire all announce their intention not to marry, and it is worth considering the arguments that they advance in support of their respective decisions. While in Rome, Bomston becomes involved in a romantic triangle with a married noblewoman (who at first conceals her marriage from him) who is in love with him, and a lovely prostitute to whom the noblewoman introduces him when he explains to her that he will not knowingly commit adultery. Bomston and Laura, the prostitute, fall deeply (and platonically) in love; he reforms her, and contemplates marrying her. But as advised by Saint-Preux, she realizes that an English nobleman cannot marry even the most repentant former prostitute, and enters a convent.[41] Bomston then decides that he need never marry.

> Until now I had regarded marriage as a debt that each person contracts at his birth toward his species, toward his country, and I had resolved to marry, less by inclination than by duty: I have changed my opinion. The obligation to marry is not common to all: for each man it depends on the state where fate has placed him; it is for the common people, for the artisan, for the villager, for truly useful men that celibacy is illicit: for the orders that rule the others, to which all incessantly aspire, and which are always only too well filled, it is permitted and even expedient (*Julie*, VI, 3, p. 654).

Ironically, Bomston's argument against marriage agrees with one of Julie's arguments in favor of marriage: the wife of a coal dealer is more respectable than the mistress of a prince. But for Bomston this is not so much because wives are superior to mistresses as it is because coal dealers are superior to princes. Those who rule over society need not rule over one another in marriage, because they do not deserve to rule. Marriage would seem to be relative to the regime; if there were a society wherein "truly useful men" ruled, presumably they would be obliged to marry. But in monarchical Europe it is fitting that rulers such as himself not marry. Bomston does not question the intimate connection that Rousseau perceives between regeneration of domestic *moeurs* and political reformation, but he does suggest that the Rousseau of the Second Preface is excessively optimistic in assigning so clear a priority to the former. For Bomston, the regeneration of domestic *moeurs* will not lead to political reformation; instead it would be truly desirable only in the context of a prior political reformation.

Bomston is a member of Parliament, and as such the one truly political figure in the novel; because he is most aware of what a good regime would be, and most concerned with its practical implementation, he is also the most pessimistic, because even improved domestic morality would not in itself achieve the most meaningful political reform. Relative to corrupt Europe, the reform of marriage may be a worthy undertaking; but such a reform seems much less significant when viewed from the perspective of a regime in which genuine citizenship flourishes. Relative to such a regime, marriage is an important but hardly the dominant social institution. Bomston is sympathetic to celibacy because of the severity of the standard by which he judges political life; marriage is too important to be left to the monarchists.

Bomston's argument suggests the limits of marriage as an agent of social reform. By contrast, Claire suggests that marriage is limited precisely because it is a social institution; she is concerned not because marriage does not adequately reform society, but because it constrains the individual. Julie wants Claire and Saint-Preux to marry one another, at least partly, it is clear, for her own personal reasons: if Saint-Preux were married to Claire, he would be much less likely to tempt Julie to be unfaithful to Wolmar, and she would be much less likely to be tempted by him. When Julie first broaches the idea of the marriage to Claire, she says that if Claire does not marry him they should "separate from [themselves] this dangerous man, always redoubtable to one of us *or the other*" (*Julie*, V, 13, p. 634; the emphasis is mine). Saint-Preux is still dangerous both to the unmarried Claire and to the married Julie. Later, she writes Saint-Preux that his marriage to Claire would "extricate you honorably from the precarious state in which you live in the world." But it is clear that his marriage would also extricate her. "It is not even enough for you to be my cousin [which he would be if he married Claire]; ah! I would like you to be my brother" (*Julie*, VI, 8, p. 691). As a married man and a cousin by marriage Saint-Preux would tempt Julie less; ideally he would be her brother, and be forbidden to her by the incest taboo. In the *Essay on the Origin of Languages* romantic love puts an end to incest, by causing men and women to seek sexual partners outside of their families;[42] in effect Julie hopes that her plan for Claire and Saint-Preux will create an artificial incest prohibition, thereby putting an end to her love.

But Claire and Saint-Preux refuse to marry one another. Claire's reasons are most interesting, and particularly so because she is a woman. For Claire makes general arguments against marriage, as well as specific arguments against marrying Saint-Preux. In other words, Claire often argues against the very idea of sexual politics; although she obviously enjoys ruling males,[43] she also argues that independence or avoidance of rule is preferable to the equality through empire that Rousseau typically portrays both as woman's fate and woman's desire. If Julie is a woman after Rousseau's own heart, Claire could be considered a woman after Mary Wollstonecraft's heart.[44]

Claire writes to Monsieur d'Orbe, then her fiancé: "As a woman I am a sort of monster, and I do not know by what peculiarity of nature friendship prevails in me over love" (*Julie*, I, 64, p. 479). They marry, which means that Claire "alienate[s] her liberty" (*Julie*, II, 18, p. 257). After Orbe's death she reflects on her marriage:

> I have told you a hundred times as a girl; I was not made to be a woman. If it had depended on me, I would not have married. But in

our sex, one purchases liberty only by slavery, and one must begin by being a servant in order one day to become mistress. Although my father did not constrain me, I was distressed at home. To extricate myself, I married Monsieur d'Orbe.

She "loved him sincerely" but sensed that "as good a husband [as Orbe] was necessary to make of me a good wife." But as a widow she does not contemplate remarrying. "Marriage is too serious a state; its dignity does not go with my disposition; it saddens me and suits me badly; without reckoning that all restraint is insupportable to me. Think . . . what in my eyes can be a tie in which I did not even laugh at my ease seven times during seven years!" (*Julie*, IV, 2, pp. 407–08).

When Julie broaches the idea of Claire marrying Saint-Preux, she responds by speaking again of her "independent disposition and [her] natural dislike of the yoke of marriage" (*Julie*, VI, 2, p. 645). Claire is "a sort of monster" as a woman, because of her "independent disposition"; unlike ordinary women, it seems that she would rather avoid rule than exercise it over another at the price of being ruled herself. She enjoys her widowhood because it, unlike marriage, involves the absence and not the interchange of rule. Marriage is a severe and restrictive state; women (and men too, we may assume) of "independent disposition," to whom "restraint" is "insupportable," are not attracted by it. In short, Claire rejects the married state because she claims to be a woman who is in some respects very similar to the sort of man Rousseau is;[45] if "all restraint [*gêne*] is insupportable" to her, he too "abhor[s] restraint [*gêne*]"; if she has an "independent disposition" [*humeur indépendante*]" and dislikes the "yoke [*joug*] of marriage," he has an "independent natural temperament [*naturel indépendant*]" and "become[s] rebellious" upon "feel[ing] the yoke [*joug*]" (*Confessions*, I, p. 37; *Reveries*, VI, p. 83).[46] In the view of people such as Claire (and for that matter also in Bomston's view) marriage is not an inherently desirable condition toward which one aspires but a social obligation that outside forces may constrain one to fulfill.

Saint-Preux's argument against marriage arises from his experience with Julie and Claire. He argues that he can never love Claire as much as he loves Julie, and that Julie's constant presence at Clarens (both in reality and in his imagination) would inevitably estrange him from Claire were she to become his wife. Thus if Saint-Preux were to marry Claire he would make her unhappy. "I love her too much to marry her" (*Julie*, VI, 7, p. 679). In the *Confessions*, Rousseau claims to have loved both Madame de Warens and Madame d'Houdetot too much to possess them (*Confessions*, V, p. 202, IX, p. 459). The tepid love of ordinary men leads them to possession and to moral involvement with others in the world of reality. The extraordinary love of a Rousseau (and of a Saint-Preux, and, as we shall see, of a Julie) leads them to flee from the world of reality, so as to avoid the destruction of the illusions of love that reality sooner or later brings about.[47] Rousseau states explicitly that Saint-Preux is based on his own character; like Rousseau, Saint-Preux prefers the preservation of the illusions of love to the active social involvement that participation in a moral institution such as marriage necessarily entails. Marriage is a social institution; like all other social institutions, it provides a remedy for humanity's dependence while also testifying to it. In marriage the two partners depend on each other, for better or for worse. Although marriage can under many circumstances justify the mutual dependence of men and women, it need not always do so; the partners' mutual dependence may be for worse, not for better. Should this be the case, if dependence could not be mutually redemptive, it would be better to avoid dependence altogether. This is the basis of Saint-Preux's argument; since his marital dependence on Claire could not be justified, it must be avoided. Thus Saint-Preux can claim to act in a socially responsible manner when he shirks the social responsibility of marriage: "If it is a duty to marry, it is a still more indispensable duty not to cause anyone to be unhappy" (*Julie*, VI, 7, p. 680). For Saint-Preux as for Bomston, there are certain classes of men who benefit the social order by not marrying; in view of their very different arguments, it is surprising that the men of whom they speak at least in one respect are quite similar. For imaginative lovers like Saint-Preux are no more likely to be "truly useful men," from a social standpoint, than are social potentates such as Bomston.

Thus the novel's defense of married life is presented with the qualifications to the defense already included. The novel begins with Saint-Preux informing Julie that "I must flee from you" (*Julie*, I, 1, p. 31). In fact, in the course of the novel he never manages to flee from her, or rather from her image. But the impact of her image upon him does cause him to escape all others, as he explains to her in his last letter in the book: "I have not been able to live with you; I will die free" (*Julie*, VI, 7, p. 681). And similarly, as we have seen, Claire flees from Saint-Preux and Bomston flees from all womanhood. Finally, Julie flees from life.

For Julie is pleased to die when she does. "I am leaving at a favorable moment, content with you [Saint-Preux] and me; I am leaving with joy, and there is nothing cruel about this departure" (*Julie*, VI, 12, p. 741). One reason she is happy to die is that her "illusion" is shattered; she believed herself to be "cured" of her love for Saint-Preux, and discovers that she is not (*Julie*, VI, 12, p. 740). In marrying Wolmar, she thought that she was leaving behind the illusions of love so as to take an active part in the world of social reality; it now develops that her participation in that world was itself based upon an illusion. Having come to this realization, henceforth her life would have required of her a struggle in order to remain virtuous; in death her virtue is guaranteed without a struggle. "Virtue, which separated us on earth, will unite us in the eternal sojourn"

(*Julie*, VI, 12, p. 743). "Virtue," as Claire remarks, "is a state of war" (*Julie*, VI, 7, p. 682); and of no one is it more true than of Julie that she would rather make love than war.

Thus Julie dies so as to avoid the necessity of struggling. Earlier, interestingly, she suggests exactly the opposite—that she would be willing to die because she has no need to struggle. "I have nothing to desire; . . . I am living at once amidst all that I love, I am sated with happiness and life: O death, come when you want! I no longer fear you" (*Julie*, VI, 8, p. 689).

When Julie considers her irrepressible love for Saint-Preux, the prospect of constant struggle frightens her; when she considers herself cured of her love for him, the prospect of a life from which struggle would be eternally absent bores her. Julie wants neither a life in which she must struggle nor a life in which she can rule without struggle. She rejects her life because she rejects the sexual politics, the struggle to rule others, and (in her case) the extraordinary success at ruling others that characterize it. Rousseau makes this clearer in a note to Julie's remarks than she does in the remarks themselves.

She speaks of her boredom with life: "I am too happy; happiness bores me" (*Julie*, VI, 8, p. 694). "To live without pain is not man's estate; to live thus is to be dead. He who could be all without being God would be a miserable creature; he would be deprived of the pleasure of desiring; every other deprivation would be more supportable" (*Julie*, VI, 8, pp. 693–94).

Rousseau explicates these complaints by placing them in a political context. "Hence it follows that every Prince who aspires to despotism aspires to the honor of dying of boredom. In all the Kingdoms of the world do you seek the most bored man in the country? Always go directly to the sovereign; especially if he is very absolute" (*Julie*, VI, 8, p. 694). We have seen Julie described as a despot; we now can understand that she is willing to die because she has been too successful at sexual politics. She no longer finds the ideal of an empire over her acquaintances to be an exciting or attractive one. Rousseau contends that women normally aspire to rule; the example of Julie suggests that rule may not be a goal to which it is worth aspiring. Those who rule absolutely "without being God" are miserable; perhaps in order truly to be divine one would have not to rule but instead to avoid rule absolutely.

Julie rejected the world of romantic illusions to live and to rule in the world of social reality, but she came to see that even this world was based upon an illusion. It is therefore not surprising that in the end she prefers the wholly ideal world of total illusion to the world of reality that is still permeated by illusion. "The land of chimeras is in this world the only one worthy of being inhabited, and such is the nothingness of human things, that outside of the Being existent by himself, there is nothing beautiful but what is not" (*Julie*, VI, 8, p. 693). As is the case with Rousseau and the girl like Sophie, Julie's dissatisfaction with the real world stems from her love of the beautiful and her conviction that the real world is devoid of beauty. Perhaps Julie, unlike most other women, is ultimately dissatisfied with sexual politics because also unlike them (and like Rousseau) she possesses so great a capacity for love. For the completion to which Julie and Rousseau aspire cannot be achieved through the domination of others. For the two of them (and for Saint-Preux as well) completion is to be achieved through the imagination of the ideal, not through the possession and domination of the real.

This is not to suggest that Julie's love leads her to betray the ideal of social service to which she is devoted. She insists that her love of God is compatible with and even helps to motivate her social service. "To serve God is not to pass one's life on his knees in chapel, as I know; it is to fulfill on earth the duties that He imposes on us" (*Julie*, VI, 8, p. 695). And even while dying, in fact, Julie fulfills duties on earth. For she dies after saving her son from drowning, hence as "a martyr to maternal love" (*Julie*, VI, 11, p. 717). Furthermore, her death leads to her husband's conversion; before her illness she declares that she "would like at the price of [her] life to see him one time convinced [of the truth of religion]" (*Julie*, VI, 8, p. 700). Julie dies while saving her son's life in this world and perhaps also her husband's soul in the next.

Nevertheless, it is clear that Julie does not find social service altogether satisfying in itself. Her devotion, Wolmar claims, "is an opium for the soul" (*Julie*, VI, 8, p. 697). Her image of a divine being (and the illusions of love of which it is a transfiguration),[48] not the power that she exercises in society, provide her with the opium she needs.

Thus in Julie Rousseau presents us with a woman who at first seems to be ordinary both in her susceptibility to error and in her propensity to rule. But she is also another woman, one who is extraordinary by virtue of her great capacity to love. With reference to the first woman, Rousseau suggests that men and women need to engage in sexual politics for the good of society. With reference to the second, he suggests that they may desire a completion which life in society is unable to provide them. We earlier observed that men make women happy as objects of women's love and subjects of women's rule. Julie's example suggests that these two routes to women's happiness to a considerable extent exist in tension with one another. Perhaps only more ordinary women, less sensible of the need to love, can take full satisfaction in sexual politics. Women who are capable of great love would certainly be more attractive to men such as Rousseau; it is not altogether clear that they would also better serve the interests of society. Rousseau writes *Julie* in praise of the sociability that the sexual division of labor engenders, but also in praise of love, the passion that elevates at least some extraordinary men and women from human partiality in society to divine completion in the imagination. Thus his praise of the one is distinct from his praise of the other. As he says in the *Letter to D'Alembert*, "Love either seduces or it is not love. . . . It overshadows everything that accompanies it" (*Letter*, p. 55). And among the things that accompany love are participation in the world of social reality. The love that individuals such as Julie and Rousseau experience testifies not to the virtues of that world, but to its limitations.

∽ 6 ∽

Conclusion
What Is Living and
What Is Dead in
Rousseau's Sexual Politics

Rousseau presents us with two different teachings about sexuality. In both teachings, in fact in all of his philosophy, Rousseau contemplates the meanings of both human nature and human freedom, and the relationship between them. Are we free because of our nature? Might we be free in spite of it? These are always Rousseau's central questions, and they are questions which figure prominently in his discussions of sexuality. In Rousseau's first teaching, he argues that freedom and sexuality are compatible, or that we can attain freedom through sexuality; in his second teaching, he contends that they are incompatible, or that true freedom could be achieved only on the basis of freedom from sexuality. In this concluding chapter, I would like to reexamine the two teachings, by considering whether Rousseau's teachings still speak to us today. To what extent does the sexual politics of the twentieth century invalidate Rousseau's thought or demonstrate its obsolescence? On the other hand, to what extent does Rousseau's thought continue to illuminate the sexual politics of the twentieth century?

In the first teaching he contends that sexuality can make us free because sexuality differentiates us yet also equalizes us; it divides us yet, in spite of and even because of our division, it also brings us together. Most importantly, sexuality gives men and women power over one another because it differentiates men from women.

Because it is so intellectually unfashionable today to insist on the importance of the differences between men and women, it is worth noting how unconventionally Rousseau presents the differentiation between the sexes. Rousseau is not a Victorian; as he portrays women, they are not insensible to sexual pleasure, they are in no way "above" sexual pleasure; in this respect Rousseau's women are closer to women as understood by Masters and Johnson than they are to women as understood by Mrs. Grundy and Mr. Bowdler. However different he thinks men are from women, he certainly does not believe that only men are sexual creatures, and that women are never sexual creatures; if anything, the reverse is closer to the truth.

Rousseau not only realizes that women have bodies and desires; he also realizes that they have both the ambition and the ability to control others, that they are in no way simply passive, submissive objects. In some respects men are able to dominate women; but in other respects, women are equally successful at dominating men.

In emphasizing the ability of each sex to dominate the other, Rousseau teaches an important truth about the male-female relationship. It is a truth of which many feminists in particular tend to lose sight, both in their descriptions of women's role in the past, and also in their prescriptions for women's role in the future. Sexual relationships are in part exercises in mutual domination; it is false to assert that domination has historically been exercised always and only by males upon females, and it is utopian to reject all human relationships which involve domination, in the expectation that in some future (and/or nonheterosexual) world "meaningful" or "supportive" relationships will evolve devoid of any element of domination. Human beings like to rule one another; there is nothing necessarily wrong with this (though there is much about absolutely unchecked rule that is dangerous), and there is much that may be positive about it.

Rousseau is not a feminist, but in emphasizing the power of women he has much to teach feminists. I say this because feminists, like those who advance the causes of other oppressed groups, often are tempted to make two different (and to some extent incompatible) arguments: they want to call attention to the extent of past and present oppression but also to anticipate the possibility, desirability, and inevitability of future emancipation. If no women had ever been in any way oppressed, obviously their liberation would be meaningless; but if *all* women have *always* been *completely* oppressed, how plausible is it to believe in their future liberation? By emphasizing (and exaggerating) the extent of women's oppression (and most importantly by emphasizing and exaggerating women's docility and submissiveness, their internalization and acceptance of their oppression), many advocates of women's liberation often sound remarkably like their traditional oppressors; one finds it hard to believe that women could ever be capable of liberating themselves if they have been so totally and mindlessly submissive for so long.

Rousseau can be useful to us, then, in reminding us that the power of men over women has never been absolute, and that the power of women over men has never been nonexistent. Rousseau's women want to benefit themselves, to make decisions and not simply have decisions made for them; his women may well need to liberate themselves, but at least one can be reasonably confident that they would be able to liberate themselves. I would argue that many feminists err strategically in universalizing male oppression and female submission: *"all men"* do not keep *"all women"* in a state of fear" through a "conscious process of intimidation."[1] All men are not born predators, all women are not born victims, and women are done no favor by those who emphasize their total inability throughout recorded history to take care of themselves.

Rousseau emphasizes that most women are able to take care of themselves most of the time; he emphasizes their power, not their powerlessness. It is true that he emphasizes their power within the context of domestic and familial relations alone, not within the economic and political world. Women for Rousseau are equal as wives and mothers (vis-à-vis husbands and fathers), not as workers or citizens.

The Impact and Implications of Technology

Why does Rousseau restrict women to equality in the familial sphere alone? To answer this question, one must begin be recalling that Rousseau wrote in an era which preceded the drastic transformation of the world occasioned by the past century's technological conquest of nature. There is no question that technological developments such as mechanization, automation, and contraception have created possibilities for contemporary women which Rousseau could not even have imagined. Women's liberation would not be seriously thinkable in the absence of these developments. For this reason, it is obvious that Rousseau's pronouncements about sexual relations (based as they are upon an analysis of the pretechnological conditions of the eighteenth century) could never be immediately and unthinkingly applied to our very different contemporary conditions. But by the very same token, Rousseau ought not to be criticized by us today, who live under one set of conditions, because he wrote about radically dissimilar earlier conditions. Thus, it is fair to say (as Okin does) that "Rousseau defines woman's nature, unlike man's, in terms of her function—that is, her sexual and procreative purpose in life."[2] But it would be fairer still to take account of one of the reasons Rousseau advances for so doing: "In order for the human species to be preserved, every woman must, everything considered, produce nearly four children; *for nearly half of the children who are born die before they can have others*, and the two remaining ones are needed to represent the father and the mother" (*Emile*, V, p. 362; the emphasis is mine).[3] For Rousseau, it was literally a matter of life and death that women be willing to bear a great many children. If this is unpleasant for us to read today, it is because a world in which the infant and child mortality rate approached fifty percent would be an unpleasant world in which to live; it is not because Rousseau's response to that world is such a prejudiced and unfair one.

Rousseau writes at a time when infant and child mortality rates were staggeringly high, when contraception was uncertain at best, when brute strength was of far greater political and economic relevance than it is today. For these reasons, he would say that *he* does not restrict women to equality in the familial sphere alone—he would argue instead that *nature* does so. It is not implausible to say that nature places women at a disadvantage outside of the family, given the greater burden that pregnancy places upon them in the sexual division of labor, and given their greater physical weakness. In the absence of any technological mastery of nature, these are handicaps which many women would surely be able to overcome. Nevertheless, they are undeniably handicaps, and any analysis of the historical (as opposed to the contemporary) oppression of women which fails to acknowledge them as natural and not merely cultural handicaps must inevitably be disingenuous or shortsighted.

Yet even if we grant that Rousseau's distinctions between men and women make considerable sense in terms of the pretechnological world of which he writes, we may still wonder what sense they might continue to make in the technologically transformed world in which we live. One might argue that today's technological transformations would make it possible for Rousseau to advocate the liberation of women as that liberation is customarily understood today. After all, he suggests that women are no less eager for power than men, but that their bodies and their sexuality require them to express their eagerness differently than do men. To the extent that today's technology minimizes the importance of the differences between male and female bodies and male and female sexuality, even on Rousseau's grounds women could conceivably begin to express their eagerness for power not only within the family but in the political and economic world outside the family as well.

The notion that Rousseau's philosophy plus the birth-control pill would yield the liberation of women is in some respects attractive, and it is not wholly false. It is mostly false, however; if we are to take Rousseau seriously, it is necessary to realize why he would not simply have welcomed the advent of a technology which minimizes the importance of the distinctions between male and female bodies.

Rousseau opposes the technological transformation of nature, or at least has grave doubts about it. His opposition is apparent in many of his writings, and is in no way specific to his treatment of human sexuality. Even the gift of fire has been less than wholly beneficial, he tells us in the *First Discourse*: "Fire burns when one touches it" (*First*, p. 48n). One could easily imagine reading this on an environmentalist (specifically, an antinuclear power) banner at a demonstration: to increase human knowledge is to increase human power as well, which may present the human race (even if it had the best will in the world) with risks it would be incapable of averting. If excessive power is inherently dangerous to humanity, one must in principle oppose the increase in power which technology makes possible, and one cannot leave it at the pious hope of using that power for good rather than for evil.

Rousseau goes so far as to criticize the introduction of the inoculation against smallpox, probably the most spectacularly successful medical innovation of his day. His argument here is of particular interest, since he more or less concedes that the vaccine is effective; his critique is not that it may not work, but that it will prove disadvantageous even if (and in fact because) it does work. "If [Emile] is given smallpox [i.e., if he is inoculated, or given a small dose of a similar disease to immunize him against the more virulent variant of the disease], one will have the advantage of foreseeing and knowing his illness ahead of time; that is something. But if he gets it naturally, we will have preserved him from the doctor. That is even more" (*Emile*, II, p. 131). Medicine may prevent us from dying, but it also emphasizes and increases our fear of death, so our gain in physical health is compensated for by a decrease in mental health (*Emile*, I, pp. 54–55).

With respect to the technology which has made possible today's sexual revolution, Rousseau could make similar arguments about the costs that have come to us along with the benefits. (Given the spectacular successes of post-Rousseauian medicine, such arguments would in fact be somewhat more plausible than is the argument above.) Because pregnancy need no longer be the likely outcome of sexual relations, women for the first time have been able to adopt what one may term a male attitude toward sexuality. The technology of birth control has enabled women to divorce sexual pleasure from sexual procreation, which men have always been able to do.[4] Thus this technology has made the natural sexual double standard,[5] one of the bases of Rousseau's first teaching on sexuality, less tenable by far.

Modern contraceptive techniques have liberated women from most of the sexual constraints naturally imposed upon them by their bodies. It is true that Rousseau would be blind to the considerable benefits women have received from this liberation; nevertheless, he was not wrong to contend that sexual liberation would also impose costs upon both men and women; his argument therefore is not simply wrong, but only incomplete. For contraceptive advances, by abolishing the double standard, have made the contemporary sexual revolution possible. One need not be a sexual reactionary (in part because one may doubt the feasibility of any possible reaction) to note that this revolution, like so many others, has indeed imposed costs: Rousseau is right to argue that promiscuity has harmful consequences, in that it almost invariably encourages human beings to treat one another as means to their particular selfish gratification. One need not support the "teenage chastity bill" to be annoyed at the superficiality of sophisticates who find the idea of chastity, even for teenagers, a subject for condescension and amusement.

Men and Women in the Polity and in the Economy

Technology has enabled women to act sexually like men, which Rousseau would oppose because it has made promiscuity more possible, which has to some extent degraded both men and women by making "sexual objects" of them both. Technology has also enabled women to act politically and economically like men. Rousseau would also oppose the transformation of women into wage earners and citizens, their entrance into what had previously been a male world. He could make two seemingly contradictory arguments in defense of his opposition: "To leave her above us in the qualities proper to her sex and to make her our equal in all the rest is to transfer to the wife the primacy that nature gives the husband" (*Emile*, V, p. 382). "The more women want to resemble [men], the less women will govern them, and then men will truly be the masters" (*Emile*, V, p. 363). One can oppose equal opportunity for women either because it would make them men's superiors or because it would make them men's inferiors; one cannot oppose it for both reasons simultaneously.[6]

Of the two arguments given, the second one seems to me to be Rousseau's real one; however mistaken one may think him, he opposes equal opportunity in order to maintain effectual equality between the sexes, not in order to deny it. His argument in favor of maintaining male superiority is a rhetorical one, addressed by him as a male to other males; he includes himself among the male "us" who would lose their privileged superiority should women be released from the occupational and educational constraints imposed upon them. In this argument Rousseau means to appeal to that male *amour-propre* which he believes essential if any heterosexual relationship is to succeed (*Emile*, V, p. 358). In relating to women men must think themselves dominant over women, but in doing so men delude themselves; objectively they are not dominant. Men who believe in their superiority to women deceive themselves, but as sexual beings they must necessarily do so; hence Rousseau does not openly challenge their self-deception. Instead he exploits it and appeals to it, with the aim of making the differentiation of the sexes attractive to men. Rousseau makes a deceptive argument (thereby acting like a woman, he might say) without himself believing it.

Rousseau's real reason for restricting women's opportunities is the second one; because of the differences between the sexes, he believes that most women could not successfully compete with most men in what he regards as the male arenas of politics and economics. He therefore believes that on balance most women benefit themselves by not attempting to compete.

This argument may have been plausible two hundred years ago; it is certainly implausible today. We have seen that technology has led to the irrelevance of many of the differences between men and women with respect to political and economic action. In addition, whatever differences remain are not vast; are at least in part the effect of the different ways in which men and women have been educated and socialized; and finally, apply only to the sexes in the aggregate, not to every individual member of each sex. To illustrate this last contention, suppose that men on the average have a greater aptitude for welding than do women on the average; this would not justify denying any particular woman the opportunity to become a welder, and would not preclude the possibility that any particular woman might be a better welder than many (or all) of the men with whom she works.

Rousseau's argument differentiating between men and women as political and economic actors is thus of little practical relevance to us today. I mean by this that regardless of whether or not the nature of women differs from the nature of men, the opportunities for women should not differ from the opportunities for men. It may nevertheless be the case that there are differences between women and men which are at least partially natural, and not entirely the result of social conditioning. Women today are certainly able to compete economically and politically with men; but Rousseau may even now not be *wholly* incorrect in suggesting that they compete at a natural disadvantage.[7] I say this because contemporary scientific investigations permit the hypotheses that women on the whole are genetically less predisposed toward success in mathematics than are men,[8] and less aggressive than are men.[9] To the extent that a technological society places a particular premium upon mathematical ability, and to the extent that it is legitimate to associate "aggressiveness" with the capacity to lead, conceivably one could contend that the overall greater success of men as opposed to women in the economic and political worlds is not altogether the result of remediable social discrimination, but is at least in part also the outgrowth of immutable biological distinctions.[10]

I realize very well that there are good reasons for disputing these contentions about genetic predispositions[11] (even if there are also less worthy politically motivated reasons for doing so).[12] My point is only that even today it may not be simply ridiculous to believe that the political and economic worlds are at least to a slight extent "men's worlds"; if only in the sense that even today it may be the case that women face small but genuine natural hormonal handicaps in competition against men—handicaps which (if they existed) could not be wholly overcome by birth-control pills, machinery, consciousness-raising, or the funding of day-care centers.

We do not know to what extent differences between men and women such as those to which Rousseau points exist by nature (undeniably they also result in large part from social conditioning); but we surely do not know that whatever differences there are exist simply as a result of social conditioning (and not at all by nature). Even if there are natural differences between the sexes, though, I reiterate that neither their extent nor their importance appears to be great. Furthermore, regardless of the size of such differences in the aggregate, no one could seriously argue that all men are mathematically more gifted or more aggressive than all women.

To be fair to Rousseau, one must acknowledge that he concedes that there are "exceptions" to his generalizations about the sexes—even if most women lack "the talents of men," he realizes that some women nevertheless possess them (*Emile*, V, p. 364; *Letter*, p. 48n). One may think Rousseau too ready to recommend that the talented woman of his day have her opportunities restricted in the name of the purported good of the average woman, and one may think him too ready to conclude that the scarcity of talented women in his day was chiefly the effect of natural and not cultural handicaps. Just the same, in assessing Rousseau's views in the context of the conditions prevailing in his era, it might be fairer to criticize him for promoting the equality of women in an insufficient manner rather than for consciously promoting their inferiority.

Rousseau advocates the exclusion of women from the world of men not only because he believes that men and women differ intellectually but also because he believes that they differ morally. For all its irrelevance to the contemporary economic and political world, Rousseau's discussion of the differing moralities of men and women has much to teach us in other respects.[13]

The Contemporary Case for Sexual Differentiation

Rousseau wishes to argue that there are moral advantages to a division of labor between the sexes, which is an argument we might do well to take more seriously than we normally do. In general, contemporary intellectual opinion is too ready to decry any conformity of behavior to the roles traditionally assigned to the sexes. The stereotypically manly man is denounced for being *macho*, the stereotypically womanly woman is denounced for falling victim to the feminine mystique. Such denunciations are not wholly unmerited, but we should condescend less to the stereotypes we are said to have left behind us, and congratulate ourselves less for our supposed progress in leaving them behind us.

To give an example of the occasional appropriateness of the sexual stereotypes, one can point out that men should not feel apologetic about being brave in battle and courageously attempting to defend the women and children dependent upon them. The case against this particular stereotype is made by a feminist author: "Unless we can effectively check the power of manly men and the women who willingly support them, we will experience new Vietnams, My Lais, Kent States."[14] But a moment's reflection suggests the inadequacy of this argument since, unless we can effectively promote the power of manly men, we will no longer experience new Battles of Britain and Entebbes.[15] Heroism in battle is not an unqualified vice; it depends upon who is fighting the battle, and how and for what purposes it is fought. Furthermore, it is at least conceivable that heroism in battle has something to do with "male bonding," with the separation of men from women, with the differentiation of men from women. It is at least conceivable that heroism in battle is best promoted by means of the conditions prevailing when participation in combat is limited to males.[16]

Whatever their faults, the male and female who act out stereotypical sex roles are social as opposed to self-centered creatures. The stereotypically manly husband and father protects his wife and children; the wife and mother under the spell of the feminine mystique cares for her husband and children. In very different ways, both dominate those who surround them, but their domination can in many respects be beneficial and is by no means inherently indefensible. To advocate the androgynous personality type, who is "free to be you and me," is not obviously to improve on the sexual stereotypes. We are told that androgyny will enable us to combine the advantages of stereotypical masculinity and femininity within each and every one of us: men will at long last learn to cry, and women will finally learn to fight back. But one can argue just as plausibly that androgyny might cancel out the advantages of stereotypical masculinity and femininity, rather than combine them. Androgyny might in reality be nothing but the lowest common moral denominator: the effectual truth of "free to be you and me" might be for you to be free to care only about you, and for me to be free to care only about me.[17] Rousseau's argument is in some ways a compelling one: if men and women are really to care about one another, men and women must really be different from one another. To say this is not to assert that friendship is impossible among people of the same sex; it is only to acknowledge that husbands and wives live with one another far more intensely than friends normally do, that fathers and mothers are involved in cooperative undertakings— by which I mean the raising of children—whose importance far exceeds the undertakings normally characteristic of friends. Even if (and in a way especially if) the "natural" differences between the male and female personalities were rather minimal, it might still be in our collective interest as men and women not to obliterate them.

The argument in favor of androgyny would seem to be that men should devote themselves less to protecting women, and that women should devote themselves less to looking after men, as both men and women learn as individuals to become increasingly self-sufficient. But as Rousseau argues so forcefully, our sexuality is the clearest testimony to our mutual interdependence. Insofar as the call to androgyny is instead a call to our individual independence, we may rightly be at least somewhat skeptical about it. To deny that men as men and women as women need each other in any fundamental way necessarily liberates our self-centeredness.[18] We are not wrong to be somewhat suspicious of sexual stereotyping, but we should also be more suspicious of our suspicions than we customarily are.

Rousseau wishes to argue that men and women are equal because of their differences from one another, and not simply in spite of them. His picture of the harmonious interaction of men and women continues to be both recognizable and attractive even today. He can quite plausibly suggest that men are more likely to acquire some virtues, women others—and that in consequence men and women can complement or perfect each other, each sex taking satisfaction in its ability to aid and be aided by the other. As we have seen, however, the interaction which Rousseau depicts takes place in the private, domestic, romantic world of personal relations alone. He does not and to some extent cannot also envision such interaction in the world of economics and politics. In that second world, to which women have of right at last been admitted, the differences between men and women to which he points are of minimal importance, and often of none at all. "Feminine intuition" may or may not mean anything, but even if it exists it is irrelevant to the career of a computer programmer who happens to be a woman. There is obviously no female way as opposed to a male way to program computers, there are only more or less correct ways. In the world of husbands and wives Rousseau argues (to my mind quite plausibly) that men and women are and should be different from one another; in the world of workers and citizens, as the example of the computer programmer is meant to suggest, such differences are largely irrelevant. The great problem in the relations of the sexes today is whether the importance of the differences between men and women in domestic life can in some way be combined with the irrelevance of those differences in most spheres of economic and political life. Because Rousseau does not conceive of women as workers and citizens,[19] he cannot help us to solve that problem. Nevertheless, insofar as he points to the advantages of sexual differentiation (as opposed to its disadvantages, of which contemporary feminism has made us so well aware), he illuminates our problem.

The Case against Sexual Differentiation

Rousseau himself, of course, is no less aware of the dangers and pitfalls of sexual differentiation than are contemporary feminists; he merely emphasizes somewhat different dangers for somewhat different reasons. If in his first teaching he celebrates sexual differentiation for the power that it gives the sexes over one another, he condemns it in his second teaching for the very same reason. It may be true that sexuality gives men power over women, and women power over men; but insofar as, ideally, no one should have power over anyone, Rousseau is led to attack sexuality even as he praises it.

His ambivalence emerges very clearly in Book V of *Emile*. There he praises sexuality because of the moderate, limited character of the rule that it establishes between the sexes. We have seen him argue that Sophie prefers limited rule over a free man to absolute rule over a slave, that woman's cleverness makes her man's companion and not his slave (*Emile*, V, pp. 439, 471). Nevertheless, his own rhetoric calls into question the distinction between political and despotic rule upon which he rests his defense of sexual relations in his first teaching on sexuality. Time and again, notwithstanding the above disclaimers, he himself points out that women are indeed enslaved by their sexuality, and that they must there-fore enslave men as well. Rousseau himself concedes that the imperative that women be modest entails their enslavement. Since husbands must know that they are the biological fathers of the children whom they support, women must be "enslaved by public opinion [and] by authority" (*Emile*, V, pp. 361–62, 364–65, 377).

If women's biology enslaves them, as Rousseau suggests, they might logically conclude that it is necessary (and at long last possible, owing to technological developments) to alter or eradicate their biology. This is the solution to the problem of sexuality offered by the most radical of women's liberationists.[20] Rousseau cannot consider this possibility; sexual enslavement cannot be eliminated, simply because the reproduction of the species requires that women be enslaved by their bodies. Instead, since women must be enslaved, all he (or rather nature) can offer them by way of compensation is the opportunity to enslave men as well. Women compensate themselves for their slavery by using their modesty "to en-slave the strong" male sex as well (*Emile*, V, p. 358). Emile in particular is said to be Sophie's slave (*Emile*, V, p. 424). Slavery cannot be eliminated, but at least it can be generalized.[21]

Women cannot be independent, and so must make men dependent on them. Women cannot be free, and so must see to it that men share women's slavery. Rousseau's depiction of women is disturbing in that it often makes them seem so ineluctably monstrous because manipulative. If Rousseau praises women because they can acquire and make use of power, he also condemns them because they must acquire and make use of power. Rousseau's second teaching about sexuality is frightening be-cause it so heavily emphasizes woman's lack of self-sufficiency (and hence her need to dominate), as opposed to man's potential for self-sufficiency (and hence his lack of the need to dominate). The second teaching in effect retells the fairy tale about Little Red Riding Hood, but radically reverses it by recasting the sexual roles: innocent (masculine) Little Red Riding Hood meets terrifying (feminine) Big Bad Wolf.[22]

Rousseau is weakest as a student of sexuality insofar as he exaggerates the extent of female dependence and the extent of the possibility of male independence. Nevertheless, even (and in a way especially) because of his great suspicion of sexuality, Rousseau tells us much about our own sexuality. Because he emphasizes the political character of sexuality, its unavoidable connection with domination, in Rousseau's own life he offers, however hesitantly, the alternative path of the ultimate rejection of sexuality, or the adoption of asexual anarchy. If dependence is painful, and if sexuality makes dependence inevitable, one may prefer to restrict one's sexual encounters to the realm of the imagination, or ultimately to avoid them altogether. Whatever his preachings to others, in his own life Rousseau emerges as the prophet of narcissism and androgyny. Rousseau articulates more starkly than do the most radical feminists the dangers and difficulties with which sexual interdependence can confront us. He is more profound than they are, however. He rejects as utopian a vision of sexuality which would eliminate these dangers and difficulties; no recasting of sex roles could ever make it impossible for men and women to make one another miserable, and no sexual relations in which men and women could not make one another miserable could be sexual relations in which men and women could make one another happy.

Because sexuality makes us dependent and can make us unhappy, at some level we will always feel the temptation to flee from sexuality. Rousseau suggests that sexuality is inherently unsatisfactory, that in a way it must necessarily arouse in us a discontent. For this reason his second teaching on sexuality suggests that we might do better to be asexual, or at least to escape from the chains of heterosexual interdependence. Nevertheless, it is clearly not a teaching that Rousseau either expects or wants a great many people to listen to. In fact, one might say that his first teaching is democratic (because it is meant for the many), and his second teaching aristocratic (meant only for few). Whatever dissatisfactions mutual interdependence may engender, he would say that the vast majority of us must inevitably depend upon one another; only the exceptionally rare individual could hope to escape from dependence. In our time, however, participants in the sexual revolution may be said to have attempted to democratize Rousseau's aristocratic teaching: the impulses toward narcissism, androgyny, and polymorphous perversity have been liberated, as part of a flight from the constraints imposed by monogamous heterosexual interdependence.[23] It is possible to regard Rousseau as a prophet of the sexual revolution, in that he speaks openly of his masturbation, masochism, exhibitionism, and homosexual experience;[24] but this is to say that he has followers because of what he says (in his *Confessions*) he did, and most definitely not because of what he says (in *Emile*) we should do.[25] But it should be apparent that Rousseau understands his liberation from ordinary sexuality as an escape from society; he would never have believed that such a liberation could instead form the hedonistic basis for a society. Rousseau is the most unlikely of prophets for a hedonistic mass-liberation movement, because he contends that the hedonism and liberation which he personified are possible only for isolated individuals, hence by definition not for the masses. Rousseau emphasizes the mutual incompatibility of the asocial liberated individual and society; the contemporary cult of personal liberation has instead attempted an untenable synthesis of Rousseau's two teachings, insofar as it advocates a society composed of liberated individuals.

Nevertheless, I do not want to seem too apocalyptic; even now most of us live in a world of heterosexual interdependence to which Rousseau's first teaching is still quite relevant. That world is, on balance, a better world than Rousseau makes it seem, because women are less like the Big Bad Wolf and men are less like Little Red Riding Hood than he suggests. Women do depend on men, but women are not as totally incapable of self-sufficiency as he suggests. Men do depend on women, but men are not as capable of achieving self-sufficiency as he sometimes suggests.

Rousseau's sexual politics is, we have seen, based on something like the Aristotelian definition of the political as the interchange of rule among equals. Interestingly enough, this is far less true of Rousseau's politics proper. There the generalized will is intended to result in the elimination of particular wills and factions within the polity. The generalized will therefore promotes not so much the interchange of rule among equals as its avoidance. The general will aims to substitute the rule of all over each for the exchange of roles between ruling and ruled parts. In politics Rousseau is uncomfortable with the rule of some over others, and does not regard the occasional exchange of roles between rulers and ruled as sufficient guarantee against the abuse of authority. One can argue that Rousseau's political writings would be more plausible were he as willing to accept the interchange of rule among political partners as he is between sexual partners. One can also argue, however, that Rousseau's sexual politics too would be more plausible were he less ambivalent about the equality of the sexual partners, and hence about the legitimacy of their interchange of rule. Women are not usually the potential tyrants he sometimes makes them seem, and men are not usually the potential solitaries he sometimes makes them seem.[26]

Rousseau's presentation of sexuality is in some respects irrelevant to contemporary conditions; in others, it seems unpersuasive. But for all of its weaknesses, I have argued that the Rousseauian presentation also has great and undeniable strengths, which continue to be relevant. Let me conclude by recalling one of them: it is often a good thing, Rousseau remarks, for countries "to be able to raise themselves back up to the level of love" (*Letter*, p. 118). This is true of us today, and in spite of all Rousseau's ambivalences, he can help us to understand why. Properly moralized, sexuality can bring us together, and sexuality can make us free.

Notes

Chapter One

1. Susan Moller Okin, *Women in Western Political Thought* (Princeton: Princeton University Press, 1979), p. 99.
2. Ibid., p. 120.
3. Brigitte Berger, "What Women Want," *Commentary*, March 1979, p. 65.
4. Perhaps the most useful source for a study of Rousseau's materialism is his discussion in *Confessions*, IX, p. 422, of a projected (though ultimately abandoned) work, "La Morale Sensitive," or "Le Matérialisme du Sage." In this work Rousseau hoped to investigate what motivates human behavior; for example, why human beings at some times resist temptation, but at other times succumb to it. He concludes that such changes "depended in great part upon the impression which external objects had previously made upon us, and that we, being continually modified by our senses and our bodily organs, exhibited, without perceiving it, the effect of these modifications of ourselves, in our ideas, our feelings, and even in our actions. The numerous and striking observations which I had collected were unassailable, and, from their physical principles, seemed to me well adapted to furnish an external rule of conduct, which, being altered according to circumstances, might place or keep the mind in the condition most favourable to virtue. . . . Different climates, seasons, sounds, colours, darkness, light, the elements, food, noise, silence, movement, repose—all affect the bodily machine, and consequently the mind; all afford us a thousand opportunities, which will almost infallibly enable us to govern those feelings in their first beginnings, by which we allow ourselves to be dominated." What affects "the bodily machine . . . consequently [affects] the mind"; this is the vital premise underlying the whole of Rousseau's discussion of the relation between the sexes.
5. The contradiction between contemporary egalitarianism and contemporary materialism is well stated by Leszek Kolakowski, in his Introduction to *The Socialist Idea*, ed. Leszek Kolakowski and Stuart Hampshire (New York: Basic Books, 1974), p. 16: "We maintain that people should be considered as material beings, but nothing shocks us as much as the idea that people have bodies: it means that they are born, they die, they are young or old, men or women and that all these factors can play a role in social processes regardless of who owns the means of production."
6. See *Second*, p. 138: "It will be understood . . . how much natural inequality must increase in the human species through instituted inequality." See also p. 155, as well as *Social*, I, 9, p. 58: "Rather than destroying natural equality, the fundamental compact on the contrary substitutes a moral and legitimate equality for whatever physical inequality nature may have placed between men."
7. See *Second*, p. 181: "Moral inequality . . . is contrary to natural right whenever it is not combined in the same proportion with physical inequality."

8. It is noteworthy that women are blamed for the corruption of artistic sensibility in a work one of whose central tenets is that artistic sensibility is inherently corrupting. On this point, see Jacques Derrida, *Of Grammatology*, trans. Gayatri Chakravorty Spivak (Baltimore: The Johns Hopkins University Press, 1976), p. 181.

9. In an editorial note in his translation (p. 72), Masters suggests that "the reference is clearly to Plato's *Republic*, especially 451c–457c." But cf. Henri Gouhier, *Les Méditations Métaphysiques de Jean-Jacques Rousseau* (Paris: Librairie Philosophique J. Vrin, 1970), p. 145n, where *Laws*, 780a–d, is suggested as the passage to which Rousseau here refers.

10. In chapter 4 below, I suggest why Rousseau thinks himself competent, as a man, to educate the women who educate men. In effect it is because he claims to transcend the distinction between the sexes by virtue of his imagination. He is neither male nor female because he is both.

11. Berger, p. 65.

Chapter Two

1. *The Politics of Aristotle*, Ernest Barker, ed. and trans. (London: Oxford University Press, 1958), 1259b. For Aristotle "the relation of the male to the female is permanently that in which the statesman stands to his fellow-citizens." Thus there is no "interchange of ruling and being ruled" between man and wife, hence theirs is not truly a political relationship. See, however, *Politics* 1277b, and *Nicomachean Ethics*, trans. Martin Ostwald (Indianapolis: Bobbs-Merrill Library of Liberal Arts, 1962), 1160b, where Aristotle acknowledges that there are spheres in which women predominate over men. One might therefore contend that, like Rousseau, Aristotle recognizes that women can rule men; it is nevertheless the case that, unlike Rousseau, he severely criticizes Sparta, because it is the one regime that he discusses in which women do rule men. See *Politics* 1269b, and the comparison between Aristotle's and Rousseau's analyses of Sparta in chapter 3 below.

2. See the discussion below of the role played by male *amour-propre* in fostering sexual desire.

3. According to Rousseau, "the moral element of love is an artificial sentiment born of the usage of society, and extolled with much skill and care by women in order to establish their ascendancy and make dominant the sex that ought to obey" (*Second*, pp. 134–35). One might therefore assume that by nature men rule women, but this is not the case. In society (as we shall see in this and subsequent chapters) women "ought to obey" men (though even this obedience is qualified). But the opposite of women's ruling men in society is not men's ruling women by nature but the absence of any rule by nature. See the conclusion of the comparison between Rousseau and Buffon below.

4. Compare the discussion of compensating sexual inequalities in the *Letter to D'Alembert*, p. 84: If women and not men took the sexual initiative, "since the power and the will, always in disaccord, would never permit the desires to be mutually shared, love would no longer be the support of nature but its destroyer and plague." Note however that the *Letter* but not the *Second Discourse* emphasizes the role of female modesty in compensating for the inequalities between the sexes.

5. On Lucretius as Rousseau's source, see Leo Strauss, *Natural Right and History* (Chicago: The University of Chicago Press, 1953), pp. 264 and 271n, and Jean Morel, "Recherches sur les Sources du *Discours de l'Inégalité*," *Annales de la Société Jean-Jacques Rousseau* 5 (1909): 163–64.

6. Lucretius, *On The Nature of Things*, trans. Cyril Bailey (Oxford: Oxford University Press, 1910), V, 962–65.

7. *Le Droit de la Nature et des Gens*, trans. Jean Barbeyrac (Leiden: Chez J. de Wetstein, 1759), 2: 1, 6.

8. See Victor Goldschmidt, *Anthropologie et Politique: Les Principes du Système de Rousseau* (Paris: Librairie Philosophique J. Vrin, 1974), p. 357: "Rousseau is not, to be sure, the first

among the theoreticians to consider love as a possible cause of dissension; but he is really the first to see in it the single argument that one could plausibly produce in favor of the thesis of natural war."

9. Goldschmidt, p. 367.

10. Lucretius, IV, 1073–1120, and Goldschmidt, p. 363. On Buffon as Rousseau's source, see Otis Fellows, "Buffon and Rousseau: Aspects of Relationship," *PMLA* 75 (June 1960): 184–96, Goldschmidt, pp. 362–64, Morel, p. 183, and Jean Starobinski, "Rousseau et Buffon," in *Jean-Jacques Rousseau: La Transparence et l'Obstacle Suivi de Sept Essais sur Rousseau* (Paris: Gallimard, 1971), pp. 380–92.

11. *Discours Sur La Nature des Animaux*, in *Oeuvres Complètes* (Paris: Chez Verdière et Ladrange, 1824–31), 16: 83.

12. On p. 183 Morel argues for the similarity between the views of Buffon and Rousseau. On p. 364 Goldschmidt notes the distinction between Rousseau's view of "moral love" and Buffon's equation of it with vanity.

13. See also the subsequent discussion of vanity, in the context of the comparison between the *Second Discourse* and the *Essay on the Origin of Languages*.

14. *Histoire Naturelle de l'Homme*, in *Oeuvres Complètes*, 13: 159–60.

15. *Histoire Naturelle des Animaux Carnassiers*, in *Oeuvres Complètes*, 18: 412: "We do not suppose in accord with a philosopher, one of the most haughty critics of humanity [a note of Buffon's here refers to Rousseau by name], that there is greater distance from man in pure nature to the savage than from the savage to us."

16. *Histoire Naturelle des Animaux Carnassiers*, in *Oeuvres Complètes*, 18: 415.

17. *Histoire Naturelle de l'Homme*, p. 160. Note however that in *Histoire Naturelle des Animaux Carnassiers*, p. 415, savage couples are said to have spoken "the language of love" to one another.

18. *Histoire Naturelle de l'Homme*, p. 160.

19. *Social*, I, 2, p. 47: "The most ancient of all societies and the only natural one, is that of the family."

20. Rousseau appends a note to the 1782 edition of the *Second Discourse*, p. 112, in which he indicates that females of certain kangaroo-like South American species essentially share the advantages possessed by the human female biped.

21. A proof offered by Rousseau (*Second*, p. 185) to demonstrate that the human animal is naturally a biped relates to the question of mothers nursing children: "The breast of a woman [is] very well placed for a biped who holds her child in her arms."

22. See John Locke, *Two Treatises of Government*, ed. Peter Laslett (New York: New American Library, 1965) II, pars. 79–80.

23. In order for the pure state of nature not to evolve toward civilization, conception there must be infrequent. Yet while Rousseau praises the pure state of nature (in which conception is infrequent), he also condemns civil society, precisely on account of the infrequency of conception in its midst. See *Second*, p. 197: "How many shameful ways there are to prevent the birth of men and trick nature." In civil society nature is tricked, whereas in the state of nature it is fulfilled, if sexual acts do not result in many pregnancies.

24. But cf. Roger D. Masters, *The Political Philosophy of Rousseau* (Princeton: Princeton University Press, 1968), p. 125, where it is argued that woman's omnivorousness was the condition of her being able to raise children without a male's assistance even in the pure state of nature. The argument about females' employing male assistance (and the explanation of how the family "becomes" natural) is to be found in Goldschmidt, pp. 255–56.

25. See Jean Starobinski's note in *Oeuvres Complètes*, 3: 1343: "Technical modifications ... precede and determine the moral and social transformation."

26. See Lucretius, V, 1011–12, where he too links the birth of·the household to the invention of the house.

27. On the distinction between romantic love and the conjugal affection characteristic of the original family, see also Goldschmidt, p. 422.

28. In the *Second Discourse*, p. 153, by contrast, the invention of agriculture is explained as an effect of other economic developments: "the invention of the other arts was . . . necessary to force the human race to apply itself to that of agriculture." (Even in the *Second Discourse*, however, we have seen that the "first revolution"—the invention of the family—preceded the second "great revolution"—the invention of private property, leading finally to the creation of the polity. Cf. *Second*, pp. 146, 152.)

Rousseau sometimes treats economic developments more or less independently; at other times he presents them in the context of, and in part as effects of, erotic developments. We learn from the *Essay*, p. 46, that this apparent discrepancy results from geographical divergences: "In southern climes, where nature is bountiful, [economic] needs are born of [erotic] passion. In cold countries, where she is miserly, passions are born of need." For this reason (p. 47), "the first words among [northerners] were not *love me* [*aimez-moi*] but *help me* [*aidez-moi*]." In view of Rousseau's claim that nature is "bountiful" more often than it is "miserly," it is not surprising that he asserts the predominance of the southern pattern of development; that is to say, he asserts that erotic developments historically have more often been causes of economic developments (hence ultimately of political developments), less often effects of economic developments. Cf. *Essay*, p. 30: "The human race originated in warm climes; . . . on two-thirds of the globe, winter is hardly known."

29. In *Corsica*, p. 295, Rousseau again indicates the importance of romantic love in creating peoples out of families. Speaking of the Swiss, he says that "Peace and concord reigned in their numerous families. Marriages were almost the only subjects of negotiation between them, and here inclination alone was consulted." On particularized love as a cause of generalized sociability, see also Goldschmidt, p. 447.

30. See also the earlier discussion of vanity, in the context of the comparison between Rousseau and Buffon.

31. Rousseau's note to the *Second Discourse*, wherein he distinguishes *amour-propre* (translated by Masters as "vanity") from love of oneself is also relevant to the distinction suggested here. The two passions have social effects comparable to the different social effects of love as described in the *Essay* and the *Second Discourse*. Love of oneself (like love in the *Essay*) "produces humanity and virtue." *Amour-propre* (like the "children of love" in the *Second Discourse*) "inclines each individual to have a greater esteem for himself than anyone else, inspires in men all the harm they do to one another." See *Second*, pp. 221–22.

32. Rousseau's argument is of course based upon the fact that sexual impotence is a problem for males, not for females; human females but not human males have the capacity to engage in many sexual acts in rapid succession. (We have already seen Rousseau's emphasis on women's unrestricted sexual capacity in the state of nature above.)

As will shortly become apparent, however, Rousseau's claim about female sexuality here differs from his assertion in the *Second Discourse*: there he refers to the infinite sexual *capacity* of women, whereas here he refers to their infinite sexual *desire*. Rousseau is hardly original in stressing the infinitude of female sexual desire; one need only think of the depictions of women in many of the comedies of Aristophanes. But the fact that precedent for an argument exists in the works of an earlier writer (and a comic poet, at that) is not, to be sure, an adequate proof for what Rousseau intends as a scientific assertion.

Rousseau's argument about the sexual capacity of women is correct; his argument that female sexual desire is in some sense stronger than male sexual desire may be correct as well. But neither of these arguments justifies his belief in the insatiability of female sexual desire. This is important, because (as we will see below) it is female desire, not female capacity, which can be said to be threatening to men. To the extent that Rousseau asserts but does not adequately support his belief in the insatiability of female desire, the biological basis of the male fear of women (and hence of the second teaching, which contends that men might be advised to be independent of women) is therefore rendered questionable.

33. See the discussion of the status of sex as a natural need towards this chapter's beginning.

34. Note the praise of "veiled desires," and compare it to Rousseau's reluctance (expressed in the *Second Discourse*, p. 198) to "tear off the veil that covers so many horrors." The veiled horrors in question are the aborted births of what would have been illegitimate children. See also the approval of the veiling of sexuality in *Emile*, IV, p. 218. What is most pleasant as well as most painful about human sexual activity should be treated circumspectly. Rousseau's praise of "veiled" sexuality, of "obstacles," should perhaps lead to a qualification of the thesis, brilliantly argued by Jean Starobinski, that Rousseau's central concern is the overcoming of obstacles separating human beings, or the achievement of full spontaneity among them. See the discussion of Rousseau's image of the veil as the obstacle to human spontaneity in Starobinski, especially chapters 1, 4, and 5.

35. *Histoire Naturelle de l'Homme*, pp. 160–61.

36. Note that in the *Letter*, p. 87, Rousseau provides himself with a "fallback position" in case the naturalness of female modesty should be denied: "Even if it could be denied that a special sentiment of chasteness was natural to women, would it be any less true that in society their lot ought to be a domestic and retired life?" See also the discussion of feminine modesty in Derrida, pp. 179–80.

37. In the *Letter*, pp. 83–84, Rousseau adds a second argument as to modesty's role in preventing sexual conflicts: "The shame which veils the pleasures of love from the eyes of others . . . is the safeguard that nature has given in common to the two sexes for a time when they are in a state of weakness and forgetfulness of themselves which puts them at the mercy of the first comer." This argument for the natural status of modesty would seem to be more applicable in Hobbes's state of nature than in Rousseau's.

38. Hobbes, *Leviathan: Or the Matter, Forme and Power of a Commonwealth Ecclesiaticall and Civil*, ed. Michael Oakeshott (London: Collier-Macmillan, 1962), chapter 13, p. 98.

39. On p. 176, Derrida makes the analogy between Rousseau's discussion of sexual relationships and Hegel's dialectic of the master-slave relationship, in commenting on a passage occurring later in Book V of *Emile* than those discussed in this chapter. The analogy is a good one, but Derrida's use of it is inadequate, because he fails to note how very dialectical Rousseau's reasoning is: he sees only Rousseau's critique, and not also his defense, of the reversal of roles through which women come to predominate over men.

Chapter Three

1. Rousseau's approval of the exclusion of women from direct political participation is apparent from his discussion of the ancient city, to be found in this chapter below. Cf. also a pronouncement of the heroine of his novel *Julie* (quoted in chapter 5 below, p. 122).

2. Rousseau rejects the validity of "the right of the strongest" to rule in *Social Contract*, I, 3.

3. Women's susceptibility to pregnancy suggests an additional reason for Rousseau's exclusion of them from the battlefield: individual females are more important than are individual males for the perpetuation of the species, hence women's lives are intrinsically more valuable than are men's. A hypothetically devastated community of fifty women and one man could repopulate itself far more easily than a community of fifty men and one woman (and about as easily, in fact, as a community of fifty men and fifty women). Given the importance Rousseau ascribes to population increase as a sign of good government, and given his fear of the depopulation of Europe, this would be a major concern for him. Cf. *Social*, III, 9, p. 96: "All other things being equal, the government under which—without external aid, without naturalization, without colonies—the citizens populate and multiply the most is infallibly the best." Cf. also *Emile*, I, pp. 44–45: "This practice [women's use of contraception], added to the other causes of depopulation, presages the impending fate of Europe. The sciences, the arts, the philosophy, and the morals that this practice engenders will not be long in making a desert of it. It will be peopled with ferocious beasts. The change of inhabitants will not be great."

4. Consider in this context Rousseau's critique of partial societies as corrupters of the general will, in *Social*, II, 3, p. 61: "In order for the general will to be well expressed, it is . . . important that there be no partial society in the State." The family can be understood as a partial society of this sort; to the extent that women have greater allegiances to their particular families than do men, it would be harder for women than for men to be citizens.

For a related reason, the *Social Contract* says as little as it does about human sexuality and the role of the family within the state. If the good citizen by definition is denatured, the citizen can be understood only if one abstracts from the more natural sexual and familial ties which might bind him in opposition to the political tie. In this context, see Judith N. Shklar, *Men and Citizens: A Study of Rousseau's Social Theory* (Cambridge: Cambridge University Press, 1969), p. 21: "The Spartan city is explicitly based on the destruction of the family and of all its emotional and social gratifications. . . . If citizens are to be denatured so as to identify wholly with the republic, then their loyalties must not be shared with a family." See also the comment of Brigitte Berger quoted in chapter 1, p. 2, above.

As we shall see, however, Rousseau has more than one understanding of the political implications of the family; the family can be thought to supplement the state, and need not always be thought to subvert it. Even according to the *Social Contract* (as we saw in note 3 above), the best government is that in which the population increases most rapidly. One could take this to mean that the best government is one under which family life is most harmonious—even if it is also the case that the best government is one in which the harmonious family is clearly subordinated to the state.

5. I have grouped hidden and personal rule together, because they both differ from the Rousseauian ideal of manifest impersonal rule, and because Rousseau links them both with the rule of women. It is obvious, however, that hidden and personal rule are not identical: a despot's rule is personal but by no means hidden. In discussing Rousseau's conception of the political impact of women, I will be emphasizing their hidden rule much more than their personal rule.

It is true that Rousseau admires the hidden rule of women; it is also true, however, that his insistence that rule be manifest also leads him to criticize what he takes to be the necessarily devious and manipulative character of their rule. Rousseau's ambivalence toward women can thus in part be explained by the fact that legitimate rule is not in and of itself efficacious rule, and by the ensuing tension between the legitimacy and the efficacy of all rule. For a related argument, cf. note 4 in chapter 4 below.

An attempt to resolve this tension would take me well beyond the scope of my argument. I therefore limit myself to noting that the tension is well illustrated by Rousseau's recognition of the need for a government as well as a sovereign. A separate government must exist, even though Rousseau contends that the "government makes a continual effort against sovereignty," which it will eventually manage to overthrow: cf. *Social*, III, 10, p. 96. The laws must be made by all (who jointly comprise the sovereign) and must apply to all. But Rousseau realizes that many decisions must deal with particulars, not generalities; these decisions, which are the province of the government, should be made by a few, not by all. Cf. ibid., III, 1, p. 78: "The executive power cannot belong to the general public in its legislator's or sovereign capacity, because this power consists solely of particular acts which are not within the jurisdiction of the law, nor consequently of the sovereign, all of whose acts can only be laws." Cf. also ibid., II, 6, p. 66. In one sense, the government is clearly subordinate to the sovereign; in another sense, however, the government actually exercises much of the power which the sovereign formally possesses.

It is illuminating in this context to observe that Rousseau associates women with knowledge of particulars and not of generalities, and that he specifically analogizes woman's rule in marriage to that of the government within the state. Cf. *Emile*, V, p. 387: "She must . . . make a profound study of the mind of man—not an abstraction of the mind of man in general, but the minds of the men around her." Cf. ibid., p. 408: "She ought to reign in the home as a minister does in a state—by getting herself commanded to do what she wants to do."

6. The interests of rulers as well as those of the ruled require that political authority be openly recognized. Rousseau generally associates the desire for political rule with the desire that one's rule be recognized by others. Political ambition is therefore a manifestation of *amour-propre*. In this respect, the male desire for the appearance of power can be said to be more political than the female desire for the reality of power. Note that the "political goods" discussed in chapter 2 above all involve the recognition by others of one's power, not simply the reality of one's possession of power.

7. Cf. also Rousseau's praise of Servius's division of the Roman populace into classes, in *Social*, IV, 4, p. 115: "In order that the people would have less understanding of the consequences of this last division, Servius pretended to give it a military appearance."

8. Cf. Shklar, p. 156: "To be truly effective political authority must penetrate to the very heart."

9. Rousseau's association of women with personal rule is also evident in the comparison between Julie and Wolmar as figures of authority in the *Nouvelle Héloïse*. Cf. chapter 5 below, note 18. Cf. also chapter 4, note 23, and the discussion in chapter 4 of Mademoiselle Lambercier.

10. *Discourses on the First Ten Books of Titus Livius*, trans. Christian E. Detmold, in *The Prince and the Discourses* (New York: The Modern Library, 1940), II, 2, p. 285.

11. We will see that the women of antiquity controlled their men to a considerable degree; this is not, however, to deny the obvious fact that they were controlled in turn by their men to an astonishing degree. Rousseau realizes very well that the women of antiquity were almost totally deprived of individual freedom; as can be seen from the discussions of the ancient city below, he readily acknowledges that the women of Sparta and Rome were "shut up" and "imprison[ed]" in their homes. But they were compensated for their lack of personal liberty by the power which they exercised over others. The women of antiquity were not free, even though they ruled to a considerable extent. In this respect, however, women are wholly comparable to the possessors of formal political authority, since Rousseau maintains that rule over others necessarily entails subjection of oneself. Cf. *Social*, I, 1, p. 46: "One who believes himself the master of others is nonetheless a greater slave than they." Cf. also *Emile*, IV, p. 244: "Kings" are "slaves of all that obey them."

12. See the discussion in chapter 2 of the political implications of romantic love.

13. From a surface reading of the story, one would conclude that the Spartan rejoices because he is such a good citizen. But see Masters, p. 299n, where he argues that Rousseau may have chosen this story not so much to illustrate as to call into question the reality of Spartan dedication.

14. In the *Second Discourse*, by contrast, Spartan child-rearing practices appear to be thought of as natural: "Nature treats [children] precisely as the law of Sparta treated the children of citizens: it renders strong and robust those who are well constituted and makes all the others perish" (*Second*, p. 106). This fact again illustrates that paternal concern for children is only ambiguously natural according to Rousseau. See the contrast between maternal and paternal love in chapter 2 above.

15. *The Republic of Plato*, trans. Allan Bloom (New York: Basic Books, 1968), V, 463c.

16. Ibid., 467a–b.

17. Rousseau explicitly acknowledges his indebtedness to Plato for his belief in public education in an autobiographical context, while excusing himself for having abandoned his children. "In handing over my children to public education, for want of means to bring them up myself, in deciding to fit them for becoming workmen and peasants rather than adventurers and fortunehunters, I thought that I was behaving like a citizen and a father, and considered myself a member of Plato's Republic" (*Confessions*, VIII, p. 367). I have altered the translation.

18. One can say that Sparta only "more or less" maintains the usual family unit because Lycurgus, like Plato, encouraged the communism of women and children (and also, as we saw in n. 14 above, because the Spartans abandoned their unhealthy offspring at birth). It is important to realize, however, that the familial communism instituted by Lycurgus was less radical than its Platonic counterpart. Lycurgus encouraged an elderly man to lend out his wife to a younger man so that the elderly man might have "a son *to himself*." Or a Spartan might ask to borrow the wife of a fellow Spartan "that he might raise . . . worthy and well-allied children *for himself*." See Plutarch's "Lycurgus," in *The Lives of the Noble Grecians and Romans*, trans. John Dryden, revised by Arthur Hugh Clough (New York: The Modern Library, n.d.), p. 61. The emphasis is mine in both cases. A wife is borrowed or lent only with her husband's permission, not by the decision of the government. Whereas in the *Republic*, it is the rulers who determine who is to procreate with whom, when, and how often. Men and women beget and bear "for the city," not for themselves. *Republic*, V, 460c. And children, of course, are raised communally, without knowing the identity of their true parents. See *Republic*, V, 457d–461e.

19. Presumably Plato's detractors wrongly criticize him for advocating the random copulation characteristic of the early stages of Rousseau's state of nature. In fact, as remarked in note 18 above, nothing could be less random than procreation in the *Republic*, which is strictly regulated by the government. Procreation is illicit unless approved by the rulers. See *Republic*, V, 461a–b.

20. It is not certain that Rousseau's argument here is correct, but I am inclined to think that it is. One might argue that even if the individual family unit were abolished, it could still be the case that all of the officers in charge of rearing the children collectively would be female. But Socrates says that "the officers established for this purpose are men or women, or both, for presumably the offices are common to women and men." *Republic*, V, 460b.

21. It is admittedly difficult to understand how Rousseau can think that the citizen is "denatured," while also believing that a "natural base" for citizenship exists in the family; cf. Okin, p. 192. But if what is most natural (for males) is not dedication to their families but solipsistic preoccupation with their individual selves, the suggested harmony between family and city becomes somewhat more comprehensible. If by nature male individuals care only for themselves, dedication to any group would be problematic; in learning to overcome natural selfishness through dedication to the family (the most natural group), individual males could be said to be provided with the preconditions for dedication to a less natural group—the city. Different as the lover and the citizen may be, the citizen can nevertheless be said to resemble the lover, in that each "detach[es] himself . . . from the baseness of the human *I*" (*Emile*, V, p. 391; the emphasis appears in the translation). The man who depends upon a woman forms only a part of the "moral person" (ibid., p. 377) which the two collectively compose; he thereby bears a certain resemblance to "civil man," who "is only a fractional unity dependent on the denominator; his value is determined by his relation to the whole" (ibid., I, pp. 39–40). In view of these similarities, it is conceivable that willingness to subordinate oneself to any group (however small) may ultimately make possible subordination to considerably larger groups. For a comparable argument (which admittedly contradicts other statements by Rousseau, e.g., ibid., I, p. 39), cf. *Geneva*, I, 2, pp. 161–62: "We conceive of the general society [i.e., the whole human race] on the basis of our particular societies; the establishment of small republics makes us think about the large one, and we do not really begin to become men until after we have been citizens."

22. Recall that Rousseau makes a similar argument about the sexual act itself: men's desire is strengthened, they become more potent, when they seem to overcome the resistance of weaker women by virtue of their superior strength. See the discussion of sex as a psychological need, not a physical one, in chapter 2 above.

23. See *Fragments*, p. 488: "If the state is well governed it must prescribe common rules to all the families and provide in a uniform manner for the authority of the father, the obedience of servants, and the education of children."

24. Rousseau also rejects the familial analogy in *Political*, pp. 209–11, in *Geneva*, I, 5, pp. 168–71, and in *Fragments*, pp. 487–88. See also Shklar, p. 193.

25. This statement occurs in the context of a comparison with the modern Genevan republic. Women actually "did . . . command" at Sparta; they deserve to [but one may infer in fact do not] command at Geneva." Thus the ancient republic is characterized not by lesser but in fact by greater feminine influence than is the case in its modern (and presumably inferior) counterpart. See also the discussion below of the decrease in the influence of modern women.

26. *Politics*, II, 1269b.

27. "Lycurgus," p. 60.

28. This portrait of a communal celebration, in which women's desire to please has beneficial consequences for the community, calls to mind the favorable description of communal celebration in the *Essay on the Origin of Languages*, discussed in chapter 2 above. For a discussion of public festivals, see Starobinski, pp. 116–21.

29. By contrast, however, see *Letter*, p. 134.

30. Rousseau's account of Spartan sexuality is an example of extreme historical revisionism. All of the ancient sources agree that the Spartans were exemplary citizens; but these same sources also portray Sparta as a city peopled largely by homosexuals and nymphomaniacs, and not by the good family men and devoted wives described by Rousseau.

Rousseau may not wholly believe in the historical accuracy of his revisionist interpretation of Sparta. I say this because he undoubtedly does not believe very much in the importance of historical accuracy. See *Emile*, IV, p. 238: "The fidelity of history is of less interest than the truth of morals and characters." Cf. also ibid., II, p. 156n. Keeping in mind Rousseau's view of the uses of history, one can perhaps understand his portrait of Sparta as a thought experiment: he may describe Spartan sexual relations as they could and should have been, regardless of whether they actually were that way. Rousseau argues that heterosexual affection and the indirect power of women can underlie republican citizenship; whether or not they actually did so to any great extent in Sparta is not ultimately very important to him.

31. Cf. Okin, pp. 104, 121, 130–31. *Sur Les Femmes* is thought to date from 1735. The *Essai Sur Les Événements* may also have been written then, but perhaps also as late as 1745, after Rousseau's service as secretary to Mme. Dupin, for whom he worked as a research assistant while she was contemplating a feminist work which she ultimately abandoned. For information on this period in Rousseau's career, together with a list of literary, historical, and philosophical works relevant to women which he read and annotated while working on this project, see Anicet Sénéchal, "Jean-Jacques Rousseau, Secrétaire de Madame Dupin, d'après des Documents Inédits, Avec un Inventaire des Papiers Dupin Dispersés en 1957 et 1958." *Annales de la Société Jean-Jacques Rousseau* 36 (1963–65): 173–290.

32. One might take this as an anticipation of Hegel's philosophy of history, because of the importance Rousseau accords to the passions as the forces motivating historical development. Hegel's doctrine, which in some respects coincides with Rousseau's statement, is as follows: "We assert then that nothing has been accomplished without interest on the part of the actors; and . . . we may affirm absolutely that *nothing great in the world* has been accomplished without *passion*." I doubt, however, that Hegel would emphasize specifically erotic passions as much as Rousseau does here. See *The Philosophy of History*, trans. J. Sibree (New York: Dover Publications, 1956), p. 23. The emphasis appears in the translation.

33. Jacques Derrida claims that, in the projected work, Rousseau planned to "recall the occasionally pernicious character of th[e] role [of women in history]." *Of Grammatology*, p. 342. He says this because, according to Rousseau's outline, the third part of the work was to have been devoted to "some observations on great men who . . . allowed themselves to be governed by women." I would question Derrida's claim, however, since there is no evidence in the fragment to indicate that Rousseau intended to demonstrate that it was necessarily bad for great men to have allowed themselves to be governed by women.

34. "All the faculties common to the two sexes are not equally distributed between them, but, taken together, they balance out" (*Emile*, V, p. 363; see also pp. 358 and 375).

35. I have restored the French *moeurs* when quoting from the *Letter*, feeling that it is less cumbersome than Bloom's translation "morals [manners]." Bloom discusses the meaning of this term and the difficulty in translating it in his note on pp. 149–50.

The secrecy of the rule of the women of antiquity is also suggested by the fact that only the male exemplar of Spartan citizenship (and not his female counterpart) has a name. Cf. the discussion of "the Lacedaemonian Pedaretus" and "a Spartan woman" in *Emile*, I, p. 40: I recount their respective stories above, in illustrating the difference between purification and denaturing. At least with respect to antiquity, Rousseau would agree with the feminist contention that "Anonymous was a woman." He would then part company with feminism because of his insistence that she should have been.

36. But see *Héros*, pp. 1271–72, in which Rousseau seems to argue the opposite position: "Temperance is still less [the virtue characteristic of the hero than is prudence]; heroism itself, which is nothing but an intemperance of glory, seems to exclude it. . . . Caesar was sober, but was he chaste, he who made unheard-of prostitutions known at Rome, and changed his sex at his taste?"

37. See *Emile*, I, p. 40: "Public instruction no longer exists and can no longer exist, because where there is no longer fatherland, there can no longer be citizens. These two words, *fatherland* and *citizen*, should be effaced from modern languages." The emphasis appears in the translation.

38. Vera Lee, *The Reign of Women in Eighteenth-Century France* (Cambridge, Mass.: Schenkman Publishing, 1975), pp. 115–16.

39. Ibid., p. 130.

40. Although the Spartan women "live[d] like the men" in that they were physically fit, unlike the men (and the women of the *Republic*) they did not go to war. Thus the strength of women was compatible with the maintenance of the distinction between the sexes. See *Emile*, V, p. 366: "The girls of Sparta exercised in military games like the boys—not to go to war but one day to bear children capable of withstanding war's fatigues."

41. *Discourses*, II, 2, pp. 285–86.

42. *Considerations on the Causes of the Greatness of the Romans and Their Decline*, trans. David Lowenthal (Ithaca, N.Y.: Cornell University Press Agora Editions, 1965), p. 189.

43. *The Spirit of the Laws*, book VII, chapter 9. See also XII, 6, XIX, 12.

44. Quoted in Peter Gay, *The Enlightenment: An Interpretation*. Vol. 1, *The Rise of Modern Paganism* (New York: Alfred A. Knopf, 1976), p. 150.

45. See also *Emile*, V, p. 392: "A young and beautiful girl will never despise her body, she will never in good faith grieve for the great sins her beauty causes to be committed, she will never sincerely shed tears before God for being a coveted object, and she will never be able to believe within herself that the sweetest sentiment of the heart is an invention of Satan. Give her other reasons that she can believe within and for herself, for these will never get through to her."

46. I noted above that Machiavelli blames not Christianity as such but rather its "false interpretation" for the modern demise of republicanism. Pressed by clerical attacks, Rousseau makes a similar response in speaking of the impact of Christianity on marital life. See *Montagne*, III, pp. 753–54: "One does wrong to make me say of the Gospel what I have said only of the Jansenists, the Methodists, and other devout people of today, who make of Christianity as terrible and displeasing a Religion as it is agreeable and sweet under the true law of Jesus Christ." He goes on to praise Jesus as a man who "fled neither pleasures nor festivities, who went to weddings, who saw women, who played with children."

47. See Denis de Rougemont, *Love in the Western World*, trans. Montgomery Belgion (New York: Fawcett, 1956), especially book II, chapter 5, and C.S. Lewis, *The Allegory of Love* (Oxford: Oxford University Press, 1975), chapter 1.

48. Rousseau does not explain why women have adopted a course of action which he

thinks runs so manifestly against their self-interest. Two possible explanations occur to me, only the second of which emphasizes women's conscious intentions. Rousseau may consider what one could call the sexual homogenization of modernity to be part of a more general homogenization which he elsewhere notes (and regrets). Increasing contacts among different sorts of people lessen the differences among them, resolving all differences in accordance with the lowest common denominator. The result is the production of a uniform type lacking distinctive character. Cf. *First*, pp. 37–38: in simpler societies, "differences of conduct announced at first glance those of character. . . . Today, . . . a base and deceptive uniformity prevails in our customs, and all minds seem to have been cast in the same mould." Cf. also *Emile*, V, p. 453. This line of argument would seem to suggest that sexual homogenization is regrettable but unstoppable; but insofar as Rousseau writes to prevent and reverse sexual homogenization, he cannot completely accept such an argument.

Since Rousseau writes in order to persuade women to act differently, he clearly believes that the effeminacy of men results largely if not entirely from women's conscious intention. Presumably he would say that women have chosen to make men effeminate because they do not like to feel themselves dependent upon men; if men are not strong, women will no longer have to rely upon them. Rousseau's contention is that such a course of action on women's part is self-defeating. Women themselves can never be strong, he would say; their alternatives are either to be weak or to borrow and manipulate the strength of others (i.e., men). Women should therefore not make men effeminate, because men must be different from women if women are to be aided by men (and are to control men). On this point, cf. the discussion of Mary Wollstonecraft's critique of Rousseau, in chapter 4 below.

49. See the contrast between the *Second Discourse* and the *Essay on the Origin of Languages* in chapter 2 above.

50. For another view of this issue, however, cf. the discussion of Rousseau's imaginative bisexuality, and its relation to his art and his quest for self-sufficiency, in chapter 4 below.

51. Compare Rousseau's similar discussion of the purpose of his novel *Julie* (*Julie*, Second Preface, pp. 23–24).

52. Gaspard Vallette, *Jean-Jacques Rousseau, Genevois* (Paris and Geneva: Librairie Plon and A. Jullien, 1911), pp. 122 and 134.

53. By saying that Geneva preserves only "some image of ancient *moeurs*," Rousseau points, however, to the differences as well as the similarities between Geneva and the classical republics. Politically, Calvinist Geneva is inferior to pagan antiquity, but superior to the corrupt Catholic monarchies of modern Europe. See Rousseau's letter to Tronchin of November 26, 1758, in *Correspondance*, 5:242: "Here [in the circles] is the middle education that suits us precisely, between the public education of the Greek Republics and the domestic education of the Monarchies."

54. See also *Letter*, p. 71n: "Formerly, [men] slew one another for a mistress; in living more familiarly with women, they have found that it was not worth the effort to fight for them." See also Burke's lament upon the death of the age of chivalry: "On this scheme of things [i.e., that of the Enlightenment], a king is but a man, a queen is but a woman; a woman is but an animal; and an animal not of the highest order. All homage paid to the sex in general as such, and without distinct views, is to be regarded as romance and folly." *Reflections on the Revolution in France*, ed. Thomas H. D. Mahoney (Indianapolis: Bobbs-Merrill Library of Liberal Arts, 1955), p. 87.

55. Strauss, p. 259. Rousseau makes similar arguments about the value of theatrical representations in particular. See *Letter*, pp. 58–60, and the Preface to *Narcisse*, pp. 972–73. In effect, these arguments serve as Rousseau's apology for his career as a dramatist.

56. On the history of *Narcisse*, see *Confessions*, III, VII, and VIII, pp. 123, 289, 350, 399–400. See also the Introduction and introductory note by Jacques Scherer in *Oeuvres Complètes*, 2: lxxxvi–lxxxix, and 1858–65.

57. *Confessions*, VIII, p. 400. Compare his remarks in the Preface to *Narcisse* (composed in 1753), p. 963: he describes his literary juvenilia such as *Narcisse* as "illegitimate children

which one still caresses with pleasure while blushing at being their father, to whom one says one's last good-byes, and whom one sends forth to seek their fortune, without very much concerning oneself with what will become of them."

58. To say this is not to assert what is obviously untrue, that Valère (or the effeminate moderns whom Rousseau criticizes elsewhere) is consciously homosexual, asexual, or onanistic. Even as a narcissist, after all, he is attracted to what he thinks is a picture of another woman. But before Angelique cures him, Valère's generalized sexual desire leads him more to want to exploit attractive women generally than to depend emotionally on any particular woman in a serious way; the unreformed Valère uses sexuality so as to avoid rather than to express an emotional dependence upon others. Understood in this way, Rousseau's analysis in *Narcisse* continues to be readily applicable to contemporary sexual politics; Tom Wolfe's portrait of "The Me Decade and the Third Great Awakening," in *Mauve Gloves & Madmen, Clutter & Vine* (New York: Bantam, 1977) and Christopher Lasch's *The Culture of Narcissism: American Life in an Age of Diminishing Expectations* (New York: W. W. Norton, 1978) would both seem to testify to this fact.

59. On the theme of effeminacy in *Narcisse*, see Arnaldo Pizzorusso, "La Comédie de *Narcisse*," *Annales de la Société Jean-Jacques Rousseau* 35 (1959–62): 12, 15–16, and in the discussion which follows the article, pp. 24–25.

60. Jean Guéhenno notes this chronological relationship in his biography of Rousseau, *Jean-Jacques Rousseau*, trans. John and Doreen Weightman (New York: Columbia University Press, 1966), 1: 56–57. He sees *Narcisse* as an imitation of Marivaux, and the *Essai Sur Les Événements* as a reflection of the influence of Voltaire, and the product of Rousseau's dream of a "work which would bring him instant fame." He does not discuss the fragment *Sur Les Femmes* in this context.

Chapter Four

1. The question of female dependence on males is discussed below in the section on the interdependence of men and women.

2. Rousseau's position is more consistent than this summary makes it seem. The same women do not have contradictory effects upon men; rather, different sorts of women have opposite effects upon different sorts of men. Sophie, who makes Emile dependent, is very different from the modern women whose influence and example, as we have seen in chapter 3, have made men effeminate. Emile himself is expressly said not to be "effeminate"—and hence to be unlike modern men generally and Rousseau himself specifically. See *Emile*, V, pp. 433 and 435.

3. See also *Emile*, IV, p. 327: "Emile is not made to remain always solitary. As a member of society he ought to fulfill its duties."

4. Yet we have seen in chapter 3 that the same citizens who are to regard their magistrates as natural forces are also to think of their state as "the tender mother who nourishes them." Again one can note the tension in Rousseau's thought, so relevant to his assessment of the political impact of women, between the distrust of personal dependence and the recognition of its necessity. Because only impersonal dependence is legitimate, animated magistrates must be seen as inanimate forces. But because only personal dependence strengthens the emotional ties of the dependent to that upon which he depends, it alone is effective; thus the inanimate state must be seen in anthropomorphic terms as an animated figure.

5. For this reason, we have seen and will see again, women's authority over men can be considered the most effective authority, because it is the most hidden and indirect authority. Cf. note 60 below for a discussion of the extent to which the tutor's authority over Emile can be considered "feminine."

6. Emile is taught nothing about religion as a small child. Only when "the progress of the

passions is accelerated" must Emile learn about God, so as to "accelerate the progress of the enlightenment which serves to regulate these passions" (*Emile*, IV, p. 259). "It is only then that he finds his true interest in being good, in doing good far from the sight of men and without being forced by the laws." Emile is taught to accept a natural religion, akin to the Savoyard Vicar's profession of faith, so as to be inspired to "love . . . the Author of his being," and hence to behave morally (*Emile*, IV, p. 314).

7. See the discussion of Rousseau's encounter with the Venetian courtesan Zulietta.

8. On the subject of the status of the imagination in the thought of Rousseau, see the very helpful work of Marc Eigeldinger, *Jean-Jacques Rousseau et la Réalité de l'Imaginaire* (Neuchâtel, Switzerland: Éditions de la Baconnière, 1962). Eigeldinger thoughtfully stresses the ambiguity of the imagination for Rousseau, although he does not consider the importance of the distinction Rousseau sees between the imaginations of men such as himself and those of ordinary men such as Emile.

9. Mary Wollstonecraft, *A Vindication of the Rights of Woman*, ed. Charles W. Hagelman, Jr. (New York: W. W. Norton, 1967), p. 68.

10. Ibid., p. 75. The emphases are in the text.

11. But cf. *Emile*, V, p. 382: "To leave her above us in the qualities proper to her sex and to make her our equal in all the rest is to transfer to the wife the primacy that nature gives to the husband." Rousseau seems to have felt it necessary to argue that sexual differentiation is beneficial from the self-interested standpoint of both males (who are anxious to maintain the appearance of predominance) and females (who are anxious to maintain the reality of equality). I discuss the relationship between these two seemingly contradictory passages in chapter 6 below.

12. Wollstonecraft, p. 107.

13. Ibid., p. 162.

14. In other respects, however, women are less political as a sex than are men, in that men and not women are concerned to have their rule recognized by others. Cf. chapter 3, note 6, where I acknowledge that women's hidden rule is less political than is men's open rule. It is also the case, however, that a potentially anarchic sex is in a sense less political than is a sex which must necessarily rule because it is necessarily ruled; in this sense, women are indeed more political than are men. Men are more political when they rule, less political in that they need not rule.

The conception of women as the more political sex may help to make more comprehensible the most misogynistic passage in the Rousseauian corpus, *Letter*, p. 103n. Rousseau argues there that women are necessarily men's inferiors in artistic endeavors: "Their works are all cold and pretty as they are. . . . They do not know how to describe nor to feel even love." Men are strong, and their strength helps to explain their warmth and their capacity to love; women are cold in that their weakness leads them to prefer domination to love. One has the impression of male *noblesse oblige*, expressed in love, as contrasted to female *faiblesse domine*. The misogynistic element in Rousseau would seem to anticipate the Nietzschean analysis of slave morality generally and of femininity in particular. Derrida, p. 342, has an interesting note along these lines.

Having said this, however, I must add that the extreme misogyny of this particular passage is unrepresentative of Rousseau's thought as a whole. Rousseau cannot believe that women are simply incapable of love; otherwise there would be no point in his presenting Sophie (and Julie) as models for young women to emulate. Sophie is not a "prodigy" (*Emile*, V, p. 393); nevertheless, "the need to love . . . devours her" (ibid., p. 397). Women's desire to rule men need not therefore exclude their love for men. Cf. the discussion below of the ways in which men complete women, and make women happy.

15. Rousseau emphasizes feminine submissiveness because of his materialism; he argues that women's submissiveness follows (or ought to follow) from their physical nature. "Heaven did not make women ingratiating and persuasive in order that they become shrewish. It did not make them weak in order that they be imperious." In this respect (and

also in others, as we shall soon see below) Rousseau compares women to small children: "Nature has made children to be loved and helped, but has it made them to be obeyed and feared?" (*Emile*, II, p. 88). In both cases Rousseau argues that a moral "ought" follows from a physical "is." (Although as I argue below, in the case of women the "ought" in question is not so much that they ought to obey because of their weakness as it is how they ought to act if they are to rule in spite of their weakness.) As we have seen, the physical or natural differences between men and women are largely irrelevant in the state of nature; paradoxically, it is only when human beings become civilized, or in some respect denatured, that natural inequalities become relevant. Furthermore, Rousseau asserts that physical inequalities can justify moral inequalities; he is therefore consistent with his own principles in arguing for the moral relevance of the physical distinctions between the sexes. On these points, see the discussion of Rousseau's materialism in chapter 1, and the references cited in notes 6 and 7 thereto.

16. Wollstonecraft, p. 58.

17. Cf. *Emile*, v, p. 386: "The quest for abstract and speculative truths, principles, and axioms in the sciences, for everything that tends to generalize ideas, is not within the competence of women." Cf. also pp. 387, 426. In addition, cf. above, chapter 3, note 5, and the discussion of the relationship between Julie and Wolmar, in chapter 5 below.

18. One must not, however, conceive of "practical reason" in Kantian terms. There is nothing a priori about women's thought as Rousseau presents it. Cf. *Emile*, V, p. 387: "It is for women to discover experimental morality, so to speak, and for us to reduce it to a system."

19. Furthermore, one should recall that Rousseau often writes as though theoretical reason were of no particular use to *anyone*. Given Rousseau's critique of theoretical reason, one is tempted to say that women are superior in practical reason, men in impractical (or useless) reason. To say this would be to exaggerate, but the exaggeration would merely magnify an important tendency in Rousseau's thought. Cf. *First Discourse*, passim. Cf. also note 60 below.

20. Cf. *Emile*, V, pp. 386–87: "All [women's] studies ought to be related to practice. It is for them to apply the principles man has found, and to make the observations which lead man to the establishment of principles. . . . Men will philosophize about the human heart better than she does; but she will read in men's hearts better than they do."

21. One story from Emile's courtship of Sophie illustrates women's combined dependence upon men and rule over men particularly well. See ibid., V, p. 437, where Emile and Sophie compete in a race. Emile gives Sophie a head start. "He pursues her, follows close on her heels, and finally catches up with Sophie who is all out of breath. Gently putting his left arm around her, he lifts her like a feather and, pressing the sweet burden to his heart, completes the course. He makes her touch the goal first and then, shouting 'Sophie is the winner,' puts his knee on the ground before her and admits that he is conquered." Sophie is weaker and slower afoot than is Emile, but gets him to bestow his greater strength and speed upon her, to enable her to triumph over him.

22. Rousseau gives as examples incidents from domestic life which illustrate this contention. His examples may seem trivial, but one must realize that his concern here is the equality between men and women in the everyday relations of familial life. In one story, in *Emile*, V, p. 371, Rousseau compares a young boy with a young girl, in order to demonstrate the latter's superiority in being served delicacies at a meal without being allowed to ask directly for them. On pp. 383–84, Rousseau compares the behavior of a wife and a husband as hosts of a dinner party, to the wife's advantage. The wife is a better hostess than her husband is a host; this means that the wife is more successful at *appearing* to be singlemindedly concerned with nothing but the welfare of her guests: "On leaving the table each guest believes that she has thought only of him. All think that she has not had time to eat a single bite. But the truth is that she has eaten more than anyone."

23. Note that Rousseau also employs the image of the "lever" in discussing the ability of rulers in monarchies and tyrannies (the governments of which he is generally the most

critical) to act upon others at a distance. Cf. *Social Contract*, III, 6, p. 89: "For a monarchical State to be well governed, its size or extent would have to be measured by the capabilities of the one who governs. . . . With a big enough lever, it is possible to move the world with one finger." Cf. also ibid., 8, p. 95. Conceivably this affinity between women and monarchs also points to the personal character of the rule of both women and monarchs.

24. On the resemblance of women to children, see also note 15 above.

25. Note that Sophie smiles "secretly"; her rule over Emile is hidden.

26. Compare the very similar discussion of the possible motives for male chastity in chapter 3 above.

27. The tension between these two manifestations of female happiness—through the love of men and the rule over men—is a central theme of Rousseau's novel, *La Nouvelle Héloïse*. See the discussion of Julie's death in chapter 5, below.

28. Note, however, Rousseau's important qualification of this statement: "A truly happy being is a solitary being." Insofar as humans cannot be self-sufficient, they must love; true happiness, however, would be found through sufficiency of self (not through dependence upon and love of others). One must keep this in mind in order to understand Rousseau's ultimate rejection of love and his search for self-sufficiency, discussed in this chapter's conclusion.

29. Compare the statement in *Dernière*, quoted in chapter 1, where Rousseau criticizes women who "disdain from the hands of virtue an empire which they want to owe only to their charms."

30. *Politics*, 1255b.

31. Compare the discussion in chapter 2 of the harmonious character of sexuality in the state of nature.

32. See also *Emile*, II, p. 162: "Without wanting to command, he will be the master." See also ibid., IV, p. 236: Emile does not "seek glory" but is instead "content to see."

33. Although Emile does not desire to rule Sophie, it would be wrong to conclude on this basis that his sexuality is apolitical. We have seen that male sexuality focuses on the appearance of rule, female sexuality on its reality. For this reason, both male and female sexuality are political in character. They differ from one another, however, in one vital respect: the appearance of rule is less essential to men than is the reality of rule to women. Thus Emile does not desire to rule Sophie, because his rule over her is less important to him than her rule over him is important to her. Also for this reason, asexual anarchy is a possibility for Rousseau, as it would not be for any woman. Cf. the discussion of Rousseau's quest for independence below, as well as notes 39 and 60.

34. On p. 428 we learn that Sophie's triumph too "costs her her freedom." Again, however, the difference is that men have more freedom to surrender than do women, which is why men are less eager to rule women than women are to rule men.

35. Cf. ibid., p. 363 (quoted in its entirety in the context of Rousseau's critique of Plato, discussed in chapter 3, above): "The good husband [is] the good citizen."

36. The analogy between Emile and the ancient citizen should not however be overstated. Like the ancient citizen, Emile's motive for political allegiance is his familial attachment. But unlike the ancient citizen, Emile is not to expect that he will be called upon to act politically very frequently. See *Emile*, V, pp. 473–75, and Rousseau's depiction of the ancient city, discussed in chapter 3 above.

37. Compare chapter 2's discussion of the political implications of romantic love.

38. See Rousseau's analysis, discussed in chapter 3 above, of the relationship in antiquity between political and romantic attachments.

39. Note that Rousseau wants Emile to be prepared to leave Sophie, whereas he would never advise Sophie to leave Emile. Rousseau believes that only males are potentially autonomous and fully independent, because only they are strong enough to be able (at least in principle) to dispense with the assistance of others. Women are necessarily social, because they require the assistance of others: for this reason Rousseau would say that women should

not aspire to the radical autonomy which he envisions. This becomes apparent in *Émile et Sophie*: Emile's departure from Sophie is regarded by Emile (and, he tells us, by Sophie as well) as a punishment for her crime, but as a test (painful though it be) of his virtue. It is a punishment for a woman to live without a man; it is a proof of virtue for a man to be able under certain circumstances to live without a woman.

40. See the discussion of the political implications of romantic love, in chapter 2 above.

41. *Émile et Sophie* is an epistolary novel, made up of letters from Emile to his former tutor. The entire first letter (the only completed portion of the text—Rousseau wrote only a part of the second letter) consists of Emile's account of his debate with himself as to how to respond to Sophie's adultery.

In view of Rousseau's insistence that women depend upon men, Emile's abandonment of Sophie (and of his remaining child) appears to be an extraordinarily heartless and callous action to take. For this reason, it is important to consider the motivation of Emile's action. His action may well be wrong, but at least it is wrong in a complicated way, not in a simple way: it is not the action of a selfish individual unconcerned about its impact upon others whose lives he affects. Emile contends that he disregards his selfish desire in abandoning Sophie; his "penchant" (*Émile et Sophie*, p. 901) dictates that he remain with her. In abandoning her, he claims to disregard his passionate inclination, and to act instead as Sophie would wish him to act. (Even Emile's act of abandoning Sophie, paradoxically, therefore testifies to his subjection to her rule.) Cf. *Émile et Sophie*, pp. 909–10: "She knew that I was rational but weak; and I knew even better how much her proud and sublime soul retained inflexibility even in its faults. The idea of Sophie restored to grace was insupportable to her. She felt that her crime was one of those which cannot be forgotten; she preferred to be punished than to be pardoned. Such a pardon was not made for her; even punishment degraded her less in her opinion." The same pride which makes Sophie seek a husband worthy of her also demands that she think herself worthy as a wife of him; when she no longer feels worthy, he must no longer retain her as his wife. Cf. also note 45 below.

42. This point is made both by Madame de Staël, *Lettres sur le Caractère et les Écrits de Jean-Jacques Rousseau*, Lettre III, in *Oeuvres Complètes* (Paris: Chez Treuttel et Würtz, 1820), pp. 55–56, and by Pierre Burgelin, "L'Éducation de Sophie," *Annales de la Société Jean-Jacques Rousseau* 35 (1959–62): 128.

43. In another sense, however, Emile's education fails him as well. He contends that Sophie has failed him as a wife because he failed her as a husband. Cf. *Émile et Sophie*, p. 901: "It is with reason that one imputes to a husband the disorderliness of his wife, either for having chosen badly, or for having governed her badly. . . . I myself was an example of the justice of this imputation. . . . If Emile had always been moderate [*sage*], Sophie would never have failed."

44. For the three sources, see Charles Wirz, "Note sur *Émile et Sophie, ou les Solitaires*," *Annales de la Société Jean-Jacques Rousseau* 36 (1963–65): 291–301. Essentially the same information is summarized in *Oeuvres Complètes*, 4: clxi–clxvii.

45. Emile states there that he did not "know . . . what excused, what perhaps justified" Sophie's "crime. . . , until after her death." Because of Sophie's pride, Emile is unaware of the extenuating circumstances at the time of his abandonment of her.

46. Wirz, p. 299. On the basis of these notes, Wirz, p. 302, concludes that it is "impossible henceforth to call into question the testimony of Bernardin de Saint-Pierre."

47. Cf. the discussion in chapter 2 of the natural sexuality of civilized human beings.

48. Cf. the discussion in chapter 3 of the ancient city's dependence upon the family.

49. This anecdote exemplifies the thesis of the *Essai sur les Événements*, discussed in chapter 3, above: politics appears to be the realm of men, but in fact political men are often controlled by the hidden influence of their women.

50. On the importance of the formative sexual experience, see also *Emile*, IV, p. 318, and V, p. 415.

51. In this quotation Rousseau depicts the personal rule of women—which need not always be hidden rule (although it is clearly possible to "lie at the feet of an imperious mistress" only in private, never in public). Whether hidden or personal (or both), women's rule always differs from manifest impersonal rule, however. On the relationship between male sexuality and submission to women, cf. the discussion in chapter 2 of the ways in which female modesty benefits males.

52. See Rousseau's self-description, in *Second*, p. 222: ". . . men like me, whose passions have forever destroyed their original simplicity."

53. See *Confessions*, V, p. 200: Rousseau recounts Madame de Warens's speech in which she persuades him to let her seduce him; in the course of his narrative Rousseau refers critically to the tactics of the tutor in persuading Emile of the attractions of chastity and true love. Compare *Emile*, IV, pp. 324, 327.

54. Rousseau also resembles Emile in his eventual abandonment of Madame de Warens. Madame de Warens was "led astray" by "false principles" (taught to her by her instructor in philosophy): she believes that sexual promiscuity is permissible. Rousseau is willing to share her favors with Claude Anet, her valet, in a *ménage à trois* (on this point, see chapter 5 below, note 33). But he is unwilling to share her with another man, Vintzenried, who lacks Anet's great virtues. When he learns of her relations with Vintzenried, he is devastated (as is Emile when he learns of Sophie's infidelity). Cf. *Confessions*, VI, p. 272: "I saw all the happy future which I had depicted to myself vanish in a moment. All the dreams of happiness which I had so fondly cherished disappeared, and I, who from my youth had never considered my existence except in connection with hers, for the first time found myself alone." Like Emile, he regards his misfortune as a test of his virtue. Cf. ibid., p. 274: "Thus . . . those virtues began to develop, the seeds of which were sown at the bottom of my heart, which had been cultivated by study, and only waited for the leaven of adversity in order to bear fruit." (The comparison between Rousseau's abandonment of Madame de Warens and Emile's of Sophie is suggested by Pierre Burgelin, in his introduction to *Émile et Sophie*, in *Oeuvres Complètes*, 4: clv.

55. Note Rousseau's emphasis on Thérèse's stupidity: "At first I tried to improve her mind, but my efforts were useless. Her mind is what Nature has made it; culture and teaching are without influence upon it" (*Confessions*, VII, p. 341). Rousseau can be like savage man with Thérèse because she is truly like savage woman. Emile, the "natural man" in "the civil state," successfully tutors Sophie. Compare *Emile*, V, pp. 425–26. See also *Confessions*, XII, p. 617: "Let us not look for perfections which are not to be found in nature; it would be the same with any other woman whatsoever [as it is with Thérèse]." In dealing with Thérèse, Rousseau is "in nature," wherein all women are "the same." Finally, Rousseau's abandonment of the children to whom Thérèse gave birth can be understood as the act of a savage man.

56. Starobinski, p. 215. The emphasis is Starobinski's.

57. Ibid., p. 214. Derrida, pp. 155–57, 340, makes the same observation. Compare *Confessions*, III, p. 111 (*supplément* is translated as "means"), with VII, p. 341 (*supplément* is translated as "substitute").

58. See the analysis of sexuality in the state of nature, in chapter 2 above.

59. Emile, the social being who must depend upon women, is specifically said not to be "effeminate." Compare *Emile*, V, pp. 433 and 435.

60. Rousseau again speaks of his sexual doubleness later in the *Confessions* (IX, p. 449): he notes that he is the author both of "effeminate books which breathed nothing but love and tenderness" (i.e., *Julie*) and also the author of "strict principles," "austere maxims," and "biting invectives" against such books (i.e., *Letter to D'Alembert*). Rousseau's sexual doubleness is also apparent in a number of other ways. He contends (*Emile*, V, p. 387) that "Woman has more wit, man more genius; woman observes, and man reasons. From this conjunction results the clearest insight and the most complete science regarding itself that the human

mind can acquire—in a word, the surest knowledge of oneself and others available to our species." The book *Emile* itself is obviously intended to supply precisely this "clearest insight and . . . most complete science regarding itself that the human mind can acquire"—which is to say that in writing it Rousseau both "observes" particulars and "reasons" from them toward generalities. Rousseau can philosophize successfully only insofar as he can somehow combine the mental abilities of both males and females. In addition, Rousseau is sexually double in *Emile* not only as its author, but also as its actor (in his capacity as Emile's governor). He is sexually double in practice as well as in theory, in that at different times he exemplifies both the male principle of manifest rule and the female principle of hidden rule. At first, his rule over Emile is hidden. Cf. *Emile*, IV, p. 234: "To make him docile, leave him all his freedom; hide yourself so that he may seek you." Later, his rule becomes manifest (ibid., p. 326), "when the moment has come, and he has, so to speak, signed the contract." (Even after this, however, the governor's rule is less than wholly manifest: cf. ibid., V, p. 434, where Rousseau speaks of "the rules which I dictate to [Sophie, for managing Emile] in secret.")

Rousseau's emphasis upon effeminacy or bisexuality may help to explain why he would contend that only men, and not women, are capable of radical individualist autonomy, or asexual anarchy. Males have a strength which must be weakened if they are to become bisexual or whole; females would have to add to themselves a strength beyond that which they possess, if they were to become bisexual or whole. It is presumably easier to subtract from what one has than it is to add to what one lacks. Men can in principle become effeminate, which is to say partially female, hence whole. Women cannot in principle become partially male. (In ibid., p. 386, Rousseau states that there is only one "known exception" to this rule. He refers critically to a "Mademoiselle de l'Enclos. . . . It is said that she had made herself a man. Wonderful. But with all her great reputation, I would no more have wanted that man for my friend than for my mistress.") Women should not attempt to become partially male; nor should they attempt to make men as unmasculine as are women. Cf. chapter 3, note 48.

61. Albert Schinz, *La Pensée de Jean-Jacques Rousseau* (Paris: Librairie Félix Alcan, 1929), pp. 421, 511.

62. On Rousseau's autoeroticism, see Starobinski's note, pp. 214–15. On the similarity between Rousseau and Valère, compare Rousseau's self-description at the age of sixteen (i.e., not very long before he first conceived of writing *Narcisse*) with Lucinde's description of Valère at the beginning of *Narcisse*. See *Confessions*, II, p. 48, and *Narcisse*, p. 977. See also Pizzorusso, pp. 11–12.

63. Starobinski, pp. 90–92, notes the resemblances between Pygmalion, Narcisse, and Rousseau.

64. In *Confessions*, X, pp. 512–13, Rousseau ascribes an autobiographical origin to the *Letter*: "Without perceiving it, I described my situation at that time: I portrayed Grimm, Madame d'Épinay, Madame d'Houdetot, Saint-Lambert and myself." One can therefore wonder whether Rousseau's self-portrait is not to be found in the foolish theatergoer. This suggestion, however, reflects my own reading of the text, which seems to me to be the obvious one—that the *Letter* celebrates civic virtue, and is as such an antierotic work, a polemical attack upon romantic love. Yet Rousseau's own conception of the work, as stated in the *Confessions*, is very different: "Hitherto, virtuous indignation had been my Apollo; on this occasion, tenderness and gentleness of soul supplied his place. . . . Alas! in what I wrote it is only too evident that love, the fatal love of which I was doing the utmost to cure myself, was not yet banished from my heart."

65. Note that Rousseau makes a very similar remark concerning Madame de Warens, in *Confessions*, V, p. 202.

66. My capitalization of "Flowers" follows Rousseau's. Rousseau wrote his botanical dictionary in 1774. Roger de Vilmorin, who annotated the Pléiade edition of Rousseau's botanical works, speaks (*Oeuvres Complètes*, 4: 1840) of the article in which this passage appears as "the gem of the dictionary of Rousseau." He adds that it "testifies clearly to the

predilection which he had for the study of the reproductive organs." Rousseau's interest in the sexuality of plants is frequently evident in the dictionary: cf. in particular p. 1205, where Rousseau asserts that Linnaeus (whom he admires) developed his system of classification as a result of his having been "replete with his sexual system and the vast ideas which it had suggested to him."

Chapter Five

1. Cf. the discussion of the informal authority of women in chapter 3 above.

2. *Julie* is not, however, the work of a citizen of Geneva. Novels are needed only for "corrupt peoples," as Rousseau declares in the Preface, p. 5. For this reason he cannot claim to have authored the book as a "citizen of Geneva," because by doing so he would "profane the name of [his] fatherland" (Second Preface, p. 27).

3. René Hubert, "L'amour, la nature et la société chez J-J Rousseau: *La Nouvelle Héloïse*, roman à thèse," *Revue d'Histoire de la Philosophie et d'Histoire Générale de la Civilisation* 7 (1939): 204.

4. See *Emile*, V, p. 430, and *Second*, pp. 146–47 and 148–49.

5. Although Julie manages to prevent it, the scheduled duel between Bomston and Saint-Preux illustrates the potentially fatal consequences of the jealousy occasioned by romantic love (*Julie*, I, 56, pp. 150–52).

6. Here as elsewhere, I have capitalized words in my translation that are capitalized in the French.

7. Rousseau's description of Wolmar is to some extent more reminiscent of his general characterization of women than of his general characterization of men. We have seen him contend (*Emile*, V, p. 387) that "woman observes, man reasons"; we have seen him describe (ibid., p. 377) woman and not man as "the eye" of the "moral person" which heterosexual union creates. But Wolmar's observation is very different from woman's observation. Rousseau claims that women observe for a practical purpose: they must observe men in order to control men, so as to get men to assist them. Observation for women is thus a means to a practical end. For Wolmar, observation is an end in itself. He does not observe in order to act; given his preference, he would instead observe and never act. Because he is solitary and impractical, Wolmar more closely approaches Rousseau's stereotype of the male than his stereotype of the female.

8. On this point, cf. the discussion of the practical character of women's reason, in chapter 4 above. It is important to note that Rousseau admits that there are exceptions to his rule about the limitations of the female intellect. "It is not to a woman that I refuse the talents of men, but to women" (*Letter*, p. 48n). Presumably some women could therefore have genius instead of wit. Rousseau in fact speaks of one woman who had genius: Madame de Chenonceaux, the "good mother who thinks for herself" for whom *Emile* was written. "By her visage she is an ornament to her sex, and by her genius an exception to it." Compare *Emile*, Author's Preface, p. 33, and *Montagne*, V, p. 783.

9. See Starobinski, p. 138, and Shklar, pp. 128, 135–36, 142, 151.

10. In discussing Wolmar's position at Clarens, Saint-Preux observes that "A father . . . is happy like God himself" (*Julie*, IV, 10, pp. 466–67). See also Saint-Preux's declaration to Wolmar: "In giving myself entirely to you, I can offer you, as to God himself, only the gifts that I take from you" (ibid., V, 8, p. 611).

11. Both Starobinski, p. 139, and Shklar, p. 136, suggest that Wolmar's atheism is an indication of his divinity—he does not believe in God because in effect he is God. But Julie's death leads Wolmar to become a believer; see *Julie*, Second Preface, p. 13, and Rousseau's letter to Vernes of June 24, 1761, in *Correspondance*, 9: 27. One can therefore reverse the argument: since Wolmar comes to believe in God he cannot truly have been God.

12. Pierre Burgelin, *La Philosophie de l'Existence de J.-J. Rousseau* (Paris: Librairie Philosophique J. Vrin, 1973), p. 455.

13. See the analyses of the *Essai Sur Les Événements* and of *La Mort de Lucrèce* in chapter 3 above.

14. Julie is not however altogether indifferent to political questions. Even in this context, in which she declares her lack of interest in politics, she says that she is "obliged to love the government under which heaven has caused me to be born." On her deathbed she goes further, thanking heaven for "having caused me to be born in a free country, and not among slaves" (*Julie*, VI, 11, p. 723). *Julie* celebrates sound domestic life, not sound political life. Yet Rousseau also indicates that domestic life is to a considerable extent relative to the regime; in a wholly corrupt regime, even sound domestic life would be impossible. See also the discussion below of Bomston's views on the extent of the obligation to marry.

15. See also *Emile*, V, p. 368: "Intelligence is more precocious in girls than in boys."

16. See also the tutor's advice to Sophie, in *Emile*, V, pp. 478–79: "'You will reign by means of love for a long time if you make your favors rare and precious, if you know how to make them valued. Do you want to see your husband constantly at your feet? Then keep him always at some distance from your person.'"

17. *De Cive*, ed. Sterling P. Lamprecht (New York: Appleton-Century-Crofts, 1949), Epistle Dedicatory, p. 1.

18. See particularly the comparison between Wolmar and Julie as governors of the servants at Clarens: "The more severe of the two is not the more dreaded. . . . They fear the grave reprimands of Monsieur de Wolmar less than the touching reproaches of Julie. The one, causing justice and truth to speak, humiliates and confounds the guilty; the other gives them a mortal regret of being guilty, in showing them her regret that she has been forced to withdraw her benevolence from them" (*Julie*, IV, 10, p. 465). Wolmar's rule of legality is less absolute than Julie's dominance exercised through the emotions.

19. Julie is also referred to as the "preacher" in I, 44, p. 124; I, 45, p. 126; II, 16, p. 243; III, 20, p. 377; IV, 2, p. 405; IV, 13, p. 506; and VI, 2, p. 638.

20. Here Julie complains about the fact that social conventions compel women to act deceitfully. She goes on to assert that young women such as herself live "under the tyranny of the proprieties. . . . But our inclinations are restrained in vain; the heart receives laws only from itself; it escapes slavery; it gives itself at its own liking."

The passage quoted in the text is of considerable interest, because in it Julie seems to criticize precisely those feminine characteristics—guilefulness and deceptiveness—which Rousseau contends are both necessary and praiseworthy. Does not Rousseau's beloved fictional creation call into question Rousseau's own proposed course of action for women?

In answering this question, it is helpful to distinguish between two different kinds of deception. To the extent that Julie complains of being forced to be attentive to wellborn suitors, and to dismiss those who are commoners (and hence to deceive others about her true feelings), her position is no different than Rousseau's: he, like she, agrees that the heart should "give itself at its own liking." (Or at any rate, Rousseau believes that natural compatibility should take clear precedence over considerations of social status—cf. *Emile*, V, pp. 399–401, 407–08.)

But Julie says more than this; she complains that she must "lie out of modesty." This would seem to suggest that she would prefer to be able openly to express her desire to her lover (notwithstanding her recognition that modesty is predominantly a feminine virtue—cf. her critique of Plato, as discussed above). Here, one must admit, Julie's position does contradict Rousseau's. For as we have seen, Rousseau denies that women can or should openly express their sexual inclinations: in a sense, he contends that women must often lie for their own good. Cf. *Emile*, V, p. 385: "According to the true inclinations of their sex, even when [women] are lying, they are not false. . . . Does not woman have the same needs as man without having the same right to express them? . . . Why do you say modesty makes women false? Are those who lose it most completely also truer than the others? Far from it."

Rousseau believes that women must act deceptively, but he also understands why an

extremely lovable and admirable woman would be uncomfortable with the policy of deception which he proposes. I therefore believe that Rousseau would contend that the policy of
deception which he advocates is the least unsatisfactory alternative which women could
adopt—but that it is very far from being a wholly satisfactory alternative. Rousseau is very
well aware of the problematic character of the "solution" which he offers to the problems
facing women; but he does not believe that any unproblematic solution to the problems of
women (or, for that matter, to the very different problems of men) exists.

21. The women of Rousseau's day reacted with extraordinary enthusiasm to his defense
of them in *Julie*. Rousseau comments on the popular reaction to the novel: "The ladies,
especially, became infatuated with the book and the author to such an extent that there were
few, even amongst the highest circles, whose conquest I could not have made if I had been so
disposed" (*Confessions*, XI, p. 564). A recent biographer of Rousseau remarks: "Women,
especially, . . . felt at once justified and avenged by [the] novel." He then quotes Sainte-
Beuve's judgment of the novel's impact: "'It was Rousseau who started this major revolution
in France, and . . . brought . . . women into the forefront. . . . The enthusiasm shown him by
the fair sex was unparalleled.'" Guéhenno, 2: 53.

22. See Starobinski, p. 122, Shklar, pp. 152–54, Marshall Berman, *The Politics of Authenticity* (New York: Atheneum, 1970), pp. 245–47, and Lester G. Crocker, "*Julie* ou la Nouvelle
Duplicité," *Annales de la Société Jean-Jacques Rousseau* 36 (1963–65): 119–21.

23. In view of this comparison, I cannot understand how M. B. Ellis can speak of the
"analogy . . . between the government of the Wolmar estate and that of the ideal republic."
See Ellis, *Julie or La Nouvelle Héloïse: A Synthesis of Rousseau's Thought (1749–59)* (Toronto:
University of Toronto Press, 1949), p. 89. On the other hand, Crocker, p. 121, surely errs as
well in saying that "the socio-political 'system' of Rousseau is fundamentally identical in all
his writings," by which he means that the citizens in the *Social Contract* are manipulated no
differently than are the servants at Clarens. It is possible to be too cynical as well as too
credulous in interpreting an author.

24. Starobinski, p. 105, suggests the etymological relationship between Clarens (as well
as Claire) and enlightenment.

25. *Emile*, IV, p. 220. Cf. Rousseau's critique of sexual precocity as a source of immorality, discussed in chapter 4 above.

26. Compare Rousseau's account of his experience as a servant in another household,
wherein he impresses his employers by explaining to them the meaning of the old French
motto of their family: "It was one of those moments, only too rare, which replace things in
their natural order, and avenge depreciated merit for the insults of fortune" (*Confessions*,
III, p. 98).

27. Berman, who presents Clarens as "an authoritarian state that is governed like an
army" (p. 246), fails to discuss this aspect of life at Clarens. Instead he maintains (p. 247) that
Clarens aims "to minimize (and, if possible, eliminate) the role of the family." See also p. 249:
"Those who live in the world of Clarens are deprived of family, friends, lovers, of inner
space."

It is perfectly legitimate for Berman to denounce Clarens, but he should denounce it for
what it is: a paternalistic household whose servants are governed like children, not an
authoritarian state whose servants are commanded like soldiers. Because it is a paternalistic
society, relations between the sexes are both more regular and less promiscuous than they
generally are in armies.

28. Rousseau does not portray Clarens as more than a relative success: "Servitude is so
unnatural to man that it could not exist without some discontent" (*Julie*, IV, 10, p. 460).

29. It is interesting to note that Tocqueville makes very similar arguments concerning
the importance of sexual morality and the means of promoting it, in discussing a highly
democratic and egalitarian society—America. Cf. *Democracy in America*, trans. George Lawrence, ed. J. P. Mayer (Garden City, N.Y: Anchor-Doubleday, 1969), p. 598: widespread

sexual promiscuity "prevent[s] the body social from being strong and alert, . . . break[s] up families and . . . weaken[s] national morality. Society is endangered not by the great profligacy of a few but by the laxity of all."

Sexual mores are stricter in America than anywhere in Europe, a fact which Tocqueville not only notes but applauds. Their strictness results from the division of labor between the sexes. Cf. p. 598: "All these separate and necessary occupations form as many natural barriers which, by keeping the sexes apart, make the solicitations of the one less frequent and less ardent and the resistance of the other easier." Cf. also p. 601: "The Americans have applied to the sexes the great principle of political economy which now dominates industry. They have carefully separated the functions of man and of woman so that the great work of society may be better performed."

It would be wrong to exaggerate the affinities between America and Clarens, since they are clearly very different sorts of societies. Nevertheless, the affinities between the overall positions of Rousseau and Tocqueville regarding the importance of sexual behavior for society are striking. Like Rousseau, Tocqueville believes that the societies of the future will emphasize private and not public life; again like Rousseau, he believes that those societies can and must be moral, and that their morality must be exemplified in the character of the relations between the sexes within them. Finally, for these reasons he, like Rousseau, emphasizes the decisive political impact of women (whom he, like Rousseau, believes are properly excluded from direct political participation). Cf. p. 601: "You will never find American women in charge of the external relations of a family, managing a business, or interfering in politics." But cf. also p. 603: "And now that I come near the end of this book in which I have recorded so many considerable achievements of the Americans, if anyone asks me what I think the chief cause of the extraordinary prosperity and growing power of this nation, I should answer that it is due to the superiority of their women."

30. For the comparison between Julie and Clarissa Harlowe, see William Mead, *Jean-Jacques Rousseau Ou Le Romancier Enchaîné* (Princeton, N.J., and Paris: Université de Princeton, Département de Langues Romanes, and Presses Universitaires de France, 1966), pp. 47, 99. For the inutility of Lucretia as a model for Rousseau's own time, see *Confessions*, VIII, p. 407: "I ventured to introduce this unfortunate woman on the stage again at a time when she was no longer possible at any French theater." Lucretia is too perfect to interest the men and women of the France in which Rousseau lives.

31. Cf. *Emile*, V, p. 397, quoted in chapter 4 above, p. 91.

32. See also *Confessions*, IX, p. 445, quoted on p. 115 above.

33. Thus Wolmar creates a *ménage à trois* composed of Julie, Saint-Preux, and himself. As the text suggests, he does this because he feels that Julie and Saint-Preux will both be better off if their love is preserved and transformed rather than destroyed. Julie and Saint-Preux must continue to love one another, because their love provides them the passion or energy motivating all of their most praiseworthy activities. But as we saw Julie suggest above (in criticizing romantic love), lovers are unable to benefit anyone but themselves, insofar as they think only of one another. Because he mediates between Julie and Saint-Preux, Wolmar forces them to think not only of themselves, but of others as well; in this way the *ménage à trois* (and only the *ménage à trois*) can overcome Julie's objections, and make romance safe for reality. Yet in another sense, the *ménage à trois* is equally important because it makes reality safe for romance. For as we have also seen Julie (and Rousseau) argue, love is an illusion destroyed by the reality of possession. Because he mediates between Julie and Saint-Preux, Wolmar also enables them to continue to imagine one another, and not to exhaust their imaginations by possessing one another. Thus the *ménage à trois* emerges in a sense as Rousseau's (not very practical) solution to the problem of love; it enables lovers both to be dutiful to others and also to preserve the illusory joys of their images of one another. For these reasons Rousseau was involved himself in *ménages à trois* with two of the women who were most important in his life—with Madame de Warens and her lover and valet Claude Anet (whose name, as can be seen in note 39 below, Rousseau bestows upon a

character in *Julie*), and with Madame d'Houdetot and her lover Saint-Lambert. Cf. *Confessions*, V, p. 184, where Rousseau says that Madame de Warens, Claude Anet, and he "lived in a union which made us all happy, and which could only be dissolved by death." Cf. also ibid., IX, p. 477, where Rousseau says that "even if I had been able to take Madame d'Houdetot from [Saint-Lambert], I should not have wished, and I should not even have felt tempted to do so. . . . Without desiring to disturb their union, all that I had most truly desired from her in my delirium, was that she should allow herself to be loved. In short, however violent the passion with which I had been inflamed for her, I felt it as delightful to be the confidant as the object of her affections, and I have never for a moment regarded her lover as my rival, but always as my friend." The arguments against love are first that it provokes jealousy (and therefore undermines social cohesion), and second that it is impermanent; the *ménage à trois* responds to both arguments, by demonstrating that love can overcome jealousy, and by separating love from possession.

34. Wolmar praises passion, and criticizes himself for being insufficiently passionate. Although he does feel some passion for Julie, he can defend his marriage to Julie only because he believes "that if someone was capable of making Julie happy, it was I. I knew that innocence and peace were necessary to her heart, that the love with which it was preoccupied would never give them to it, and that it was only the horror of crime which could drive love from it" (*Julie*, IV, 12, p. 493). Wolmar can justify his marriage to Julie only because Baron d'Étange prevented her marriage to Saint-Preux.

In short, Wolmar feels considerable guilt about his response to a predicament which was largely not of his making. He simply is not a villain, which Berman insists on portraying him to be. See p. 257: Wolmar is "a cold, unfeeling, manipulative 'Husband.'" For Berman Saint-Preux is a hero and Wolmar a villain, and he attacks Rousseau for reversing their roles. Berman criticizes Rousseau, in other words, for writing the wrong melodrama. This is to say that Berman misunderstands Rousseau's purpose, because *Julie* is not a melodrama, since it has no villains. Rousseau states that the book contains "not one bad action, not one wicked man" (*Julie*, Second Preface, p. 13).

35. See the tutor's advice to Sophie (subsequent to the advice quoted in note 16 above), in *Emile*, V, p. 479: "'Whatever precautions anyone may take, enjoyment wears out pleasures, and love is worn out before all others. But when love has lasted a long time, a sweet habit fills the void it leaves behind, and the attraction of mutual confidence succeeds the transports of passion.'"

36. Wolmar's coldness must be distinguished from the coldness of women of which Rousseau speaks in the *Letter to D'Alembert*, p. 103n. (Cf. chapter 4 above, note 14.) If my interpretation is correct, Rousseau there contends that women are cold because they are manipulative. Wolmar, by contrast, is too cold even to be manipulative: his predilection is instead to be a wholly disinterested theoretical observer.

37. Julie's faith serves her not only as an outlet for her passion but also as a restraint upon it. She discovers her love for God on her wedding day, when she is to be united to a man she does not love. Her strengthened faith in God enables her to be faithful to Wolmar: "It is in the contemplation of this divine model that the soul is purified and elevated, that it learns to despise its base inclinations and to surmount its vile passions" (*Julie*, III, 18, p. 358). Religion is needed to consecrate and secure the marital tie. Compare Rousseau's somewhat ironic remark in *Second*, p. 179: "How necessary it was for public repose that divine will intervened to give sovereign authority a sacred and inviolable character which took from the subjects the fatal right of disposing of it." Compare also *Julie*, IV, 12, p. 494 (where Wolmar urges Julie to rely on herself to ensure her fidelity to him) with V, 5, p. 593 (where we learn that Julie relies not on herself but on the presence of God between her and Saint-Preux to ensure her fidelity).

38. *Julie* is a romance or defense of reality that also suggests the shortcomings or limits of reality. The defenses of the novel's morality do not pay sufficient heed to this latter element (any more than the criticisms of it pay sufficient heed to the former). Denis de Rougemont

praises the work because in his view it attacks romantic love. See de Rougemont, pp. 227–28: "Evidently Rousseau was no more taken in by the 'religion' of love than Petrarch had been at the end of his life. . . . Rousseau ends [the novel] with marriage—that is to say, with the triumph of the world as sanctified by Christianity." But in fact Rousseau ends not with Julie's marriage, but with her death terminating her marriage. By contrast, Madame de Staël praises Rousseau for having "attracted men to virtue" by means of "love," the "passion" that is closest to "virtue." See de Staël, p. 26. But in fact Julie is eager to die because on earth virtue opposes her love for Saint-Preux (*Julie*, VI, 12, p. 743). Julie's willingness to die demonstrates the limits to Rousseau's romanticization of reality.

39. One minor character, the servant Claude Anet, does listen to Julie, and returns to his wife Fanchon, whom he previously abandoned, when Julie is on her deathbed (*Julie*, VI, 11, pp. 721–23). This is not insignificant; I do not mean to suggest that in spite of appearances *Julie* is really an attack upon marriage. Nevertheless, *Julie's* argument in favor of marriage is much more qualified than Rousseau's defenses of the novel's moral utility would suggest.

40. One could of course argue that the novel does not really give marriage a fair chance, in that the marriage between the two people who most passionately wanted to marry one another (Julie and Saint-Preux) is prevented from taking place. But it is hard to believe that Julie's marriage to Saint-Preux would have been more successful than her marriage to Wolmar. One exaggerates only slightly in saying that the sum of their relations prior to her marriage to Wolmar consists in Saint-Preux's offending Julie and subsequently asking (and receiving) her pardon. See *Julie*, I, 9, 11, 17, 29, 50, 52, 57; II, 7, 15, 26, 27. It is hard to discern in this pattern the formula for a successful marriage over the long term.

41. The story of Bomston's romantic involvements is alluded to in ibid., V, 12, and VI, 3. But the story is told in full only in an appendix to the novel: *Les Amours de Milord Édouard Bomston*, pp. 749–60. Rousseau explains that he separates Bomston's story from Julie's so as not to "spoil" the latter's "simplicity." See *Julie*, V, 12, p. 625, and *Les Amours*, p. 749.

42. See the discussion of the political implications of romantic love, in chapter 2 above.

43. For Claire's love of rule, see *Julie*, IV, 9, p. 435 (Claire speaks of her "pride of soul"), and VI, 5, p. 661 (she speaks of the delight she has taken in mocking and discomforting her suitors).

44. Wollstonecraft would approve of Claire because of Claire's success at achieving independence from men. See the discussion of Wollstonecraft in chapter 4 above.

In addition to being more independent than is Julie, Claire is also both wittier and more charming than Julie, whose preaching is often unforgivably moralistic. If enough people read *Julie* today to make such a count worthwhile, it would be interesting to see what percentage of readers prefer the female supporting character to the principal female character. It would also be interesting to know whether a shift in sentiment away from Julie to Claire has occurred in the two centuries since the novel's publication.

45. We have seen that both Claire and Julie call to mind elements of Rousseau—Claire his desire for self-sufficiency, Julie his need to love. The duality within Rousseau and his literary creations is reminiscent of our discussion of Pygmalion (with whom, as we saw in chapter 4, Rousseau compares himself in his capacity as creator of Julie and Claire). Pygmalion's two desires, we noted, are to be "apart from his creation" and "a part of her." The first (like Julie) represents Rousseau's need to love; the second (like Claire) his desire for self-sufficiency.

46. Rousseau's presentation of Claire is a second indication of his awareness of the problematic character of his recommendations for women. (For the first, cf. note 20 above.) Rousseau clearly realizes that it is difficult and often unpleasant for women to have to depend upon men. He also believes, however, that women generally must depend upon men (and hence must also rule men). By her own admission, Claire is "a sort of monster," who "was not made to be a woman." Rousseau presumably does not mean her to serve as a "role model" for his female readers.

Taken together, Claire and Julie suggest the variety of which women are capable, in spite of women's uniform interest in controlling men and ability to control men. It is nevertheless interesting to note one element common to Claire and Julie: both ultimately come to reject the rule over men, although for very different reasons—Claire in the name of independence, Julie in the name of love. Their examples might seem to suggest that the work necessary to the perpetuation of society is ultimately unsatisfactory to society's most interesting and attractive members. This may be true of men as well as women. To the extent that Rousseau believes that women are necessarily more social than are men, however, women would be more torn between conflicting duties to society and self than are men. The intensity with which superior women feel this conflict helps to explain their susceptibility within the Rousseauian corpus to deaths which verge upon suicide—the girl like Sophie (in *Emile*), Sophie herself (in *Émile et Sophie*), and Julie.

47. For the affinity between Saint-Preux and Rousseau, see *Confessions*, IX, p. 444: "I identified myself with [Saint-Preux] as far as it was possible for me; but I made him young and amiable, bestowing upon him, in addition, the virtues and defects which I was conscious of in myself." See also ibid., III, p. 106. On reality's destruction of the illusions of love, see the discussions in chapter 4 of Emile's need to be able to be independent of Sophie, and of Rousseau's relationship with Madame d'Houdetot.

48. For an explicit statement of the kinship between religious and romantic ecstasy, see *Julie*, Second Preface, pp. 15–16: "Enthusiasm is the last degree of passion. When it is at its height, it sees its object as perfect; then it makes of it its idol; it places it in Heaven; and as the enthusiasm of devotion borrows the language of love, the enthusiasm of love also borrows the language of devotion. It no longer sees anything but Paradise, the Angels, the virtues of the Saints, the delights of the celestial sojourn." Rousseau observes that lovers do not write "Letters," but "Hymns."

Chapter Six

1. Susan Brownmiller, *Against Our Will: Men, Women and Rape* (New York: Simon and Schuster, 1978), p. 15. The emphases are Brownmiller's.

2. Okin, *Women in Western Political Thought*, p. 99.

3. The emphasis is mine. Cf. Okin, pp. 298–99, where she herself speaks of "the freeing of human beings—and primarily women, because of their biology—from the lifelong constraints of the need to reproduce. The scientific breakthroughs that have prolonged life, eradicated epidemics, and drastically reduced infant mortality, mean that there is *now* no need for women to spend more than a tiny fraction of their lives in bearing enough children to maintain the population level." (The emphasis is mine.) Because this has come to be the case only "now," Okin ought to consider the fact that the authors she criticizes wrote "then"—before this was so, or when women did indeed "need . . . to spend more than a tiny fraction of their lives in bearing enough children to maintain the population level."

4. For Rousseau's critique of an earlier feminine attempt, based on more primitive contraceptive methods, to attain sexual pleasure while avoiding procreation, cf. *Emile*, I, p. 44: "[Women] want to perform a useless act so as always to be able to start over again, and they turn to the prejudice of the species the attraction given for the sake of multiplying it."

5. Although I speak of the "double standard," to do so is to be somewhat unfair to Rousseau. It is true that he argues that a woman has a natural bodily incentive to be modest which a man lacks, and that the biological certainty of maternity as opposed to paternity rightly imposes constraints upon the behavior of a wife (who must convince her husband that he is the biological father of the children to whom she gives birth), but not upon that of a husband. It is not, however, the case that Rousseau treats the promiscuity of men at all indulgently. Cf. ibid., V, p. 361, where Rousseau severely criticizes the marital infidelity of

males (while contending nevertheless that the marital infidelity of females is even worse). Emile certainly sows no wild oats before his marriage; his behavior as an adolescent is in no way any more promiscuous than is Sophie's.

6. In a sense, of course, the contradiction between the two passages can be resolved. Women will be superior to men (the first passage suggests) if they can somehow be both similar to men and different from them; they will be inferior to men (the second passage suggests) if, through striving to be similar to men, they cease in any significant way to differ from them. In explicating Rousseau's position below, I assume that in fact he does not believe that women can be both similar to men and different from them; Rousseau could not think sexual homogenization to be so dangerous, if he did not believe that it would preclude sexual differentiation. In presenting my own position, I argue that the sexes can be different in some respects, similar in others—and that this partial similarity and partial differentiation need not entail the predominance of either sex.

7. In view of the highly controversial nature of the discussion which I have just begun, I must emphasize the extreme limits of the claims that I am making. I do *not* claim that contemporary science "proves" that Rousseau correctly argues for the natural inferiority of women to men (among other reasons, because Rousseau himself does not believe that women *are* naturally inferior to men). I wish only to rebut the preconception which many of my readers (who, like me, are likely to have little knowledge of modern natural science) will possibly have—that contemporary science has proven that *all* measurable psychological and intellectual differences between the sexes are *exclusively* the result of differences in environment and conditioning. In other words, I introduce the findings of contemporary scientific research only to point out that they do not unequivocally refute the view that there are significant innate differences between men and women with respect to their moral and intellectual predispositions. I do not suggest that they unambiguously support this view; even if they did, by no means would they wholly support the specifically Rousseauian variant of the view. Finally, and most importantly, for all of its incomparably greater sophistication, contemporary scientific research addresses fundamentally different and fundamentally more limited questions than does Rousseau: contemporary scientific research can tell us whether or not there is a natural basis for sexual differentiation, but (unlike Rousseau) it cannot tell us whether it is socially and psychologically beneficial that such a basis does or does not exist.

In view of some of the available scientific evidence concerning sexual differentiation, I shall suggest that it *may be* that men on the average are to a small extent genetically advantaged in comparison with women on the average as economic and political actors; to suggest that something hypothetically *may be* so is not, however, categorically to assert that it *is* so. Furthermore, economics and politics are not (happily) all of life; one can speak of a hypothetical male advantage with regard to economics and politics, while also believing in a hypothetical female advantage with regard to other spheres. For a related argument, cf. Judith M. Bardwick, *Psychology of Women: A Study of Bio-Cultural Conflicts* (New York: Harper and Row, 1971), p. 201: "While many feminists conceive of the vocational achievement-oriented society as an ideal, other ideals are possible. There is rather an implicit assumption that the charitable and community-directed efforts of women are a poor second choice, since they are rewarded with little status, no money, and no power. That is true if you assume that the 'natural' goals are status, money, and power. We have already indicated that in addition to the goals and values of the masculine achievement model, women also value intrapsychic development and their contributions to others, their help in improving the welfare of others." Cf. also note 19 below.

8. Cf. Daniel B. Hier and William F. Crowley, Jr., "Spatial Ability in Androgen-Deficient Men," *New England Journal of Medicine* 306 (1982): 1202: "There are several reasons to suspect that the gonadal steroids may influence certain cognitive skills: . . . sex differences can be demonstrated for a variety of cognitive skills, with . . . men performing better on spatial and mathematical measures; . . . these sex differences do not generally emerge until

after puberty." Cf. also Camilla Persson Benbow and Julian C. Stanley, "Sex Differences in Mathematical Ability: Fact or Artifact?" *Science* 210 (1980): 1262–64.

9. Cf. Eleanor Emmons Maccoby and Carol Nagy Jacklin, *The Psychology of Sex Differences* (Stanford, Calif.: Stanford University Press, 1974), pp. 242–43: "Let us outline the reasons why biological sex differences appear to be involved in aggression: (1) Males are more aggressive than females in all human societies for which evidence is available. (2) The sex differences are found early in life, at a time when there is no evidence that differential socialization pressures have been brought to bear by adults to 'shape' aggression differently in the two sexes. . . . (3) Similar sex differences are found in man and subhuman primates. (4) Aggression is related to levels of sex hormones, and can be changed by experimental administrations of these hormones." Cf. also p. 247: "We have been presenting a fairly detailed case for a biological contribution to the sex difference in aggression. It seemed incumbent upon us to establish this case as explicitly as possible, since many readers will no doubt address this issue initially with an assumption that any psychological difference between human groups is entirely a result of differences in experience and training."

10. Steven Goldberg presents an argument correlating male aggressiveness with the social predominance of males, in *The Inevitability of Patriarchy* (New York: William Morrow, 1974). Goldberg begins with the scientific evidence which links the male hormone testosterone to the greater male proclivity for aggression. Because *"the hormonal renders the social inevitable"* (p. 93—the emphasis is Goldberg's), "human biology precludes the possibility of a human social system whose authority system is not dominated by males and in which male aggression is not manifested in dominance and attainment of positions of status and power" (p. 78). The basis for this claim is Goldberg's very broad definition of aggression. Cf. pp. 257–58: "When we refer, in our everyday use of the word, to the aggression of the businessman, politician, or individual whose vocation is left unspecified . . . we are usually referring not primarily to pugnacity or belligerence . . . nor to hostility, but to: 1. a tendency to compete . . . 2. a single-mindedness of purpose . . . ; 3. a willingness to sacrifice . . . pleasure and affection . . . ; 4. an unusually great tendency to ('need for') assertion of the ego; 5. a general tendency to impose will on environment . . . ; 6. a relatively great resistance to doing what one has been told. . . ."

11. Note that each of the two articles mentioned in note 8 above appears with a companion piece which calls its conclusions into question. Cf. Jerome Kagan, "The Idea of Spatial Ability," *New England Journal of Medicine* 306 (1982): 1225–27, and Gina Bari Kolata, "Math and Sex: Are Girls Born with Less Ability?" *Science* 210 (1980): 1234–35. One can hypothesize about a correlation between genetic masculinity and mathematical skills but one cannot at this point regard such a correlation as a proven fact.

It is reasonably certain, by contrast, that males are indeed genetically more prone to be aggressive; in this case, not the fact itself but its significance is very much open to question. Thus the argument advanced by Goldberg (outlined in note 10 above) is at best controversial, for two reasons: first, it is hard to believe that testosterone and only testosterone can account for "single-mindedness of purpose" and "willingness to sacrifice . . . pleasure"—that is to say, the equation of the simple biological notion of aggression with its complex social meaning is not convincingly argued for; second, it is hard to believe that leadership involves *only* a component of aggression, and not also a component of cooperation (one doubts that there are many leaders who at some point in their careers have not had to manifest the exact opposite of "a relatively great resistance to doing what one has been told"). On these points, cf. Maccoby and Jacklin, pp. 368–69, and Philip Green, *The Pursuit of Inequality* (New York: Pantheon, 1981), pp. 127–29, 144–47. (Having said all this, I nevertheless add a caveat: even if the male "edge" in aggressiveness must be less significant than Goldberg thinks it is, it is still possible that it is more significant than those most committed to the complete irrelevance of all distinctions between the sexes think it is.)

12. Cf. David Gelman et al., "Just How the Sexes Differ," *Newsweek*, 18 May 1981, p. 83: "Women researchers [who investigate the possible differences between the sexes] have had

the toughest going at times. Some have found themselves under Lysenkoist pressure to hew to women's-liberation orthodoxy, whatever their data show. University of Chicago psychologist Jerre Levy, a pioneer in studies of brain lateralization, withdrew from public discussion of her work after she was bombarded with hostile letters and phone calls. Harvard's [anthropologist Sarah Blaffer] Hrdy recalls sitting on a panel that was cautiously examining the 'hypothesis' of male math superiority when a feminist seated next to her whispered, 'Don't you know it's evil to do studies like that?' Says Hrdy: 'I was just stunned. Of course it's not evil to do studies like that. It's evil to make pronouncements to say they're fact.'"

13. It is interesting to note in this context the recent appearance of a work which both points to the differences between the moral perceptions of men and women and also defends the adequacy of women's moral preceptions. I refer to Carol Gilligan's *In a Different Voice: Psychological Theory and Women's Development* (Cambridge, Mass.: Harvard University Press, 1982). In a manner very reminiscent of Rousseau, Gilligan contends that women's moral judgments tend to be more particular and concrete, men's more universal and abstract. Women focus more on their social conection with others, men more on their individuated isolation from others. Cf. p. 69: "The moral judgments of women differ from those of men in the greater extent to which women's judgments are tied to feelings of empathy and compassion and are concerned with the resolution of real as opposed to hypothetical dilemmas." Cf. also p. 100: "The moral imperative that emerges repeatedly in interviews with women is an injunction to care, a responsibility to discern and alleviate the 'real and recognizable trouble' of the world. For men, the moral imperative appears rather as an injunction to respect the rights of others and thus to protect from interference the rights to life and self-fulfillment." (Note, however, Gilligan's important qualification on p. 2: "The different voice I describe is characterized not by gender but theme. Its association with women is an empirical observation. . . . But this association is not absolute. . . . No claims are made about the origins of the differences described or their distribution in a wider population, across cultures, or through time.")

Gilligan's work argues that women differ from men, but are not for this reason inferior to men; those readers who are persuaded by Gilligan's defense of women's "different voice" ought to find much of Rousseau's argument equally persuasive. Perhaps the reception of Gilligan's work indicates something which would be very welcome: a greater willingness to consider possible differences between the sexes in a manner that is neither defensive nor offensive. Cf. Robert May, *Sex and Fantasy: Patterns of Male and Female Development* ([United States]: Wideview, 1981), p. xi: "With rare exception sex differences have come to be seen as a *problem*, an affront to human dignity and social progress. Our sore need is for a language and a space in which to talk about the distinguishing characteristics of men and women without its being demeaning to either." (The emphasis is May's.) Cf. also p. 77: "In most instances people matter more to [women] than things and they will put a faithfulness to human ties above dedication to 'principle' or pure 'independence' of judgment. It is a testament to the male bias of our society that such qualities are often referred to with the demeaning names of 'dependence' or 'conformity.'"

14. Carolyn Heilbrun, *Toward a Recognition of Androgyny* (New York: Alfred A. Knopf, 1973), p. xvi.

15. Heilbrun herself appears to have had second thoughts on this issue. See her review of two books by Michael Gilbert in *The New York Times Book Review*, 12 September 1982, p. 24: "As a woman, a liberal, and a feminist I still welcome Mr. Gilbert's nostalgic presentation of certain old-fashioned ideals. His heroes fight without hope of reward, because they hate bullying; they honor, albeit with regret, the slow processes of democracy and law; they are loyal to those who have fought at their side, and they do not think trust a mug's game."

16. Cf. Eliot A. Cohen, "Why We Need a Draft," *Commentary*, April 1982, pp. 38–39: "The large-scale introduction of women into the armed forces subverts discipline and morale—not the superficial discipline of the parade ground or the 'ice-cream' morale of troops who have unlimited supplies of beer and easy access to dubious entertainments, but

the discipline and morale that enable men to do their duty despite fatigue and discomfort, despite fear of capture, fear of mutilation, and fear of death. The building blocks of such discipline and morale are intangible. They include fear of disgracing oneself before one's buddies, 'machismo,' and even hate. The point is that group cohesiveness of this peculiar kind is best fostered in all-male groups, for in mixed groups various extraneous and destructive impulses begin to work—sexual desire or envy, pity, and misogyny among them. If men and women are different, and their differences extend beyond the obvious ones of muscular strength and reproductive capacity, women have no place among America's field troops." Green, p. 160, speaks of the opposition to "the proposal of some of America's military leaders to give women a combat role in the military" as "the one serious effort the sexual inegalitarians have made to apply their ideology to public policy." Speaking for myself (and not for the "sexual inegalitarians"), I regard the controversy over women's possible role in combat as the one (and only) issue of contemporary public policy to which Rousseau's philosophy of masculinity and femininity is conceivably applicable. Green, no friend of "the sexual inegalitarians," takes a rather more sanguine view of the prospect of women engaging in combat. Cf. p. 161: "Surely if women cannot compete with men on the battlefield, . . . we will find that out as soon as maneuvers start." Unfortunately, Cohen's argument suggests that perhaps we could not really "find . . . out" until a real war had begun; and by then it might be too late.

17. For an excellent critique of the perils of the quest for androgyny, cf. May, pp. 163–77. He describes the androgynous ideal (in May's wonderful phrase, the "Person For All Seasons") as (p. 173) "the individual who combines the best of each of us and has no apparent blemishes or even limitations." The question, of course, is why anyone should believe that such an ideal is attainable. Its attainment would be possible, he goes on to observe (pp. 174–75), only as a result of the separation of the "idea of 'self' from our bodies and the consequent downgrad[ing] or delimit[ation of] the sphere of the body. For instance [he quotes an advocate of androgyny]: 'We envision that the future effect of sex on behavior will become as innocuous as current reactions to hair color.' This simile reduces our physical maleness or femaleness to something cosmetic which can be, and often is, changed with only a trip to the drugstore." To accept the androgynous ideal is therefore ultimately (p. 177) to "play a cruel trick on ourselves—cruel because the hopes we raise are unlikely to be fulfilled."

18. Cf. May, p. 168: "The existence of two separate and different sexes is an insult to our dearly held narcissistic image of ourselves and our own limitless possibilities." Cf. also p. 176: androgyny "is a promised land only to be reached through the overthrow of our bodies, since our physical existence is the most concrete and persistent reminder we have of our own limitations. While being the source of our most intense pride and pleasure, the body also speaks to us of what we most probably cannot have. The tasks we cannot accomplish, the people we cannot entice to love us, and our certain aging and death—all these are thus embodied." (In this context, cf. also the discussion of materialism and egalitarianism in chapter 1 above.)

19. I have already offered one explanation for Rousseau's exclusion of women from the political and economic worlds, which focused on his perception of the comparative short-comings of women. To balance this explanation, one would also have to focus on his perception of the absolute shortcomings of the modern political and economic worlds. We saw in chapter 4 above that Rousseau regards the familial world as in all likelihood the sole locus of moral decency in the modern bourgeois world. By contrast, the polity and the economy are almost universally sites of mutual exploitation and corruption. When one keeps this in mind, the relative positions of women and men in the Rousseauian universe can seem to be radically reversed: it is not women who are disadvantaged because their nature restricts them to the familial world; instead it is men who are disadvantaged because their nature does *not* restrict them to the familial world. (For a related argument, cf. chapter 4 above, note 19.)

20. Cf. especially Shulamith Firestone, *The Dialectic of Sex* (New York: William Morrow,

1970), pp. 232–33: "Nature produced the fundamental inequality—half the human race must bear and rear the children of all of them." As a result, Firestone's "first demand" is "*the freeing of women from the tyranny of their reproductive biology by every means available.*" The emphasis is Firestone's.

21. It is interesting to observe that in this sense the moderate wing of the women's liberation movement can be said to be Rousseauian. Moderate feminists contend that child rearing is in considerable measure drudgery or work suited for slaves rather than for free persons, and therefore insist that this unavoidable drudgery be apportioned equally between the parents of the two sexes. Since the slavery entailed by parenthood cannot be eliminated, it is only equitable to demand that men be slaves part of the time, so that women need not be slaves all of the time.

22. To see this, compare *Emile*, IV, p. 333, with *Emile*, V, p. 364: in the first passage, Rousseau denies that sex is a true need for men. He speaks as a man to other men, hypothesizing what would have happened "if no lewd object had ever struck our eyes." "A solitary man . . . without women, would die . . . a virgin." He says nothing about a solitary woman without men, because he cannot conceive of a solitary woman without men. Men can be solitary, whereas women must be social, because (as we learn on p. 364) "we would survive more easily without them than they would without us." Men depend on women only because of their "desires," not because of their "needs": and if men's desires are aroused only by women's (avoidable) impact upon men's imaginations, even the limited dependence occasioned by desire could be overcome. In Rousseau's second teaching, men depend upon women only because women can and must entrap men into dependence.

23. Rousseau envisions such a flight as a possibility, although we will see that it is not a possibility of which he approves. In this respect, it is interesting to compare Tocqueville with Rousseau for a second time in terms of their respective understandings of sexuality. I pointed above (chapter 5, note 29) to their agreement regarding the importance of a moralized sexuality, and their joint support of the resultant indirect political power of women. Their positions are not wholly congruent, however; Rousseau envisions darker possibilities for the future of the family and sexuality than does Tocqueville. Cf. *Democracy in America*, p. 506: "Individualism is a calm and considered feeling which disposes each citizen to isolate himself from the mass of his fellows and withdraw into the circle of family and friends; with this little society formed to his taste, he gladly leaves the greater society to look after itself." For Tocqueville, democratic individualism causes individuals to withdraw from political concerns and to focus on familial concerns; it seems that Tocqueville, unlike Rousseau, did not anticipate a still greater individualism that would cause individuals to withdraw from familial concerns as well, which would be seen as obstacles to personal development. In this respect Rousseau was a better prophet than Tocqueville. To put this another way, there is a Tocquevillian counterpart only to Rousseau's first teaching, not to his second one.

24. I discuss Rousseau's masturbation and masochism in chapter 4 above. Rousseau speaks of his exhibitionism in *Confessions*, III, pp. 90–92, and recounts his homosexual experience in ibid., II, pp. 67–70.

25. On the other hand, one can also regard Rousseau as the sponsor of a more moderate sexual revolution, in whose social utility he believed. Rousseau denies that sexuality is either shameful or a matter of indifference; instead he believes that sexual union should be a source of pleasure to married couples. Cf. *Emile*, V, p. 374: "So much has been done to prevent women from being lovable that husbands have become indifferent. . . . I would want a young Englishwoman to cultivate pleasing talents that will entertain her future husband with as much care as a young Albanian cultivates them for the harem of Ispahan." (It is true that Rousseau says nothing here about husbands providing their wives sexual pleasure; but as we have seen, Rousseau believes that women inherently find sexuality more enjoyable than do men. Cf. chapter 2 above, p. 36.)

26. This criticism is more fundamental than it may appear to be. It ultimately suggests

the difficulties inherent in Rousseau's political conception of sexuality altogether. By emphasizing women's necessary dependence upon men (while at the same time pointing to men's potential independence of women), Rousseau can explain sexual interdependence only by means of women's manipulation of men. In this way he often seems to offer a remarkably convoluted (although admittedly ingenious) solution to a problem which is perhaps quite easily resolved. Because Rousseau begins with the premise that males are by nature individually independent, it is difficult for him to arrive at the conclusion of ultimate conjugal interdependence; to do so, he must rely on the feminine need to rule and the masculine susceptibility to being ruled. It would at least be simpler (I do not say self-evidently truer) to deny the premise of male individual independence, and instead to assert (with the Bible) that the family is divinely ordained or (with Aristotle) that the family is more unambiguously natural than Rousseau believes it to be. (Or to express my objection differently: for all of the criticisms directed at Rousseau's depiction of women, this depiction is quite arguably far closer to believability than is his depiction of men.) Women and men do indeed need one another and complete one another; but there are more commonsensical (as well as traditional) ways of arguing this case than the one Rousseau feels compelled to propound.

It is true that Rousseau more closely approaches a classical understanding of the family and sexuality to the extent that he equates love with the search for individual completion; cf. the discussion in chapter 4 above of the ways in which men and women make one another happy. But rather than solving the problem of reconciling independence with interdependence, this element of Rousseau's thought simply poses it in a different way: in view of Rousseau's belief in individual self-sufficiency, it is hard to see how he can justify a concomitant belief in the perception of individual deficiency and the consequent desire for perfection and completion with the aid of another.

Bibliography

Works of Rousseau

Rousseau, Jean-Jacques. *The Confessions of Jean Jacques Rousseau.* New York: The Modern Library, n.d.

————. *Correspondance Complète de Jean Jacques Rousseau.* Ed. R.A. Leigh. Vols. 5 (1967), 9 (1969). Geneva: Institut et Musée Voltaire.

————. *Emile, or On Education.* Trans. Allan Bloom. New York: Basic Books, 1979.

————. *Essay on the Origin of Languages.* Trans. John H. Moran. In *On the Origin of Language.* New York: F. Ungar, 1967.

————. *The First and Second Discourses.* Trans. Roger D. and Judith R. Masters. New York: St. Martin's Press, 1964.

————. *The Government of Poland.* Trans. Wilmoore Kendall. Indianapolis: Bobbs-Merrill Library of Liberal Arts, 1972.

————. *Letter to D'Alembert.* Trans. Allan Bloom. In *Politics and the Arts.* Ithaca, N.Y.: Cornell University Press, Agora Editions, 1960.

————. *Oeuvres Complètes.* Paris: Gallimard, Bibliothèque de la Pléiade, 1959–69.

————. *On the Social Contract with Geneva Manuscript and Political Economy.* Trans. Judith R. Masters. Ed. Roger D. Masters. New York: St. Martin's Press, 1978.

————. *Political Writings.* Trans. and Ed. Frederick Watkins. New York: Thomas Nelson and Sons, 1953.

————. *The Reveries of the Solitary Walker.* Trans. Charles E. Butterworth. New York: New York University Press, 1979.

Commentaries on Rousseau

Berman, Marshall. *The Politics of Authenticity.* New York: Atheneum, 1970.

Burgelin, Pierre. "L'Éducation de Sophie." *Annales de la Société Jean-Jacques Rousseau* 35 (1959–62): 113–37.

————. *La Philosophie de l'Existence de J.-J. Rousseau.* Paris: Librairie Philosophique J. Vrin, 1973.

Crocker, Lester G. "*Julie* ou la Nouvelle Duplicité." *Annales de la Société Jean-Jacques Rousseau* 36 (1963–65): 105–52.

Bibliography

Derrida, Jacques. *Of Grammatology*. Trans. Gayatri Chakravorty Spivak. Baltimore: The Johns Hopkins University Press, 1976.

Eigeldinger, Marc. *Jean-Jacques Rousseau et la Réalité de l'Imaginaire*. Neuchâtel, Switzerland: Éditions de la Baconnière, 1962.

Ellis, M. B. *Julie or La Nouvelle Héloïse: A Synthesis of Rousseau's Thought (1749–59)*. Toronto: University of Toronto Press, 1949.

Fellows, Otis. "Buffon and Rousseau: Aspects of Relationship." *PMLA* 75 (1960): 184–96.

Goldschmidt, Victor. *Anthropologie et Politique: Les Principes du Système de Rousseau*. Paris: Librairie Philosophique J. Vrin, 1974.

Gouhier, Henri. *Les Méditations Métaphysiques de Jean-Jacques Rousseau*. Paris: Librairie Philosophique J. Vrin, 1970.

Guéhenno, Jean. *Jean-Jacques Rousseau*. 2 vols. Trans. John and Doreen Weightman. New York: Columbia University Press, 1966.

Hubert, René. "L'amour, la nature et la société chez J-J Rousseau: *La Nouvelle Héloïse*, roman à thèse." *Revue d'Histoire de la Philosophie et d'Histoire Générale de la Civilisation* 7 (1939): 193–214.

Masters, Roger D. *The Political Philosophy of Rousseau*. Princeton, N.J.: Princeton University Press, 1968.

Mead, William. *Jean-Jacques Rousseau Ou le Romancier Enchaîné*. Princeton, N.J., and Paris: Université de Princeton, Département de Langues Romanes, and Presses Universitaires de France, 1966.

Morel, Jean. "Recherches sur les Sources du *Discours de l'Inégalité*." *Annales de la Société Jean-Jacques Rousseau* 5 (1909): 119–98.

Okin, Susan Moller. *Women in Western Political Thought*. Princeton, N.J.: Princeton University Press, 1979.

Pizzorusso, Arnaldo. "La Comédie de *Narcisse*." *Annales de la Société Jean-Jacques Rousseau* 35 (1959–62): 9–27.

Schinz, Albert. *La Pensée de Jean-Jacques Rousseau*. Paris: Librairie Félix Alcan, 1929.

Sénéchal, Anicet. "Jean-Jacques Rousseau, Secrétaire de Madame Dupin, d'après des Documents Inédits, Avec un Inventaire des Papiers Dupin Dispersés en 1957 et 1958." *Annales de la Société Jean-Jacques Rousseau* 36 (1963–65): 173–290.

Shklar, Judith N. *Men and Citizens: A Study of Rousseau's Social Theory*. Cambridge: Cambridge University Press, 1969.

Staël, Anne Louise Germaine de. *Lettres Sur Le Caractère et Les Écrits de Jean-Jacques Rousseau*. In *Oeuvres Complètes*, Vol. 1. Paris: Chez Treuttel et Würtz, 1820, pp. 1–101.

Starobinski, Jean. *Jean-Jacques Rousseau: La Transparence et l'Obstacle Suivi de Sept Essais sur Rousseau*. Paris: Gallimard, 1971.

Strauss, Leo. *Natural Right and History*. Chicago: The University of Chicago Press, 1953.

Vallette, Gaspard. *Jean-Jacques Rousseau Genevois*. Paris and Geneva: Librairie Flon and A. Jullien, 1911.

Wirz, Charles. "Note sur *Émile et Sophie, ou les Solitaires*." *Annales de la Société Jean-Jacques Rousseau* 36 (1963–65): 291–303.

Other Works

Aristotle. *The Politics of Aristotle.* Trans. and Ed. Ernest Barker. London: Oxford University Press, 1958.

———. *Nicomachean Ethics.* Trans. Martin Ostwald. Indianapolis: Bobbs-Merrill Library of Liberal Arts, 1962.

Bardwick, Judith M. *Psychology of Women: A Study of Bio-Cultural Conflicts.* New York: Harper and Row, 1971.

Benbow, Camilla Persson, and Julian C. Stanley. "Sex Differences in Mathematical Ability: Fact or Artifact?" *Science* 210 (1980): 1262–64.

Berger, Brigitte. "What Women Want." *Commentary*, March 1979, 62–66.

Brownmiller, Susan. *Against Our Will: Men, Women and Rape.* New York: Simon and Schuster, 1978.

Buffon, Georges Louis Leclerc de. *Oeuvres Complètes.* Paris: Chez Verdière et Ladrange, 1824–31. Vols. 13, 16, 18.

Burke, Edmund. *Reflections on the Revolution in France.* Ed. Thomas H. D. Mahoney. Indianapolis: Bobbs-Merrill Library of Liberal Arts, 1955.

Cohen, Eliot A. "Why We Need a Draft." *Commentary*, April 1982, 34–40.

Firestone, Shulamith. *The Dialectic of Sex.* New York: William Morrow, 1970.

Gay, Peter. *The Enlightenment: An Interpretation.* New York: Alfred A. Knopf, 1976. Vol. 1.

Gelman, David, et al. "Just How the Sexes Differ." *Newsweek*, 18 May 1981, 72–83.

Gilligan, Carol. *In a Different Voice: Psychological Theory and Women's Development.* Cambridge, Mass.: Harvard University Press, 1982.

Goldberg, Steven. *The Inevitability of Patriarchy.* New York: William Morrow, 1974.

Green, Philip. *The Pursuit of Inequality.* New York: Pantheon, 1981.

Hegel, Georg Wilhelm Friedrich. *The Philosophy of History.* Trans. J. Sibree. New York: Dover Publications, 1956.

Heilbrun, Carolyn. Review of *End Game*, and *Mr. Calder & Mr. Behrens*, by Michael Gilbert. *The New York Times Book Review*, 12 September 1982, 9, 24.

———. *Toward a Recognition of Androgyny.* New York: Alfred A. Knopf, 1973.

Hier, Daniel B., and William F. Crowley, Jr. "Spatial Ability in Androgen-Deficient Men." *New England Journal of Medicine* 306 (1982): 1202–05.

Hobbes, Thomas. *De Cive.* Ed. Sterling P. Lamprecht. New York: Appleton-Century-Crofts, 1949.

———. *Leviathan: Or the Matter, Forme and Power of a Commonwealth Ecclesiasticall and Civil.* Ed. Michael Oakeshott. London: Collier-Macmillan, 1962.

Kagan, Jerome. "The Idea of Spatial Ability." *New England Journal of Medicine* 306 (1982): 1225–27.

Kolakowski, Leszek, and Stuart Hampshire, eds. *The Socialist Idea.* New York: St. Martin's Press, 1974.

Kolata, Gina Bari. "Math and Sex: Are Girls Born with Less Ability?" *Science* 210 (1982): 1234–35.

Lasch, Christopher. *The Culture of Narcissism: American Life in an Age of Diminishing Expectations.* New York: W. W. Norton, 1978.

Lee, Vera. *The Reign of Women in Eighteenth-Century France.* Cambridge, Mass.: Schenkman Publishing, 1975.

Lewis, C. S. *The Allegory of Love.* Oxford: Oxford University Press, 1975.

Locke, John. *Two Treatises of Government.* Ed. Peter Laslett. New York: New American Library, 1965.

Lucretius. *On the Nature of Things.* Trans. Cyril Bailey. Oxford: Oxford University Press, 1910.

Maccoby, Eleanor Emmons, and Carol Nagy Jacklin. *The Psychology of Sex Differences.* Stanford, Calif.: Stanford University Press, 1974.

Machiavelli, Niccolò. *Discourses on the First Ten Books of Titus Livius.* Trans. Christian E. Detmold. In *The Prince and the Discourses.* New York: The Modern Library, 1940.

May, Robert. *Sex and Fantasy: Patterns of Male and Female Development.* [United States]: Wideview, 1981.

Montesquieu. *Considerations on the Causes of the Greatness of the Romans and Their Decline.* Trans. David Lowenthal. Ithaca, N.Y.: Cornell University Press Agora Editions, 1965.

———. *The Spirit of the Laws.* Trans. Thomas Nugent. New York: Hafner Publishing, 1966.

Plato. *The Republic of Plato.* Trans. Allan Bloom. New York: Basic Books, 1968.

Plutarch. *The Lives of the Nobel Grecians and Romans.* Trans. John Dryden, revised by Arthur Hugh Clough. New York: The Modern Library, n.d.

Pufendorf, Samuel. *Le Droit de la Nature et des Gens.* Trans. Jean Barbeyrac. Leiden: Chez J. de Wetstein, 1759. Vol. 2.

Rougemont, Denis de. *Love in the Western World.* Trans. Montgomery Belgion. New York: Fawcett, 1956.

Tocqueville, Alexis de. *Democracy in America.* Trans. George Lawrence. Ed. J. P. Mayer. Garden City, N.Y.: Anchor-Doubleday, 1969.

Wolfe, Tom. *Mauve Gloves & Madmen, Clutter & Vine.* New York: Bantam Books, 1977.

Wollstonecraft, Mary. *A Vindication of the Rights of Woman.* Ed. Charles W. Hagelman, Jr. New York: W. W. Norton, 1976.

Index

References to characters in Rousseau's fictional works are followed by a parenthetical notation of the work in which they appear.

Index

Index

Index

Tronchin, letter to, 165 n.53

Valère (*Narcisse*), 71–72, 107–8, 166 n.58; compared to Emile, 81; compared to Rousseau, 172 n.62
Vanity, 32, 157 nn.12, 13, 158 n.31; in *Narcisse*, 71
de Vercellis, Mme., 127
Vernes, letter to 173 n.11
de Vilmorin, Roger, 172 n.66
Violence. *See* State of Nature

de Warens, Mme., 102, 137, 171 nn.53, 54, 172 n.65, 176 n.33
Wirz, Charles, 170 nn.44, 46
Wolfe, Tom, 166 n.58
Wollstonecraft, Mary, 85–86, 89, 136, 178 n.44
Wolmar (*Julie*), 116–17, 118–21, 127, 128, 130–34, 136, 173 nn.7, 10, 174 n.20, 176 n.33, 177 nn.34, 36

Zulietta, 103–6, 111